Popular Music and National Culture in Israel

Popular Music
and National Culture in Israel

MOTTI REGEV AND EDWIN SEROUSSI

University of California Press

BERKELEY   LOS ANGELES   LONDON

University of California Press
Berkeley and Los Angeles, California

University of California Press, Ltd.
London, England

© 2004 by the Regents of the University of California

Library of Congress Cataloging-in-Publication Data

Regev, Motti.
   Popular music and national culture in Israel / Motti Regev and Edwin
Seroussi.
       p.   cm.
Includes bibliographical references (p.   ) and indexes.
Discography: p.
   ISBN 0–520-23652-1 (cloth : alk. paper)—ISBN 0–520-23654-8 (pbk. :
alk. paper)
   1. Popular music—Israel—Social aspects.   2. Popular culture—
Israel.   3. National characteristics, Israeli.   I. Seroussi, Edwin.   II. Title.

ML3502.I75R44   2004
306.4′8423′095694—dc22   2003022856

Manufactured in the United States of America
13   12   11   10   09   08   07   06   05   04
10   9   8   7   6   5   4   3   2   1

Contents

Preface

The study of Israeli culture is one of the most challenging fields of inquiry among those relating to the investigation of nation-states that arose during the twentieth century. Irrespective of a scholar's field, be it the social sciences or humanities, the extreme complexity of the Israeli case always calls for an interdisciplinary approach. The intricate web of contrasting human factors, backgrounds, memories, ideologies, and wills that shaped Israeli society and its modern culture (what we call "Israeliness") can be better interpreted if approached simultaneously from various disciplinary perspectives. This is certainly true of our topic: Israeli popular music.

Our interdisciplinary collaboration began in the early 1990s, when Regev, a sociologist, had completed his doctoral dissertation, which was the first attempt to interpret the rise of Israeli rock by using the theoretical tools of the sociology of art. Seroussi, an ethnomusicologist, had, in collaboration with other colleagues, studied only one aspect of Israeli popular music, "oriental ethnicity." We arrived at the study of Israeli popular music from widely different perspectives and believed that the study of popular music would be enlightening for the understanding of contemporary Israeliness. Concluding that only a major ethnographic undertaking could possibly map out the complex field of Israeli popular music in its entirety, we embarked on this project around 1993. A major grant from the Israel Science Foundation (formerly managed by the Israel National Academy of Sciences) for the years 1994–97 and the assistance of several colleagues and graduate students enabled us to accomplish some of the significant goals of this encompassing ethnographic endeavor. Additional grants came from the Shein Institute and the Silbert Foundation for Israel Studies, both at the Faculty of Social Sciences of the Hebrew University of Jerusalem. The research project was administered through Bar-Ilan University. We are grateful to the Research Authority of Bar-Ilan University for their support and for an additional intramural grant, which enabled us to complete our fieldwork. Grants for final editing of this book were provided by the Research Authority of the Open University of Israel and by the Research Committee of the Faculty of Humanities of the Hebrew University of Jerusalem.

This book, therefore, represents the conclusion of a research effort that spanned several years. Even so, this text is by no means a definitive study of all aspects of Israeli popular music; it is, rather, a starting point for reflection and a basis for future in-depth studies of the topic. We hope that the extensive raw materials we collected, a fraction of which are presented here, will nourish such future enterprises.

Throughout this project, we interviewed many of the leading lights of Israeli popular music and we are grateful to all of them for their patience when sharing their lore with us. Three major figures among them, Moshe Vilensky, Alexander "Sasha" Argov, and Yair Rosenblum, passed away only a few months after we interviewed them. We carry with us these memorable encounters that took place at their homes. We also thank the following composers, lyricists, arrangers, producers, and critics, who granted us extensive interviews during the various stages of this project: Shimon Cohen, Yehoram Gaon, Hanoch Hasson, Haim Heffer, Nahum Heiman, Nurit Hirsh, Ehud Manor, Hanan Yovel, Yoni Rechter, Arieh Levanon, Shem Tov Levy, Meir Noy, Yaacov Orland, Naomi Polani, Amalia Rosen, and Yoram Tehar-Lev. Many other musicians, lyricists, producers, and critics talked with us in informal conversations. Space constraints prevent us from mentioning them individually, but we extend our sincere thanks to all those in the Israeli popular-music community who assisted us.

Many students worked with us at various stages of this project, and they deserve our most heartfelt recognition. Some students completed their theses and dissertations under our guidance in the framework of this project, and their studies are extensively reflected in the present text. First of these all, we would like to thank Dr. Talila Eliram, who coordinated the research project with patience and efficiency and worked with us on most of the ethnographic research. Chapter 3, "Songs of the Land of Israel," would not exist without her key contribution. Eliram also assisted at the different stages of the preparation of this manuscript. Shulamit Marom contributed a detailed study of the role of the Histadrut (the General Federation of Hebrew Workers in Eretz Yisrael) in the creation of an Israeli musical culture; her work is reflected in Chapter 2. Dr. Carmela Topelberg's study of popular music in Tel Aviv between the 1920s and the 1950s served as the basis for Chapter 4. Shifra Fürst studied the phenomenon of the popular-music festivals in Israel; Chapter 6 relies heavily on her findings. Other students who participated in this project were Alona Sagui, who studied the evolution of jazz in Israel; Galit Saada, who investigated Sderot's rock scene; Miriam Kelmer, who examined the work of Naomi Shemer; and Yael Zilbershlag, who assisted us in the early stages of our research on the IDF ensembles. We thank Shmulik Tessler of Tel Aviv University for sharing his recent findings on the IDF ensembles, as well as Shoshana Levi for allowing us to quote from her ethnographic work on *musiqa mizraḥit*. Our thanks also go to Dr. Marina Ritzarev for her bibliographical research on our behalf.

We are also grateful to the colleagues who assisted us at various stages of our work, in particular Dr. Dan Almagor, a leading scholar and author of the Israeli song and the musical stage, for allowing us to explore substantial sections of his private archive on the history of IDF ensembles and for his conversations with us; and Dr. Nathan Shahar for his willingness to share his vast resources and enormous knowledge on the Israeli song. Thanks also to music journalists Dalit Ofer, Yoav Kutner, Gidi Avivi, and Amit Shoham for being helpful with their knowledge and contacts. And finally, we send our gratitude to the late Meir Noy for his clarifications about the early history of the Israeli song and for compiling and leaving his vast and unique collection of Israeli songs to subsequent generations of scholars.

We benefited from the special collections of the Music Department and the National Sound Archives of the Jewish National and University Library in Jerusalem, especially the Noy-Wachs Archive of Jewish and Hebrew Song. We would like to thank the director of the department, Dr. Gila Flam, and the members of her staff, Daria Israeli, Ruti Fried, Roni Goel, Avi Nahmias, Yaacov Mazor, and Efraim Yaacov, who were at all times patient with our endless requests. We also thank the authorities of ACUM, Israel's Society of Composers and Lyricists, for allowing us to use their database for our research. We are grateful to Gila Haimovic for her dedication to the style editing of the manuscript. Special thanks to Lynne Withey, Mary Francis, Colette DeDonato, Kate Warne, and Alex Giardino at the University of California Press, who handled the manuscript and guided it to fulfillment. We thank Fern Seckbach for preparation of the indexes. Finally, we would like to thank Simon Frith and two anonymous reviewers for reading the manuscript and contributing a number of illuminating and useful comments.

Parts of the Introduction and Chapter 1 were previously published in the article "To Have a Culture of our Own: On Israeliness and its Variants" (*Ethnic and Racial Studies* [2000] 23: 223–47). We would like to thank Routledge Journals and the Taylor and Francis Group (http://www.tandf.co.uk) for permitting us to use these sections.

Motti Regev and Edwin Seroussi
Tel Aviv and Jerusalem, May 2002

Introduction

Popular Music and National Culture

On May 1, 1998—the fifth day of the Hebrew month of Iyar—Israelis celebrated fifty years of statehood. Throughout the day, the two major national popular-music radio stations broadcast hit parades, and audiences selected the "most beloved" or "most popular" song in Israeli history. Reshet Gimmel (the "third network" of Israel radio) called its poll the "jubilee song"; Galei Tzahal (the army radio station) dubbed its own project, in which only soldiers participated, the "jubilee parade." In addition, Israel television conducted an "expert" poll to select the "best" song ever in Israeli popular music. The media polls were not the only events in this context during 1998. Others included the launching of comprehensive sets of CDs. Most notable among these were *Gadalnu yaḥad* (We grew up together), a lush, box set of eleven CDs with annotations, containing "240 greatest Israeli songs" (excluding the ones for which the company was unable to gain copyright), produced by Hed-Artzi, the largest and oldest record company in the country; and *'Avoda 'ivrit* (Hebrew labor), subtitled "A Tribute to Fifty Years of Original Creation," a four-CD box that contained new interpretations by a wide range of Israeli artists of 51 "classic" Hebrew songs.

All these events and projects took advantage of the fiftieth anniversary of the state and served as a general opportunity for summaries and recapitulations of what Israeliness is all about. Public ceremonies, books, television programs, exhibitions, all were devoted to descriptions, examinations, and assessments of Israeliness. Particular attention was given to the issue of indigenous, native "national" culture. Public discourse was filled with debates and discussions of questions such as "Does an indigenous Israeli culture exist? And if so, what are its typical contents and meanings?" and "What, in

1

different art fields, are the individual works that constitute the 'canon' of Israeli culture?"

The preoccupation with culture and national identity during 1998 reflects a key belief held by culture professionals in all fields in Israel—a belief that has dictated and determined artistic and cultural practices in Israel for nearly a century, since the early days of Zionist settlement in Palestine. This belief holds that Israel, as a national cultural community, should have a culture of its own. That is, it should have a set of cultural practices and artworks that, as an exclusive body of contents and meanings, expresses the uniqueness and specificity of Israeliness, and that it is through routine practice of and intimate acquaintance with this unique world of contents and meanings that Israeliness at both individual and collective levels comes into being. However, Israeliness needed to be constructed or "invented," because for the early Zionist pioneers in Palestine, this culture had to be different from traditional Jewish cultures forged in the Diaspora. Moreover, since the cultures of the different Jewish groups that immigrated to the new country were diverse in their contents and meanings, the construction of Israeliness was a constant source of ideological contest and struggle; hence, the preoccupation with the measure of the success of the construction of Israeliness on the occasion of the state's fiftieth anniversary.

We can see that in Israel the idea of a new nation is thoroughly interwoven with the creation of a new culture and arts. Moreover, as the polls and CD projects described above indicate, popular music is a particularly important locus where the definition of the new culture is both constructed and contested. Another belief shared by many media commentators and music professionals is that popular music is the cultural form that most strongly signifies Israeliness (second, perhaps, only to the reemergence of Hebrew as a living language), and that it represents convincing "proof" of the existence of Israeliness as an indigenous cultural entity.

Having accepted the cultural significance of popular music, a major argument of this book is that popular music in Israel should be understood primarily as a leading area in the symbolic representation of Israeliness. We perceive popular music in the Israeli context as an arena of contest and struggle among several musical genres and styles that represent the music cultures of Jews of different ethnic and social backgrounds. This is a struggle for legitimacy and dominance as each of these different musical styles seeks recognition as "the" true Israeli national music. Thus this book describes the changes in Israeli popular music during the past five decades as attempts to construct and invent indigenous and authentic Israeli music.

THE FIELD OF NATIONAL CULTURE

Two major sets of problematics dominate the study of modern national cultures: their connection to earlier, premodern entities from which they supposedly evolve; and the regional, ethnic, class, religious, and other forms of cultural diversity that exist within any given nation-state.

Scholars of nationalism disagree about the extent to which modern nations and national cultures are natural transmutations of earlier, premodern ethnic entities. Primordialists tend to view nations as having strong roots in such entities (Smith 1986, 1991; Armstrong 1982), while for modernists, nations and national cultures are totally modern phenomena, constructed and invented in recent history (Gellner 1983; Hobsbawm and Ranger 1983; Anderson 1991; Hobsbawm 1990). However, "since primordialists concede that the 'past' is a selective and interpretive *present* construction, and since modernists concede that the 'present' must make use of available *past* cultural repertoires of the collectivities in question, the gulf between the two is indeed minor" (Ram 1995: 93).

Thus, in both cases, the existence of a constructed national culture in which narratives of ancestry and origin are presented as objective history is widely accepted. In this framework of thought, culture consists of the material and immaterial assets through which the existence of a nation as community is "imagined," practiced, and believed, that is, one "correct" language, canons of works in the various arts, and specific forms of food and dress that are consecrated as embodying the "true," "traditional," and "native" character of the nation.

Although the notion of one, singular national culture is widely acknowledged, a number of studies have pointed to two interrelated phenomena that seem to be eroding the singularity of national cultures in recent decades. These are the intensification of the globalization of culture and the (re)emergence of subnational groupings. At the core of what has recently been called the globalization of culture, which is in fact the intensification of a centuries-old phenomenon, is the dissemination of products and materials of the international culture industry: films, television series, popular music, and the hardware gadgets for consuming them; all types of manufactured foods; fashions in clothing, cosmetics, cars, glossy magazines; and the advertisements for all these products. Sometimes this process has been considered "cultural imperialism" that homogenizes world culture and destroys local cultures (Mattelart 1979; Ritzer 1993). It has also been argued and demonstrated that the work of the globalization of culture is more subtle and complex in two major ways. First, the flow of cultural materials is multidirectional—not only from the West to the rest of the world, but in other directions as well. Second, these cultural materials are used and decoded differently in different countries. That is, they are localized or nationalized by typical uses and interpretations (Appadurai 1990; Featherstone 1990; Hannerz 1992; Liebes and Katz 1993; Regev 1997b; Tomlinson 1999). Consequently, the current global flow of cultural materials—for which the terms "global culture" and "world culture" are commonly used—should be viewed primarily as having the effect of increasing the amount and variety of cultural materials present in a given national cultural setting, available for the construction of a contemporary sense of that national culture.

The modern construction of nations has typically excluded from its invented, singular, and homogenized national culture at least some traditions, arts, or languages of various groups that exist within the nation-state. The cultural materials of certain classes and regional, ethnic, or religious groups have been relegated by dominant national cultures to marginality and secondariness. In addition, a recent form of migration—most notably of workers and former colonials—has created new forms of minority cultures within nation-states. Some of these more traditional subnational groups tend to struggle for cultural or political autonomy, or indeed for separation and construction of a different nation-state. Yet, in many cases, the struggle is for recognition, legitimacy, acceptance, and integration within the existing national culture. In these cases, "minority," "alternative," or "ethnic" discourses of the national history are constructed, as well as "alternative" canons of art, accompanied by claims for inclusion in, or even for redefinition of, the singular-dominant national culture. (The discourse of "black" culture within the United Kingdom is paradigmatic in this context. See Hall 1991, 1996; Gilroy 1987, 1993; see also Soysal 1994.)

Taken together, then, contemporary national cultures consist of three major variants, each of which is in fact a construction, an invention, or an imagined version of the collective identity. One is a pure or traditional variant, typically constructed and invented at the formative period of the "imagining" of the nation. The second is a globalized variant, in which elements of contemporary global culture are mixed with traditional elements to produce a contemporary, (post)modernized national culture. The third is a variety of subnational variants, in which old or recently formed collectivities within the nation-state invent a different, separate identity vis-à-vis the traditional one (this type might also contain global influences, albeit in a different mode than the former). Thus each of the three is also a hybrid, a mixture of cultural materials borrowed, confiscated, appropriated, adjusted, and adapted from various sources (the major source being the ethnic, prenational entities believed to be the origin of the nation).

The existence of these variants can be viewed simply as pluralism, or as an indication that the nation, as a single cultural community, does not really exist. But the collective and individual actors that represent such variants do share, in many cases, a common belief in the ideology of nationalism, in the idea of congruence between the state and the cultural community. As such, they are engaged, manifestly or implicitly, in a constant struggle over the definition of the dominant national culture. The arena of contest over the definition of the dominant and legitimate national culture, and its underlying doxa, the ideology of nationalism, can be therefore understood as a field, in Bourdieu's meaning of the concept (Bourdieu 1985; Bourdieu with Wacquant 1992).

The field of national culture is then a space with a number of positions, each occupied by a set of collective actors. Each position is taken up by a specific variant of the national culture, whose representatives struggle to gain recognition, legitimacy, and dominance (or separation, when the variant defines itself as a different nation altogether). The issue at stake, around which the field of national culture as an arena of struggle is organized, is the repertory of practices, tastes, sensibilities, elements of knowledge, and canons of art forms and artworks—in short, the specific cultural capital and habitus—that defines natural membership in the given national culture. Or, to use a different concept, at stake are the contents of the institutionalized cultural repertory through which national culture is experienced as a reality (Lamont 1995). Typically, the contents and meanings of the traditional variant compose the taken-for-granted national cultural capital, while other variants struggle for legitimacy and recognition. In the fields of art—both "high" and "popular"—this means that art forms and artworks associated with the traditional variant tend to be consecrated as national art, while those associated with other variants are engaged in a struggle for national legitimacy.

POPULAR MUSIC AND NATIONAL CULTURE

It has been widely acknowledged that music in general, and popular/folk music in particular, is a major cultural tool in the construction of modern national, ethnic, and other collectivities and in the evocation of a sense of place. In fact, this argument is one of the essential premises of anthropologically oriented ethnomusicology (Merriam 1964; Nettl 1985; Slobin 1993;

Stokes 1994). Live performances of music and dance, radio broadcasting, music education, the recording industry, and home playing of phonograms (vinyl records, cassettes, CDs) are elements of a complex of practices and institutions that use popular music as a major cultural form through which place and identity are experienced. Nations are no exception. Popular and folk music have been extensively in use as cultural symbols of nations—of their particularity and uniqueness, of their unity and homogeneity. National educational systems, the international tourist industry, and Hollywood films make use of such institutionalized typical music forms in order to signify particular places and ethnic or national identities. However, the emergence in the second half of the twentieth century of local, contemporary popular-music styles—especially pop/rock—has undermined the homogenized images of national music cultures employed by such bodies. Moreover, these recent forms of popular music often claim recognition and legitimacy as national music as well.

At the basis of the claim that popular and folk music can represent the constructed national or ethnic collectivities lies the unique potential of music as a system of symbolic representation (Monelle 1992; Tagg 1982). Music is an important vehicle for the construction of the objective reality of the external social world. As Shepherd and Wicke (1997: 205–6) argued, "Sound can act as homologous and iconic means of signification in relation to phenomena which themselves are not comprised of sound. . . . That is, the relationship between the sound and the phenomenon evoked is established and determined purely by convention." These conventions emerge from "actual and concrete practices of sonically grounded signification and communication . . . couched within an understanding, categorization and formulation of these practices in terms of the ways a society or culture may reflect on them through an extension of these very same practices" (Shepherd and Wicke 1997: 210).

The semantic power of music is thus the basis for the widespread claim that popular music can represent constructed national or ethnic collectivities (Monelle 1992; Tagg 1982). Certain musical works may accumulate long-standing, widely accepted connotations, ones that, for all practical purposes, eventually arise from the works themselves. Thus music's semiotic powers may be stabilized through the ways in which they are constituted and reinforced through discourse, through consumption practice, and through patterns of use over time (De Nora 1986). Meanings can be constantly attached to certain sound constellations through the everyday uses of specific musical materials in specific contexts of meaning. But music does not only convey or communicate meanings, it also has the power to influence what people experience and how they feel. Since music has the power to affect the shape of social agency, control over music in social settings is itself a source of power (De Nora 2000).

One major point in this book is that Israeli national identity is not inherent in the specific sonic structures of the music perceived by Israelis as "Israeli" or as connoting "Israeliness." There is, rather, an accumulated collection of items in diverse musical styles that over time and at specific historical and social junctures of Israeli existence acquired the signification of one or more variants of Israeliness. Our ethnographically oriented work thus tries to offer a pragmatic theory of how music can represent national identity. In this endeavor we follow Hennion (1993) and Middleton (1990), who suggest that particular configurations of meaning in music can be stabilized through ritual procedures and practices over time. Music may be reappropriated, reclaimed for different interpretative uses (for example, representing Israeliness) according to the configurations of the mediators (the creators of Israeli culture and the institutions that contributed to nurturing this culture). Our case shows how music's semiotic force cannot be fully specified in advance of actual reception because musical affect is contingent on the circumstances of its appropriation (De Nora 2000).

In general, musical representation of nonmusical ideas is a complex phenomenon, subject to multiple interpretations, even within a relatively homogenous community at a specific point in history. Thus we may speak of national fields of popular music, wherein various music cultures are engaged in contests and struggles over the repertory of musical practices, tastes, and sensibilities and over the canon of musical works that will be institutionalized as the dominant national music. Or, put differently, it is a struggle over which musical habitus and body of musical works will become natural, taken-for-granted components of the legitimate national cultural capital.

These are complex struggles in which appropriations of styles, claims of authenticity and continuity, and accusations of "imitation" go hand in hand with issues of power within and control over music education systems, broadcasting media, and music industries. In accordance with the general field of national culture, the positions in national fields of popular music are typically occupied by three types of popular music: "folk/traditional"; "pop/rock"; and "ethnic," regional, or other sectarian forms of popular music. "Folk" music typically claims a sort of cultural purity and historical depth of the nation; pop/rock is strongly associated with late modernity and the most recent cultural changes; "ethnic" music—which may take a traditional or rock form—is believed to represent various minority cultures within the nation-state.

But these differences are more in the sphere of ideology than in the actual musical components of each type of popular music. Intercultural flow of musical and music-related components, and especially the "Western impact on world music" (Nettl 1978, 1985), have greatly blurred the distinctions between folk and popular music and placed in doubt the very existence of pure musical heritages. Moreover, the emergence of the transnational style of popular music, which is mainly based on Anglo-American pop/rock, has influenced many of the local and national styles of popular music (Wallis and Malm 1984). Consequently, nearly every type of twentieth-century popular music is essentially a hybrid. That is, like the variants of the national culture, each musical style contains elements borrowed, confiscated, appropriated, adjusted, and adapted from various sources and constructed together through various practices to become what its producers and audiences claim it to be—a national/authentic/indigenous form of music.

Thus even popular music that producers claim is the folk or traditional music of given nations, thereby implying historical depth and local authenticity, is often a modern construction created from various sources to fit the needs and interests of modern nation-states. Baily (1981, 1994), for example, has demonstrated how radio-broadcasting practices brought together folk music from different regions and ethnic groups in Afghanistan, synthesized them by using Hindustani music theory, and performed them with a variety of instruments, including Western, to create the *kiliwali* style as the national popular music of the country, signifying modern Afghan nationhood.

In a similar way, the Indonesian hybrid style of *kroncong* (Becker 1981; Manuel 1988), or modernized traditional Arab music in mid-twentieth-century Egypt (Danielson 1996; Racy 1982), although they contain various Western elements, came to signify the national uniqueness, indigenous heritage, and cultural separatism of the state—that is, concepts strongly advocated by and associated with traditional variants of national cultures.

But where folk-derived popular music still claims some sort of cultural purity and uniqueness—especially when it comes to issues of national and other collective identities—other forms of popular music do not. That contemporary, late-twentieth-century styles of pop/rock are hybrids is a given, almost taken-for-granted feature of their existence. Less obvious, however, is the claim made by musicians, producers, and audiences associated with pop/rock cultures for legitimacy and recognition as national music, despite their Anglo-American components.

Facing accusations of imitation of American music and of abandoning the national heritage, speakers for national rock cultures in many countries insist on the local authentic nature of their specific form of rock music. Pointing to the use of local language in the lyrics and to fusions with folk styles, they argue that rock is no less of a national type of music than any other, thereby demanding legitimacy and recognition. For example, in his study of Chinese popular music, Jones quotes an appraisal of the song "I Have Nothing" by Cui Jian, the prominent Chinese rock musician, in the Chinese *People's Daily:*

> What the song exposes, is the feeling of a whole generation: their sadness, their perplexity. . . . The song's use of the deep, desolate tone of the folk music of the Northwestern plateau, and its coarse rhythms are well suited for this purpose. . . . "I Have Nothing" can also be called the seminal work of Chinese rock. It fuses European and American rock with traditional Chinese music, creating a rock music with a strong Chinese flavor. (Jones 1992: 134)

In other words, local commentators relating to national styles of rock music interpret them as expressions of a collective will for change, a demand to open up what they perceive to be conservative and rigid national cultures to contemporary artistic innovations and to progressive cultural trends (on the "rock nacional" movement in Argentina, see also Vila 1987; on rock in the former communist bloc in Eastern Europe, see Ramet 1994; and on rock in Russia, see Cushman 1995). Local and national styles of rock tend to go hand in hand with globalized variants of national cultures.

Ethnic, regional, and other sectorial forms of popular music within given nation-states are sometimes expressions of movements for separation and independence. Nevertheless, in many cases, such music cultures are part of a larger demand for legitimacy and recognition, for inclusion within the context of the given national culture. Thus in Turkey, the popular-music culture of *arabesk* emerged among migrants who, after the 1950s, came to the country's major cities from the rural southeast and found themselves living in squatter towns. The music came to express resentment of the rapid urbanization, modernization, and Westernization of the country and a demand to retain an "Eastern" Turkish culture associated with Arab and Muslim culture (Stokes 1992).

Similar demands to redefine "Britishness" in light of the large Asian sector in the United Kingdom can be found in musicians' and audiences' discourse on *bhangra* rock (Banerji 1988; Sharma, Hutnyk, and Sharma 1996); and to reformulate "Frenchness" or "Italianness" in the ethnic and regional rap and hip-hop cultures that emerged in those countries in the 1980s and 1990s (Gross, McMurray, and Swedenburg 1994; Mitchell 1995).

As comparative studies of contemporary popular music have pointed out, the global flow of musical materials—that is, structures of melody and harmony, patterns of rhythm, use of musical instruments—does not diminish the belief of musicians and audiences in the national authenticity of the popular music that they produce and consume in their countries (Frith 1989; Taylor 1997). On the contrary, the rise of the transnational music culture, and its omnipresence within most countries of the world, increases the efforts of local popular-music communities to redefine and insist on the existence of their own national music styles. This is done either by pop/rock musicians who "indigenize" transnational music by fusing it with elements perceived as local (language, melodies, modes of vocal delivery, instruments) to produce new national or contemporary ethnic music (Campbell Robinson et al. 1991), or by purists who attempt to preserve and conserve what they believe is their traditional folk music. The resulting struggle over what type of music is national determines the logic of national fields of popular music.

THIS BOOK

Our contention here is that in Israel the struggle for institutionalized national music can be defined in terms of musical representation because the social forces at work created and promoted musical styles that are different enough in their inner components to be singled out for study. This book considers popular music to be a field of national music. We examine the Israeli field of popular music as a cultural site in which three major types of Israeli popular music are engaged in a cultural contest and a struggle for the formulation of Israeliness in music, and the construction of Israeli popular music. They are Shirei Eretz Yisrael (Songs of the Land of Israel—SLI), the "folk" music of Israel; Israeli rock; and musiqa mizrahit, the major ethnic popular music. We present each of these in its historical perspective, discuss its evolution and transformations, and examine the complex relationships among them.

Part I of this study consists of two chapters: one, a general introduction to the major positions and strands in Israeli culture; and two, a review of the major institutions and organizations within which popular music is and has been produced, disseminated, and consumed in Israel. Part II examines the phenomena most clearly connected to nationalist ideology, the music that parallels the "invented tradition" strand of the national ideology: Shirei Eretz Yisrael, the "folk" music of Israel (Chapter 3); the early, prerock popular music (Chapter 4); the unique phenomenon of *lehaqot tzvayiot*, the army ensembles (Chapter 5); and the festivals and contests that encourage local production of popular music (Chapter 6). Part III focuses on the music most clearly belonging to the globalized variant of Israeli culture: Israeli rock. Chapter 7 discusses the first generation, in particular the founders of Israeli rock in the 1970s; further developments and strands of rock in the 1980s and 1990s are examined in Chapter 8. Part IV looks at musiqa mizrahit, ethnic popular music in Israel that was initially labeled as "other," and its struggle for legitimacy and recognition. The emergence of the genre is traced in Chapter 9; its rise and success is described in Chapter 10. We conclude with a general discussion of popular music and Israeliness.

Two things should be emphasized at the outset. First, we are well aware that this book does not deal with all the forms, styles, and scenes of popular music in Israel. Among the expressions of popular music excluded from this text or only treated briefly are music associated with the religious expressions of the various ethnic Jewish communities, such as Klezmer music, or the *piyyutim* (religious poetry) of the Sephardi and *mizrahi* Jews; popular music among Palestinian citizens of Israel; the extensive scene of "world music" in Israel; and some other micromusic associated with various local communities (Slobin 1993). The book intentionally concentrates on the major music cultures that have participated in the attempts to invent and construct indigenous Israeli popular music. In other words, we focus on those individual and collective actors whose music making has been aimed at, or appropriated by, the central Zionist project of inventing a new, "native" Jewish national culture in Israel. Second, this book has no pretensions at being an encyclopedic source of knowledge regarding popular music in Israel. Indeed, we mention a large number of names and facts—songs, albums, authors, performers, and others—and examine the careers and works of selected musicians as paradigms of crucial phenomena. Yet the book does not discuss all the personalities that may have some claim to having made important contributions to the history of popular music in Israel. This task remains a desideratum for future publications.

PART I

Cultural and Institutional Contexts

1   A Short Introduction to Israeli Culture

Zionist settlement in Palestine (as the country was called during the centuries when it was part of the Ottoman Empire and later the British Mandate) began in the last two decades of the nineteenth century and continued with further waves of Jewish immigration during the thirty years of British rule after World War I. These are conventionally known as the five waves of *'aliyah*—that is, the "first 'aliyah," the "second 'aliyah," and so on. By 1948, when the State of Israel was established as a Jewish state and fought its War of Independence, there were some 600,000 Jews in Israel, the overwhelming majority of whom came from countries in Eastern and Central Europe. By 1952, the Jewish population had almost tripled with the arrival of more European Jews (many of them Holocaust survivors) and, most significantly, large waves of immigration from Arab and Muslim countries (Yemen, Iraq, and Morocco were among the largest). The 1948 war forced the majority of the Arab Palestinian population to leave that part of their country in which the State of Israel was established. Those who stayed became an Arab minority that, by the late 1990s, comprised approximately 20 percent of the total population.

By 1998, the Jewish population of Israel numbered approximately five million, and the Arab-Palestinian minority, one million. Defined as a "Jewish state," Israel has adapted Jewish religion, tradition, symbolism, and mythology to its modern, secular nationalistic purposes; therefore, for the "primordial" school of nationalism research, it exemplifies the perfect case of "Diaspora nationalism" (Smith 1995). But Zionism, as a set of cultural practices in Palestine and later in Israel, evolved around two major, interrelated themes: the rejection of the culture of the Jewish Diaspora (the *galut*, that is, the existence of Jews in scattered communities in many different countries) and the invention of a "new" Jew, the Hebrew person, the Israeli.

Zionist vocabulary referred to normalizing the Jewish way of life: as opposed to the "abnormal" mode of national existence in Diaspora, a "normal" mode was sought in Israel, with the model of normalcy taken directly from nineteenth-century European nationalism (Schweid 1984; Raz-Krakotzkin 1993–94; Even-Zohar 1981; Ohana 1995). That is, the construction of Israeli separatism, its exclusion mechanism, aimed not only at the neighboring Palestinians for whom Israel/Palestine was also a homeland (Eyal 1996), but also at Diaspora Jewish culture. In contrast, within the mechanisms of inclusion, it emphasized Jewish-Hebrew nativeness. Thus, from an early stage, the dominant cultural practices among Zionist settlers in Palestine were aimed at inventing a locally specific, native Jewish culture, different from traditional, galut Jewish cultures.

> In the case of Jewish nationalism . . . it was not a preexisting national culture that aroused and created a national revival but the opposite: the nationalist movement was the major generator of the new national culture. . . . [T]he cultural revival was perceived as a comprehensive process incorporating not only the "high" culture of literature and the arts but also the recreation of norms, values and aesthetics. (Shimoni 1996: XIV, summarizing Shavit 1996)

Initially, in the formative period—the prestate *Yishuv* period (Yishuv, or settlement, is the term commonly used to denote the autonomous Jewish community in Palestine before 1948)—and the first ten to fifteen years of statehood, until approximately 1960, this logic resulted in the successful invention and public imposition of a dominant cultural package known as "Hebrew culture" *(tarbut 'ivrit)*. In subsequent decades, Hebrewism was challenged by emerging variants of Israeliness. Most prominent of these were what we call "globalized Israeliness," which embodied a mixture of Hebrewism and the effects of the globalization of culture, and the variant known in Israeli public culture as "oriental Israeliness" *(Israeliyut mizraḥit* or *mizraḥiyut)*, in which Israelis of oriental origin—that is, originally from Arab and Muslim countries—insisted on the Israeliness of their specific cultural hybrid. Additional variants such as "Religious Israeliness" and one that can awkwardly be termed "Palestinian Israeliness" (or "Israeli Palestinianness") also emerged as self-proclaimed contenders for the definition of Israeliness.

The existence of these variants as different entities was expressed in various fields of cultural production in both "popular" and "high" art forms. Despite occasional claims to "native" or Jewish authenticity, each of the variants should be viewed as a hybrid, a mixture of elements taken from various readily available sources. Their claim to Israeliness was largely based on the locally specific nature of these mixtures and on the use of Hebrew as their natural language.

HEBREWISM *('IVRIUT):* TRADITIONAL ISRAELINESS

Hebrewism is a set of cultural practices and works in various fields of art invented during the formative years of Israeli society. It was mainly created by the first generations of locally born or educated Jews, with the manifest purpose of comprising the cultural material through which the new Jewish entity in Israel would be experienced and practiced. Its producers called it "Hebrew culture" (tarbut 'ivrit), and, following them, we will refer to it as Hebrewism *('ivriut).*

The core of Hebrewism was the institutionalization of the routine daily use of Hebrew as a native tongue, as the vernacular. Modern, secular use of Hebrew in literature, poetry, and song began in the nineteenth century among Jews in Europe—that is, writers for whom Hebrew was not a native tongue. Their work was "realism without vernacular" (Alter 1988). For the Israeli context, the crucial event regarding the use of Hebrew occurred among Zionist high-school teachers in Palestine in the second decade of the twentieth century. This was labeled the "conflict of languages" and debated which language should be used in teaching. The victory of those favoring Hebrew over the supporters of European languages determined Hebrew as the native tongue for the locally born generations to come.

By 1947, there were some 80,000 locally born Jews in Palestine between the ages of ten and twenty-five, the children of Zionist settlers. (This figure is based on data drawn from the Population Registry of the State of Israel, as part of a study of first names of Israeli-born Jews; see Weitman 1982, 1987.) Encouraged by their parents' view of them as the "generation of the resurrection," they began to cultivate a sense of difference, an ideology of Hebrew "nativeness," during the 1930s. This sense of identity evolved into the image of the *sabra,* the prototype of the Hebrew person, the somewhat Nietzschean image of the "new Jew" (see Almog 2000; Ben-Eliezer 1998). It materialized through various forms of cultural production, including secular adaptations and reinterpretations of Jewish religious and traditional elements, rituals invoking a mythic connection to the landscape and biblical history, and attempts to design indigenous styles of painting and sculpture (Zerubavel 1995; Ben-Yehuda 1995; Katriel 1991).

Two genres of art forms were institutionalized in Israeli culture as the great signifiers of the period and spirit of Hebrewism. The first is the generation of writers and poets collectively known as *dor ba-aretz* (generation in the land), mainly because of their representation and appraisal of the sabra (Shaked 1987; Alter 1994). The other, which will be treated extensively in Part II, is the body of popular music known as Shirei Eretz Yisrael (Songs of the Land of Israel) and its accompanying typical performance ritual, *shira be-tzibbur* (lit., communal singing; singing in public).

In the 1950s, during the first decade of statehood, Hebrewism became the major component of the official, state-supported culture. The educational system, the army, all types of state ceremonies, the tourist industry, and the public media all worked to present and impose Hebrewism as the "One Israeli Culture." Hebrewist works of art—high and popular—as well as the vocabulary of everyday cultural practices became the dominant national cultural capital and habitus. The masses of immigrants who arrived in the country during this period were expected to become "Israelis," to become culturally "absorbed" into Israeliness. Veterans were also expected to remain faithful to Hebrewism, to an ideologically mobilized, collectivist mode of cultural performance and artistic practice.

> It was perhaps within this framework that the specific Israeli problem of conservatism versus "innovation" was most pronounced, caused by the continuous weakening of adherence to the ideology which was, in turn, paradoxically due to the successful institutionalization of some of the major values and symbols implied. These included strong collective identification and the widespread acceptance of the "pioneering" ideal and of most of the Zionist premises. At the same time, the acceptance of these values often created lack of patience with fully crystallized ideological formulations which began to seem obvious and trite. (Eisenstadt 1967: 385)

Thus after the 1960s came the slow emergence of globalized Israeliness, not as a straightforward revolt against Hebrewism, but as an attempt to modernize it, to make Israeliness less separatist and more open to contemporary world culture.

From the 1970s, Hebrewism lost much of its dominant presence in everyday public culture. Yet state agencies and the educational system secured its status as traditional culture. As a signifier of rootedness, of early beginnings, Hebrewism remains an active cultural actor in the Israeli field of national culture. Moreover, some of its practices reemerged as contemporary factors in public culture when they were appropriated by the younger generations of the national-religious groups, the "neo-Zionists" (Ram 1996), in the 1980s. In other words, Hebrewism never lost its forceful position in the Israeli field of national culture.

GLOBALIZED ISRAELINESS

The term "globalized Israeliness" is used here to refer to the set of cultural materials associated with the local adaptation of the effects of the globalization of culture. It refers to the emergence of Israeli consumerism, a strong sense of critique in the arts, and a pervasive culture industry. In contrast to the emphasis of Hebrewism on Israeliness as a separate universe of meanings, different from others, globalized Israeliness insists on and constructs Israeliness as a local extension of contemporary world culture. In the arts, globalized Israeliness is practiced with close affinity to the "transnational culture of critical discourse" (Hannerz 1990) and as an integral part of contemporary "mediascapes" and "ideoscapes" (Appadurai 1990). Israeliness, or ideology of nativeness, interprets the adoption of the cultural materials previously perceived as foreign and not fitting local culture, as the accomplishment of a normalization theme in Zionist ideology. That is, if constructing a new, native Jewish culture means normalizing Jewish life, making it a nation like any other, then Israeli culture should be in line with enlightened national cultures of the world. Globalized Israeli culture, as a hybrid, is therefore basically a mixture of materials and meanings inherited from Hebrewism and materials borrowed, adapted, and adjusted from contemporary world culture. As in other countries on the periphery of the West, the internal impetus for the emergence of this variant was a sort of revolt against a state-supported traditional culture that coincided with admiration for and fascination with the contents and meanings of modernist Western culture, especially post–1960s culture (Bar Haim 1990). The aim was to produce a cultural entity that would be, at one and the same time, an extension of global culture and a variant of local-national culture. The change from Hebrewism to globalized Israeliness is often perceived as part of the move from a collectivist mode of conduct to an individualist mode (Roniger and Feige 1992).

In the arts, globalized Israeliness is best represented in the works of the literary generation known as *dor ha-medina* and in the emergence of Israeli "personal cinema" and Israeli rock (treated extensively in Part III). The conscious ideological critical stance taken by the auteurs of Israeli "personal cinema," combined with their affinity for international art cinema, characterizes the high-culture work within globalized Israeliness in other art forms as well (Shohat 1989). While trying to be modernist and well connected to recent trends and developments in their respective art fields, and thus universalist in orientation, they remain committed to national culture, using their art to constantly examine and explore what Israeliness is, was, and should be. At the popular level, Israeli rock is the one of the most salient examples of this variant.

When it emerged, globalized Israeliness tended to present its works of art as reflecting a heretical break with Hebrewism. Criticizing the insistence of the latter on cultural separatism of the nation, on cultural purism, on ideological mobilization, globalized Israeliness emphasized openness to and participation in contemporary trends of global culture. Globalized Israeli artworks, produced mainly within a market-oriented culture industry, gained recognition and eventually dominance. In the process, the critique of Hebrewism was gradually replaced with an emphasis on respect for Hebrewism as the formative phase of Israeliness. In other words, after heresy was successfully employed as a cultural strategy for gaining a presence and later legitimacy in the field of national culture, it was replaced by a strategy of "honoring the elders," in order to produce and sustain a belief in the continuity of heritage for this variant of the national culture.

MIZRAḤIYUT (ORIENTALISM): ETHNIC ISRAELINESS

A sense of difference between oriental Jews, that is, those who lived in Muslim countries, sometimes collectively known as Sephardim (from Sepharad, medieval Spain, from where many of the Jews in Muslim countries originate), and Western Jews, those who lived in Christian countries (except Spain), sometimes called Ashkenazim, existed long before Zionism. Except for a few places (most notably Latin America, Italy, Holland, or the pre-Zionist community in Palestine), these two categories of Jews had almost no opportunity to live together. After the Holocaust, oriental Jews consisted of about 20 percent of world Jewry. During the first two decades of Israeli statehood, the majority of oriental Jews (especially from the largest communities of Morocco, Yemen, and Iraq), immigrated to Israel, coming thereby to comprise about 50 percent of the Jewish population of the country (Dellapergola and Cohen 1992). Their encounter with the local cultural reality was characterized by the demand made on them to join Hebrewism. Viewed by the Hebrewist cultural establishment through its European "orientalist" prism (in Said's 1978 connotation), oriental Jews were perceived as premodern and "primitive." They, or rather the second and third generations, born and educated in Israel, were expected to modernize and become "Israelis": to adopt the image of the "new Jew," the sabra. But these same perceptions produced institutional mechanisms of discrimination and stratification that first caused and then reproduced the obvious failure of these immigrants or most of their subsequent generations to become Israelis of the Hebrewist variant. Sociopolitical and economic power relations in Israel were thus determined for generations to come. (On Israeli ethnicity in the spheres of politics, stratification, and inequality, see, for example, Ben-Rafael 1982; Cohen 1972, 1983; Smooha 1978; Swirski 1989; see also the work of early Israeli anthropology on the cultural practices that emerged among the first generation of mizrahi immigrants in response to the absorption policies of the state, especially in rural areas: Shokeid 1971; Deshen and Shokeid 1974; Goldberg 1977; Weingrod 1985.)

However, by the 1970s and into the 1980s, the second and third generations of these immigrants—that is, those born and educated in Israel—had articulated their sense of difference, their local identity, into a set of cultural practices and products usually referred to in Israel, by those representing this variant and by others, as mizrahiyut, or orientalism. The term implies a position of ethnicity vis-à-vis Hebrewism and globalized Israeliness, which are generally regarded as Western or Ashkenazi variants. Speakers for mizrahiyut tend to parallel the stance of this variant of Israeliness toward globalized Israeliness to former colonial and other ethnic minorities in the West, and to the stance of Third World cultures vis-à-vis Eurocentric dominant and colonial cultures (Shohat 1988).

Mizrahiyut, as a variant of Israeliness, is a cultural context in which materials from several sources fuse to construct its specificity as a hybrid. These sources include traditional Jewish culture from Arab and Muslim countries, various Arab national cultures, Hebrewism, and contemporary global culture. Since the 1970s, cultural producers of and speakers for mizrahiyut have been insisting on the "nativeness" and Israeliness of their particular cultural hybrid, demanding recognition and legitimacy and rebelling against what they perceive to be the stigmatizing label of "ethnicity."

Like other "new ethnicities" in recent decades (Hall 1996), the cultural endeavor of mizrahiyut began with the rejection of its racial representation in hegemonic culture, together with the acceptance of the homogenized image portrayed in it. That is, acceptance of mizrahiyut as a collective entity, as an experience of sameness (despite the obvious differences between, for example, Moroccan, Yemenite, and Iraqi Jews), but rejection of the meanings and connotations attributed to the entity as a whole. Using this collective image to construct an affirmative sense of difference, mizrahiyut evolved into reexamination of its roots and its relations with the dominant culture.

Class connotations have connected mizrahiyut to primarily popular cultural forms, of which musiqa mizrahit is the most prominent (and is treated extensively in Part IV). Another form associated with mizrahiyut is the *burekas* film genre of the 1970s (named after an oriental pastry of Turkish origins that was associated with mizrahi Jews). Usually a stereotypical representation of mizrahi protagonists and culture by Ashkenazi directors and scriptwriters, and critically dismissed as lacking artistic value, the genre is nevertheless retrospectively appraised as including in its portrayal of mizrahiyut a strong element of "carnivalesque" social criticism of dominant Ashkenazi culture (Shohat 1989). In the 1990s, several films of a more artistic nature reaffirmed the Arab elements of mizrahiyut, demanding, in effect, their legitimacy within Israeli culture. A similar stance toward cultural politics can be found in the literature and poetry of mizrahiyut (see the special issue of *The Literary Review* 37, no. 2 [1994]).

Relegated by Hebrewism and by globalized Israeliness to the inferior position of ethnic culture, mizrahi cultural practices initially accepted this inclusive ethnic identity, in order to be able later to insist on the native-Israeli nature of their specific hybrid. Against the honor afforded by the traditional status of Hebrewism, and the contemporary dominance of globalized Israeliness, mizrahiyut presented itself as a major alternative, as the "other," which is, in fact, "true" Israeliness.

RELIGIOUS ISRAELINESS

In some way and to some extent most Israeli Jews observe the Jewish religion (Kedem 1991). In this regard, even those who observe the minimum of religious edicts enforced by state legislation can be categorized as belonging to one of several patterns of Israeli Judaism (Deshen 1978). Conventionally, however, in Israel the term "religious" is conferred on those who conscientiously observe the totality of Jewish religious practices (partial observance is referred to as being "traditional," and "secular" is the term used for the occasional or minimal observance practiced by the majority of Israeli Jews). Religious Israeliness is therefore used here to refer to the clusters of cultural practices that have one major theme in common: the belief, and indeed the wish, that Israeli culture should completely overlap Jewish religion.

The commitment to culture as religion, to religion as totality, produces within this variant an emphasis on "Jewishness" more than on Israeliness—especially among the ultraorthodox factions of this variant. The scanty discussion of religious Israeliness here stems from the relative absence of distinct artistic production within this variant and its resulting absence from the arena of national culture so far as the production of national artistic canons is concerned. It should be stressed that in other cultural spheres, such as the construction of historical myths and narratives, political ideology, or public culture of everyday life, this variant has a salient presence. This is especially true of the two factions of religious Israeliness that can properly be called "Israeli," because they are indigenous hybrids of Jewish religion within the Israeli-Zionist context. These are the Religious Zionist (or National-Religious) faction and the orthodox mizrahi faction.

Religious Zionism became a significant presence in the ideological and cultural fields during the 1970s and 1980s, in the wake of the Six-Day War of 1967 and the consequent movement of Israeli settlement into the territories occupied in that war. Leading that movement, the younger generation of the religious faction of Zionism adopted the image of being the true inheritors of the pioneering spirit and practice of Hebrewism. They appropriated various aspects of sabra culture and merged them with the practice of modernized Jewish orthodoxy. The result, known in Israel as the culture of the mitnahalim (settlers, mostly on the West Bank) or Gush Emunim (the Bloc of the Faithful), emerged as an indigenous hybrid of Israeli religious nationalism (Ram 1996; Aran 1986, 1988).

The second religious faction, the orthodox mizrahim, also arose in the 1970s and 1980s. Revolting against their subjugation to the patterns of Ashkenazi orthodoxy in the earlier decades of statehood, they created an indigenous hybrid of religious practices in which some of the already incorporated patterns of Ashkenazi orthodoxy merged with elements of mizrahi religious practices. The resulting hybrid became a major movement within religious Israeliness and within Israeli politics.

ISRAELI PALESTINIANNESS/PALESTINIAN ISRAELINESS

Approximately 20 percent of Israeli citizens are Palestinian Arabs. Surveys and other research demonstrate that they perceive themselves as an integral part of the Palestinian people (Smooha 1992; Rouhana 1997). Yet their constant and continuous contact with Israeliness as a Jewish national culture, their citizenship in the State of Israel, and their relative disconnectedness from the rest of the Palestinian people (especially between 1948 and 1967) have produced a specific cultural setting, different from that of Palestinians in the territories occupied by Israel in 1967. Their identity as Israeli Palestinians is not merely a legal-administrative status enforced on them by historical circumstances, but an actual sense of difference and uniqueness (Rabinowitz 1997). Their position in the field of national culture is therefore marked by a certain dualism. On the one hand, there is insistence on autonomy and Arabness, on being an Israeli variant of a larger Palestinian identity. On the other hand, there is a demand for presence and legitimacy within Israeli culture, for being a Palestinian variant of Israeliness. The language of their literary work is one indication of this dualism. Distancing itself from Israeliness, Palestinian Arabic literature in Israel is characterized by strong opposition and resistance-based themes that attempt to undermine the hegemonic control of the Jews (Snir 1995).

Yet a group of poets and writers who choose to write in Hebrew represents a position that places itself within Israeliness. The cultural-political meaning of the use of Hebrew is in fact "to un-Judaize the Hebrew language . . . to make it more Israeli and less Jewish" (Shamas 1989, quoted in Snir 1995: 165; see also Hever 1987). In other words, cultural practices that represent Palestinian Israeliness have one major consequence for the existence of Israeli culture: they add a non-Jewish variant to the local field of national culture, and thus contest the Jewish exclusiveness of that culture.

THE FIELD OF NATIONAL CULTURE IN ISRAEL

Various events, processes, and phenomena of the 1990s led to debates among academic and media commentators as to whether Israeliness, as it is traditionally understood, still exists. A major phenomenon in this context is the arrival, during the 1990s, of approximately one million immigrants from the former Soviet Union. Many maintain strong connections with Russian culture and, from a cultural elitist standpoint, reject all variants of Israeli culture as "vulgar," "shallow," "uncivilized," and so on. Consequently, the new Russian community in Israel constructed a segregated cultural context of media, literature, and music—all in the Russian language.

Another salient phenomenon is the emergence, in recent years, of a large population (estimated at 250,000) of foreign workers from countries such as Ghana, Nigeria, Colombia, Chile, Romania, Thailand, China, and the Philippines. Their visible presence and emerging social demands have also affected traditional perceptions of Israeli culture (see Kemp et al. 2000).

Finally, the ideological differences between "right" and "left" regarding the relationship with the Palestinians, and the divergent civil and religious perceptions vis-à-vis the nature of law and public culture, intensified following the assassination of Prime Minister Yitzhak Rabin on November 4, 1995.

In light of these developments, one common feature of commentaries on Israel in the late 1990s is its portrayal as consisting of a series of subcultures, or quasi-separate communities. These are characterized as "possessing more or less separate institutional and territorial bases (residential quarters, towns, and even regions) . . . distinctly located in terms of social stratification, possessing autonomous educational systems, communication networks, cultural institutions, different kinds of authorities and leadership" (Kimmerling 1999: 29).

One implication suggested by such descriptions is that the commitment to Israeliness as a national culture is being eroded and is even disappearing. Indeed, the vocabulary of the ensuing debate on Israeli society and culture centers on the phrase "post-Zionism" as a descriptive concept for the current situation of Israel. It also includes a reexamination of the so-called major narrative of Zionism by a group of critical academics who came to be known as the "new historians" (see the special issue of *History and Memory* 7 [1995]; Ram 1996).

Whether these new phenomena will indeed undermine the commitment to Israeliness as an underlying doxa has yet to be seen. But currently, the struggle for recognition, legitimacy, and dominance between Hebrewism, globalized Israeliness, mizraḥiyut, religious Israeliness, and Palestinian Israeliness includes practices of borrowing, adoption, adaptation, appropriation, and co-optation of cultural materials between the different variants. That is, as part of one variant's attempt to gain legitimacy, claim continuity of heritage, and demonstrate commitment to the nationalist idea, cultural producers associated with it sometimes use works originally associated with another variant in a mode typical of their own. Initially, most variants do this by using works and meanings associated with Hebrewism, the traditional variant. But the logic of the quest for Israeliness encourages other appropriations as well. Thus globalized Israeliness appropriates elements of mizraḥiyut, mizraḥiyut adopts materials from globalized Israeliness, Palestinian Israeliness borrows from all Jewish variants, and all Jewish variants appropriate Palestinian cultural elements. As a result, a body of cultural elements and specific works in various fields of art has come to exist within different variants of the national culture, albeit with a slightly different meaning attributed to them within each variant. This body of elements and works has come to be identified as "all-national," as the core of national culture.

2   Israeli Institutions of Popular Music

Production, distribution, and consumption of popular music are embedded within an institutional complex. The major organizations acting within this complex are the music industry, the media, and certain state and public bodies. The structure and interests of these organizations create certain confinements, or institutional constraints, on the cultural dynamics of popular music. These constraints are sometimes interpreted as major explanatory variables of changes in style, genre, and meaning in popular music (Peterson and Berger 1971, 1975; Peterson 1990). Therefore, insofar as our study of popular music in Israel focuses on nationalism, identity, ideology, and artistic beliefs as the major concepts determining changes of style and meaning in Israeli popular music, the role of the music industry, the media, and relevant institutions cannot be underestimated. The Israeli record industry and the media (especially radio), as well as the educational system and other public bodies, have played a major role in the attempt to shape the national repertory of local popular music. By providing the material infrastructure for the existence of popular music, determining the extent of public exposure to various genres, styles, and musicians, and evaluating musical practices of all types, Israel's popular-music institutions have been the organizational tools through which the various cultural interests were pursued and achieved. Generally speaking, the organizational field of popular music in Israel has moved from a locus for massive state and public involvement in the early years, to a highly complex, sophisticated, and independent culture industry in the 1990s. From a sociological perspective, this change exemplifies a logic of organizational isomorphism (DiMaggio and Powell 1983) and imbrication within the structure of the global music industry, that is, a logic of adoption and imitation of organizational and professional patterns and practices from larger, transnational organizations of popular music that set international cultural standards in this field (Meyer 1997).

MUSIC EDUCATION

The construction of a new native Hebrew culture was one of the main aspirations of the Zionist enterprise. Music, embedded in both Hebrew songs and dances, was perceived as a promising field for the symbolic fulfillment of these aspirations. To lead the heterogeneous immigrant Jewish society in Palestine toward consumption of and identification with the new music, institutions of music education and distribution needed to be established.

Institutionalized music education during the Yishuv period related to the teaching of Hebrew songs and dances as a vehicle for socialization into the new Hebrew culture and became a pivotal ideal of the leaders of the Zionist movement. Aware of the difficulties involved in creating a new musical culture from scratch, the Zionists admitted that diasporic (or, galuti) and foreign musical elements should be incorporated into the emergent native Hebrew music and dance (Even-Zohar 1981). The purpose of institutionalized music education was therefore to find the mechanisms to transmit, through music and dance, the idea of a new Hebrew national culture to the young sabra generation. At the same time, employing Jewish or foreign musical elements denoted a link to the Jewish past or to non-Jewish cultures. This tension between the "original" and the "foreign," characteristic of the early debates on music education in the Yishuv and in the state, is the embryo of the dilemmas found in later discourse on popular music in Israel. The perception of global popular music as an "enemy" of Hebrew culture was a common theme as early as the 1930s.

A clear line divides the organization of centralized music education in the prestate and the statehood periods. During the early Yishuv period, that is, up to the third 'aliyah (1919), music education was meager and private, in the sense that almost no institutions of music education or mechanisms for the mass distribution of music existed (on different aspects of music education in the early period, see Hirshberg 1996). Moreover, the scarcity of dedicated musicians, professional or amateur, limited the invention of new Hebrew songs. Many of the new songs created in this period were actually Hebrew translations or adaptations of new Hebrew texts to diasporic Jewish songs or foreign, mainly Yiddish and Russian, folk songs.

With the third and fourth 'aliyot (1919–26), the situation of musical culture changed rapidly and dramatically. Two centers of musical activity evolved: in the urban center of Tel Aviv, and in the communal agricultural settlements, the *kibbutzim*. Music education in the kibbutzim was supported by the Music Section of the Center for Culture (Merkaz le-Tarbut) of the Histadrut (the General Federation of Hebrew Workers in Eretz Yisrael), the powerful Israeli labor union established in 1919 (Marom 1997). In the city, musical conservatories and academies dedicated to the training of musicians in the Western art-music tradition emerged. In both the city and on agricultural settlements, a major venue for the introduction of the public to the new Hebrew song was shirah be-tzibbur (communal singing), an institution that exists in Israeli society to the present day.

Communal singing was organized by the labor movement or by local councils. It consisted of more or less formal gatherings held in public auditoriums (in Tel Aviv) or in the communal dining room (on kibbutzim) with the purpose of singing and of learning new songs. These events were directed by leaders who accompanied themselves on a piano or accordion. A similar setting existed for learning folk dances (Rubin 1981). The crucial importance of communal singing is stressed by influential music educator and critic Menashe Ravina (Rabinovitch 1899–1968) in a letter to the Ministry of Education dated March 31, 1949: "Singing in public is one of the best means to unify the masses and to inculcate the new melos being created in our country. Singing in public has also a great value of teaching the Hebrew language to the new immigrants. There is a need to create a group of leaders who will know not only the melody but also the meaning of the lyrics" (quoted in Hirshberg 1995: 236).

This ideological use of new folk songs and dances as a means of socialization into the new Hebrew culture was never strong enough to resist alternative sources of musical enculturation. Of particular significance were the emergent mass media (for example, films, records, or radio broadcasts after 1936) and popular venues of entertainment, such as the musical theaters and cabarets imported from Europe by bourgeois immigrants from Poland and Germany. Even in the most ideological and centralized of all social settings, the kibbutz, there were varied approaches to musical education. For example, in the geographical vicinity of the Jezreel Valley in the 1930s, there was a polemic between the "originalists," who advocated the exclusive use of new Hebrew songs in the schools and at public events, versus the "universalists," who advocated the use of the best that Western classic music had to offer, to be performed in Hebrew translation (Shafran 1996).

After statehood, centralized state support for music education and musical production became the formal policy of the first Israeli government. This policy was institutionalized with the establishment of the Office of the

Inspector-General of Music Education at the Ministry of Education, within the framework of the adoption of a universal public education system for the new country. The first inspector was Dr. Barukh Ben Yehuda. In addition, the High Council for Music was established in 1950 with pianist, conductor, and composer Frank Peleg (1910–68) as its first chairman (Hirshberg 1999: 237–38). The office of the inspector exists to this day, though its power to affect Israeli musical culture has lessened in the last three decades. The council evolved into the Music Department of the Council for Culture and the Arts and is still the advisory body of the government on the allocation of state support to musical performers and composers.

The early programs of music education designed by the Music Inspectorate reveal a cosmopolitan, yet elitist, approach. Although basically oriented toward acquiring the tools of Western art music, the programs also recommended teaching Israeli folk songs (of which, by 1948, there was already a well-defined repertory), Arabic and Hindu modes, and traditional Jewish music, particularly biblical cantillation (Schiff Wingrad 1954). Despite its high ideals, the actual effects of this idealistic program for music education on the Israeli population appear to have been tangential.

According to Mizrahi (1983), despite the centralization of official music education, its actual development was diversified along different ideological perceptions of Israeli culture. Three contrasting views of the goals of music education in Israel evolved between 1948 and 1980: socialization, acculturation, and individualization. The first approach was intended to create a balanced "common musical denominator" for Israelis of different ethnic backgrounds. The second view attempted to repress the particularity of the music of the different ethnic Jewish groups (especially the oriental Jews) by forcing everybody into a Western-oriented musical culture. The third approach, unlike the first two, stressed the individual skills of gifted children as the focus of musical education, leaving aside socializing or acculturative goals. Mizrahi also found differences in the approach to music education among the three official branches of the Israeli public education system: secular urban, kibbutz, and religious schools.

The reality of elementary school life was, however, that much of the music education during the 1950s and 1960s consisted of lessons of shirah be-tzibbur by pupils and the teacher. Thus these lessons were conventionally referred to in the vernacular language of both pupils and teachers as a *shi'ur le-zimrah* (singing lesson) and the teacher was known as *ha-morah le-zimrah* (the singing teacher).

In both the Yishuv and the early state periods, one feature that related to the public discourse about musical education stood out: the perception that global popular-music styles are a real threat to the successful implantation of the new Hebrew musical culture among Israeli youth. Already in the late 1930s, Binyamin Omer (Hatuli), a folk-song composer and music educator from kibbutz Merḥavia in the Jezreel Valley, expressed his dismay at the "spirit of the film hits and the street songs" that pervaded the gatherings of the labor youth movements (Hatuli 1940, quoted in Hirshberg 1995: 155–56).

We can see that there was an attempt in the early stages of the history of Israel to recruit music education as a means for socializing new immigrants into the ethos of the new Hebrew culture. As time progressed, this attempt to manipulate music education lost ground in the face of the growing domination of the mass media over the national soundscape. Eventually, the recognition of the power of the mass media as a vehicle for musical enculturation, and of multiculturalism as a feature of contemporary Israeli society, led to major changes in the music education system, including the incorporation of mainstream Israeli popular songs and ethnic music into school curricula.

The Histadrut

The Histadrut, the General Federation of Hebrew Workers in Eretz Yisrael, played a key role in the shaping of music education in the Yishuv. The Histadrut was a unique case in the history of Western labor movements. During the Yishuv period, it developed quasi-state institutions and thus functioned for a large sector of the Jewish community in Palestine as a state within a state. Not only was the Histadrut dedicated to protecting the rights of workers, but it also became the major employer in the country, as well as a major force in education and health care. The Histadrut retained its power after the establishment of the state until the institution's decline in the 1980s (see Grinberg 1991). It clearly perceived cultural activities in general, and musical ones in particular, as a major tool for the promotion of its ideological goals: the metamorphosis of the Diaspora Jew into the "new" Hebrew person on the basis of a socialist platform. The Histadrut based its activities on the precepts of Marxist ideology regarding cultural production, that is, that the role of the labor movement was to educate the masses of workers (the majority of whom were new immigrants) through collective cultural activities that would transmit the ideals of the Zionist "revolution" (Marom 1997). The fact that the Histadrut put its socialist ideology and organizational power to national purposes led scholars to criticize, in retrospect, the true socialist character of this powerful organization, arguing that, in fact, it was more a nationalist movement than anything else (Sternhell 1995).

In any case, the Histadrut established institutions dedicated to the promotion of cultural activities. The Center for Culture of the Histadrut was founded in 1935 following a resolution by the fourth General Assembly of the Histadrut in 1934 to dedicate a fixed percent of the profits of Histadrut industries to cultural activities (Histadrut 1952: 408). The musical branch of this center emerged from two existing bodies: the Institute for the Dissemination of Music among the People (established in 1926 by Menashe Rabinovitch and Dr. David Shorr in Tel Aviv) and the Inter-Kibbutz Committee for Musical Activities. The musical activities of the kibbutzim thus became the basis for the concerted attempt to centralize musical activities and production on a national basis. In 1945, the committee became the Music Section (Mador le-musiqa) of the Center for Culture, under the direction of Nissim Nissimov. The department was formally dissolved in 1995, although in practice, it had already ceased its activities in 1987. But as late as 1975, the newly appointed director of the Department of Music, Henri Klauzner, insisted, in an example of anachronistic rhetoric for his time, that the Histadrut should play a major role in shaping an independent Israeli musical culture:

> The independent musical activity of the workers in Israel has been in decline during recent years. The consumer's society with all its ramifications turned our public to a great extent from creator in the fields of culture and innovator of traditions of holidays, song and dance, into a consumer of sophisticated mass media and of light entertainment. This process hurt the youth in particular. If we add to this process the aging of the founding generation and the way of life between the wars, we can understand some of the problems that weigh upon, or impede the creation of an independent cultural atmosphere. And there are, of course, many other factors, perhaps even more serious ones, such as the ingathering of the exiles, the gap between social classes, etc. (Henri Klauzner, *Megamot ve-sikuyyim ba-peʿilut ha-musiqalit* [Trends and prospects of musical activity], *Dapim le-peʿilei tarbut ve-ḥevrah* [July–August 1975]: 4)

The Histadrut did not create new musical activities but rather recruited existing ones for its purposes. Two such major activities were the promotion of choirs and communal singing. Institutionalized communal singing was established in Tel Aviv by Menashe Ravina in the framework of the Oneg Shabbat (Rejoice in the Sabbath) meetings held at the Ohel Shem Hall beginning in 1919 and continued by Daniel Samburski at Beit Brenner from 1935 until the 1950s (Hacohen 1985: 59, 105). This was adopted by the kibbutzim as a major form of cultural activity. The Histadrut subsidized the appearances of Israeli composers who taught their songs (also published by the Histadrut) during communal singing. The vital role of choirs is concisely expressed by Abraham Levinson, one of the leaders of the Histadrut:

> The choir is the primary cultural expression of the basis of cooperation, of unity, discipline, the sharing of a goal and the enthusiasm of creativity. The choir is the collective tool for the dissemination of song. . . . The choir is the cheapest and most natural collective art. . . . It is imperative that a choir is established in each settlement, city and village, and that [each choir] will be added to a developed network of worker's choirs throughout the country. . . . The role of the choir is not confined to the field of music; it is [also] an excellent tool for the ingathering of the exiles, for the teaching of the [Hebrew] language and for the creation of a collective social life. . . . The choir will serve to encourage the creativity of the composer and of the Hebrew poet, the urban and the rural, and as a tool for the dissemination of the Song of the Land of Israel, and of Jewish [song] in general, the classic and the folk. (Levinson 1951: 59)

Thus vocal music performed on a popular basis (with pretensions to an artistic level of performance) was the primary goal of the Histadrut's musical institutions. The model for the recruitment of choral activities by the workers' union appears to be the choral activities of the German labor movement during the Weimar Republic (in particular the concerted encounters of choral multitudes envisioned by conductor Franz Heyde and brought to Israel in 1935 by Henri Klauzner). The rise of Jewish choral activities in Palestine in the early 1930s coincides with the waves of Jewish immigration from Germany following the dismantling of the Weimar Republic and the rise to power of the National Socialists. The early Hebrew choral repertory distributed by the Institute for the Dissemination of Music consisted of translations of German songs (from Bach chorales to socialist hymns) and songs in other foreign languages. The commissioning of original Hebrew songs developed alongside the formulation of the ideology of a national Jewish culture in Eretz Yisrael by the Histadrut.

Following its educational goals in the field of music, the Histadrut became one of the major entrepreneurs of music, especially during the British Mandate period and in the early years of statehood. The Department of Music acted as a generator of music, by commissioning songs from composers, as a publisher, by printing the songs (what became known the Musical Library of the Histadrut that by 1970 had published 457 choral sheets including more than 300 Israeli pieces by more than 150 composers and poets), and as a distributor, by creating a network that supported performances of music produced by the department.

Eventually the Histadrut also became the main agent for musicians and lyricists. In 1949 the Artists' Bureau of the Histadrut was established. This was a union that was dedicated to the protection of the artists' rights, while, at the same time, functioning as a cartel that set prices for performances and demanded that its members pay dues. Settlements and cultural institutions associated with the Histadrut could not engage artists who were not affiliated with the union. In 1963, the union established a Repertoire Committee to monitor its members' programs. Thus at the peak of its power in the 1960s, the Histadrut was a major player in the field of cultural production in Israel.

The Histadrut also engaged in training choir and orchestra conductors, organizing music courses and workshops, as well as training singers and instrumentalists. It also organized large assemblies of choirs from all the Jewish settlements during the summers, beginning in 1929 with the first meeting of Hebrew choirs at Mikveh Israel, an agricultural school on the outskirts of Tel Aviv. These encounters expanded and reached their peak in 1945–52. Kibbutz Giv'at Brenner hosted the national assembly of choirs in 1952, with the participation of forty-seven choirs with more than two thousand singers. The Histadrut also engaged in the production of concerts and lectures on music held at the workers' clubs in agricultural settlements, villages, and cities.

The role of the Histadrut in the creation of the canon of Israeli "folk" songs should not be underestimated. Although the Department of Music of the Histadrut allowed local conductors to select the repertory according to their own tastes and technical capabilities, by 1952, more than half of the repertories distributed to the choirs consisted of Israel and Jewish songs in Hebrew. Although the power of the Histadrut in the field of culture in general, and of music in particular, steadily decreased after the 1960s, its early activities were instrumental in creating the perception that a national Israeli type of music was indeed emerging. This "national music" was slowly absorbed and transformed by the popular-music industry, particularly after the 1960s, into the genre called Shirei Eretz Yisrael (Songs of the Land of Israel), which became a component of the modern discourse about Israeliness.

THE MEDIA

Radio and Television

Over the years, television and especially radio were the most important sites of the contest over popular music and Israeliness. In addition to the obvious reason, that these broadcast media serve as the platform within which any public popular-music culture exists, there is the fact that Israeli broadcast media were, until 1990, practically a state monopoly and had only few popular-music channels. Therefore, programming of popular music carried with it the implicit connotation of being a reflection of national cultural orientations.

The major official broadcasting body is the Israeli Broadcasting Authority (IBA), which operates the various channels of Israeli radio and television. Official radio broadcasting began in Palestine under the auspices of the British Mandate in 1936. The PBA (Palestine Broadcasting Authority) broadcast in English, Hebrew, and Arabic. In 1948, the emergent State of Israel inherited this British institution and created Kol Israel (The Voice of Israel), which later developed into the Israel Broadcasting Authority within the prime minister's office. Early broadcasting on Israeli radio leaned heavily to educational goals, such as the dissemination of the Hebrew language. Little space was allotted to popular music until it was included in the programming of the second network, Reshet Bet, a commercial channel established in 1960 (Caspi and Limor 1998).

Hence, from 1960 to 1977, Kol Israel's popular-music programs were concentrated in Reshet Bet, which was therefore also known as *ha-gal ha-kal* (the light wave). Not exclusively a popular-music station, the channel included popular-music programs among other radio formats. In 1976, with the expanding market for popular music, Kol Israel established a third station, Reshet Gimmel, as an all-popular-music commercial channel, much like the BBC's Radio 1. In fact, like Radio 1 in the United Kingdom, Reshet Gimmel was a response to the Voice of Peace, an unauthorized "pirate" station that operated between 1973 and 1993, according to its slogan, "from a ship somewhere in the Mediterranean," modeled after European stations of the 1960s such as Caroline, London, North Sea, and Veronica. Through the 1980s, Reshet Gimmel was the premier pop station of Israel and the major source of recent international pop hits and trends for Israeli audiences.

Another highly influential state-controlled radio station is the army station, Galei Tzahal (Israel Defense Forces Waves, sometimes known as Galatz). Established in 1950, it initially broadcast for three and a half hours in the evenings. In 1962 it expanded to include two and a half hours of popular-music programs that aired around noon. It was further expanded in 1969 and finally became a twenty-four-hour station in 1973, during the Yom Kippur War in October of that year, but also under pressure from the Voice of Peace. Indeed, although it included in its roster news and current-affairs programs, by 1973 the station was primarily a popular-music station. As an army station, the personnel of Galei Tzahal is largely composed of soldiers, for whom working in the station as music editors or DJs is their obligatory military service. Considered highly desirable and prestigious military service, Galei Tzahal traditionally recruited its personnel from the ranks of high-school graduates equipped with the most recent and sophisticated cultural capital.

A cultural hierarchy was established between Galei Tzahal and Reshet Gimmel, where the former came to be considered as having a serious approach to popular music and the latter a "lighter" one. Yet the two popular-music stations developed similar programming patterns for popular music. Despite being state-controlled bodies, music editors and managers in both stations were given autonomy to pursue their own professional ethical or aesthetic-ideological commitments in order to keep Israeli audiences informed about and acquainted with global popular-music trends. Therefore, about half of the popular music on Israeli radio was foreign popular music.

Both stations also had their own weekly Israeli hit-parade programs *(mitz'ad pizmonim)*. Unlike similar radio programs in other countries, these were not based on sales figures of singles (45 rpm, 7" vinyl records with one song on each side), since a market for such phonograms did not exist in Israel. Rather, they were based on ranking of songs by the public who sent postcards to the editors of the hit parades. For a short period in the 1960s, the hit parades included both Israeli and foreign songs, but later the stations separated them into two hit parades: one of foreign songs and one of Israeli songs. Although the number of participants in these polls was relatively small (several thousand at the most), the Israeli hit parades nevertheless gained a high profile in the field, approaching any other market-based "top twenty." The hit parades determined careers and star status, but, most importantly, which hits would be played on other programs, thus influencing the public musical space. Of particular importance were the annual Hebrew charts, broadcast on Rosh ha-Shana, the Jewish new year, usually sometime in September. In addition to choosing the "song of the year," audiences voted for the female and male Israeli "singer of the year" and "band of the year."

Further the stations perceived it their duty to initiate special projects for the preservation of the Israeli song heritage and to encourage the writing and recording of new "authentic" music. Preservation was achieved mainly by keeping in the roster various types of nostalgia programs, completely devoted to early songs. Galei Tzahal, for example, for many years had an "oldies parade" *(mitz'ad ha-marganit, the Daisy Parade)*. New music was fostered through special song contests, which were festivals of various sorts. Thus in 1960 Kol Israel inaugurated the Israeli Song Festival, an annual competition of original songs. The live radio broadcast of this event on Independence Day was later joined by television, making it a major national annual ritual. In the late 1970s, the Song Festival merged with the contest for choosing the Israeli song for the Eurovision song contest. Galei Tzahal responded in the 1970s with three "Evenings of Songs by Poets," for which prominent composers were asked to compose music to words of major poets.

With these three mechanisms—programming policy, distribution, and judging—Kol Israel and Galei Tzahal were highly influential in the Israeli field of popular music for several decades. Individual music editors such as Yoav Kutner (Galei Tzahal) and Menahem Granit (Reshet Gimmel), and radio DJs such as Dori Ben-Zeev (Galei Tzahal) and Shosh Atari (Reshet Gimmel) played crucial roles in the introduction of music genres and radio formats. Decisions as to what new songs to put to the audience vote in the hit parades, which genres deserved special programs, and what type of foreign music to play, proved highly decisive for the overall development of popular music in Israel. In shaping the public musical soundscape, the mood of the public sonic sphere, these channels granted implicit recognition and legitimacy to genres, songs, and singers and determined the cultural hierarchy in the local field of popular music.

That the Israeli Song Festival and later the pre-Eurovision contest could become major national events was directly connected to the fact that between 1969, when it first began transmission, and 1990, IBA's Israel Television was the only television channel in Israel. With practically all viewers watching exactly the same programs at the same time, Israel Television functioned as a sort of modern-day, national ritual of collective gathering. This function had its strongest expression in news and current-affairs programs. Yet weekend entertainment shows on Friday nights (the weekend in Israel begins on Friday afternoon and ends on Saturday night), with their mélange of interviews, comedy, and popular music, set the national (popular) cultural agenda. Indeed, appearances on shows like *Sha'ah tovah* (A good hour) or *Sibah le-mesibah* (A reason for a party) gave singers the highest possible exposure and were perceived by many of them as a major career achievement. These programs represented almost the sole impact of television on Israeli popular music in the years 1970–90. Other programs were *'Od lahit* (Another hit) and *'Ad pop* (Up to pop). Modeled after existing U.K. and U.S. pop programs, they contained lip-synching performances of Israeli musicians in the studio and foreign music videos. However, since they were thirty-minute shows broadcast weekly and included very few performances per show, they had only a passing impact on the field.

The year 1990 stands out as something of a great divide in the history of the broadcast media in Israel. In that year, cable television transmission began and within a few years reached a high penetration level of 60 to 70 percent of Israeli households. Television volume in Israel further expanded in 1993, when a commercial channel, Channel Two (Arutz Shnaim), began broadcasting. Within two years, this channel achieved higher viewing rates than Israel Television (Channel One) for most prime-time programs. In the mid-1990s, the volume of radio broadcasting increased enormously when both Kol Israel and Galei Tzahal inaugurated their own traffic reports channels, consisting mostly of popular music; commercial regional radio stations began broadcasting (in 1994); and unauthorized, "pirate" stations began to proliferate, the most prominent of which were Channel Seven (Arutz Sheva', a religious-nationalist station, voicing the ideology and interests of the settlers in the occupied territories), Radio One in Haifa, and Voice of the Orient (Qol Ha-mizraḥ, a Jerusalem-based station devoted to all types of oriental music).

For the field of popular music in Israel, cable television had one important implication: it brought MTV (Europe) into all households. In the two years following its introduction, sales of foreign pop records increased from their traditional 50 percent of the market to approximately 67 percent. Israeli music later regained its share of the market, but MTV's influence was felt in the long run, in the increase of music-video production, of Israeli music-video programs on local cable channels, and other changes in marketing and publication practices for Israeli music (Regev 1997c). In addition, the roster of television programs on Channel Two showed an increase in the number of entertainment shows that included popular-music performances.

Paradoxically, the transition of Israeli radio to a free-market orientation had a mainstreaming effect. The traffic reports channels, especially the one operated by Galei Tzahal (Galgalatz), came up with a programming formula of "known, beloved, and relaxing" Israeli and foreign pop. Proving successful among audiences, the new regional stations adopted this formula for their own popular-music programs. Having lost audiences to all these new channels, Reshet Gimmel restructured its programming and in November 1997, at the time when ceremonies to mark the fiftieth anniversary of the state commenced, became an all-Israeli music channel. This declaration of confidence in the wealth and variety of Israeli popular music also left the musical public space of Israel—given the mainstream formula of the other leading stations—with very few slots for acquaintance with new foreign popular music.

Music Press

A professional popular-music press almost never existed in Israel. The few attempts to establish serious magazines—that is, magazines modeled after *Rolling Stone, NME,* and so on—were short lived. Six issues of *Volume* published during 1983, and seven issues of *E-Ton* (1987–88) were the closest thing to critical and autonomous popular-music magazines that ever appeared in Israel. *Musiqa,* which appeared for two years, 1987–88, was a slightly more successful venture, mainly because most of its pages were devoted to classical music.

The most successful of the music magazines in Israel was *Lahiton.* It appeared in 1969 as an early attempt to create a serious magazine. Lacking the knowledge, skills, and know-how for serious, critical popular-music journalism that was taking shape in the world centers of popular music at the time, within two years its editors and writers were swept into the niche of a gossip and glossy-picture type of popular-music magazine. Later the magazine merged with *'Olam ha-qolno'a* (The world of cinema) to become a general entertainment magazine, narrowing its popular-music coverage. In this format, it lasted until 1989. Another type of glossy magazine that thrived throughout the 1980s and 1990s were the youth magazines, *Rosh 1* and *Maariv la-no'ar.* The latter was originally—in the 1960s and 1970s—a highly educational pedagogically oriented youth weekly. In later decades, it was transformed into a glossy fashion, gossip, and entertainment magazine, with a large popular-music section.

Lacking a serious and sustained independent magazine on popular music, the daily and weekly newspapers filled the void and became the most important site for popular-music journalism in Israel. Three daily newspapers have dominated the press in Israel since the 1950s: *Maariv, Yedioth Ahronoth,* and *Haaretz.* The first two are wide-circulation newspapers, rivals since the 1950s. *Haaretz* is the Israeli "thinking people's" newspaper, read by intellectuals, academics, and professionals. Other notable newspapers included *Davar,* published by the Histadrut between 1925 and 1995; and *Ḥadashot,* a short-lived (1984–93) yet highly influential newspaper in its introduction of new journalism practices, and with them a young generation of journalists, most of whom later became prominent in other newspapers.

Coverage of popular music in daily newspapers was scattered and occasional until the mid-1960s, when all three major newspapers inaugurated weekend magazines. These magazines included a popular-music section, which featured news, interviews, record reviews, charts of the local foreign and Israeli hit-parades, as well as the U.S. and U.K. top twenty. From time to time, the magazines also published longer features about prominent musicians, albums, and other popular-music-related topics and extensive interviews with musicians. Although they certainly did not place popular music at the focus of their concerns, the magazines of *Maariv, Yedioth Ahronoth,* and *Haaretz* were, through the 1970s, almost the only influential and consistent sites for the review of popular music in the Israeli print press.

In the 1980s, with the growth of the field of popular music and the culture industry as a whole, all newspapers expanded their coverage of popular music. Record reviews, popular-music news, and interviews became a regular feature on weekdays as well as weekends, and the space devoted to popular music on weekends grew. *Ḥadashot* especially, with its young image, placed strong emphasis on popular music in its pages.

Yet the increase in the space and attention given to popular music in the press in the 1980s is associated mostly with the *meqomon* (local), city, and regional weekly newspapers that emerged during this decade. Schocken, the publisher of *Haaretz,* led the way by launching *Kol Ha-'Ir* (a play on words in spoken Hebrew, meaning both "All of the city" and "Voice of the city") in Jerusalem and *Ha-'Ir* (The city) in Tel Aviv. Other newspapers soon followed, together with some independents, and by the end of the decade most towns and regions in Israel had their own weekly newspapers (Caspi and Limor 1998).

The impact of the local weeklies—especially in Tel Aviv, the cultural center of the country—was immense. Looking to similar newspapers abroad for inspiration (New York's *Village Voice* was a strong influence), these newspapers developed unprecedented systematic, detailed coverage of popular music. Fostering the image of Tel Aviv as a culturally thriving city, *Ha-'Ir, Tel Aviv* (the *Yedioth Ahronoth* local newspaper) and *Zman Tel Aviv* (Tel Aviv time, published by *Maariv)* produced stories, columns, reviews, opinions, lengthy interviews, and gossip about club culture, personnel changes in bands, recording plans, albums, and so on. Popular musical life in Jerusalem was given similar expression by its local newspapers.

Thus, after 1980, popular-music journalism underwent a process of professionalization and diversification. Whereas before 1980 there was little division of labor between news, review, criticism, and so on, and all these were produced by one or two people in each newspaper, after that year, the national and local newspapers engaged special teams for their coverage of popular music.

For our research, we utilized newspaper articles as sources in order to document, with relative accuracy, current developments on the popular-music scene, as well as reflections of the critical views and perceptions in vogue on a vast array of ideological and aesthetic issues.

THE RECORDING INDUSTRY

The record market in Israel has always been relatively small. With the total population growing from 1.5 million in 1950 to 6 million in 1998, and with a 17-fold real increase in the total GND between the 1950s and the 1990s (in the mid-1990s reaching approximately $80 billion; $15,000 per capita), vinyl records, then cassettes, and later CDs became an affordable, routine commodity for most of the population only in the 1980s.

Nevertheless, the market grew immensely between 1960 and 1998. Thus, for example, in 1963, the total sales of phonograms in Israel—of all music styles combined—was 460,000, including a large share of singles (Regev 1990). By the mid-1980s, at the peak of the vinyl era, the figure reached approximately 2 million units annually, the vast majority in LP format. In 1997, approximately 11.5 million units were sold, 95 percent of them in CD format. About 70 percent of these CDs are manufactured in Israel, in local plants. The rest are imported. Before the advent of the CD, local manufacture of phonograms was approximately 80 to 90 percent. Since the early 1970s, with occasional fluctuations in both directions, sales have been more or less equally divided between Israeli and foreign music. Israeli titles, however, typically sell more copies than foreign titles. This is best illustrated by the award of "golden record." The local industry certifies an album as "gold" for sales of more than 20,000 copies. Foreign albums hardly ever achieve this status in Israel. Israeli albums, by contrast, often do.

Before 1970, Israeli music captured less than 30 percent of the market and the production of music was divided between Israeli and foreign companies. Several foreign companies (EMI, Philips, Columbia, Pax, RCA, Decca, and others) maintained branches in Israel that administered the import and local manufacturing of the foreign music they found profitable to distribute in Israel. Almost none of these were involved in Israeli music for the local market. The tiny market for Israeli music of that period was maintained by a few local companies.

Starting in the late 1960s, the organizational field of the music industry was gradually restructured, adjusting to the growing concentration of the international music industry (Gronow 1998; Wallis and Malm 1984; Negus 1992; Burnett 1996) and to the growth of the local market for Israeli music. By the 1980s the music industry consisted of two sectors: three major local record companies that produced approximately 70 percent of Israeli music and between them represented the six major international record companies; and a second sector consisting of various smaller companies, which produced specific styles of Israeli music or represented smaller foreign companies. The structural change was accompanied by changes in professional practices influenced and inspired by the global music industry. The history of the Israeli music industry is therefore the story of its gradual intertwining with and becoming embedded into the transnational music industry.

Beginnings of the Recording Industry

The first recordings of Hebrew songs were made in Europe at the end of the nineteenth century, on cylinders for Edison's Phonograph. These were either traditional religious chants or recently composed Zionist songs. During the first half of the twentieth century, as the repertory of Hebrew/Zionist songs written in Palestine steadily grew, a number of recording projects took place, mainly in Europe. In 1922, Polyphone in Germany produced sixteen records with thirty-nine songs performed by amateur singers in Jerusalem, all recorded by Abraham Zvi Idelsohn; in 1930 in Paris, Columbia issued a record with two songs by Yedidiah Gorochov-Admon; in 1934–35, HMV London produced sixteen records of Israeli songs. The most successful of these were five records containing eleven songs by singer Yossef Spindel. In Palestine, Ahva, the first Israeli record company, produced in 1933 records with thirty songs recorded by singer Yossef Goland in Berlin. The Ahva plant on the outskirts of Tel Aviv pressed the songs on records made of shellac-coated cardboard. Their poor quality caused quick deterioration, and in 1935 Yossef Goland traveled to London with composer-arranger Moshe Vilensky to re-record his repertory and some new songs, which were issued on a series of nine records by Decca. There were a number of other projects as well, the most significant of which were recordings made by Yemen-born singer Bracha Zefira of her performances with composer and pianist Nahum Nardi, issued by Columbia Phonograph in 1937 (Hirshberg 1995: 193; for more on Zefira, see Chapter 9, below; see also Hacohen 1993).

The Local "Majors"

During the first twenty to twenty-five years of statehood, the production of records of Israeli music was dominated by Hed Artzi, a firm established in 1947. Its catalog for 1952 (which consisted entirely of two-song singles) included major names such as female singers Yaffa Yarkoni and Shoshana Damari and male singers Israel Yitzhaki, Shimshon Bar Noy, and Freddy Dura. They all sang a mixture of Shirei Eretz Yisrael, original songs in trendy pop styles (rumba, swing, tango, and so on) and translations of foreign songs in the same vein. Interestingly enough, the catalog also includes Jewish cantorial singing (by famous cantors such as Moshe Koussevitzky or Samuel Malavsky and his family) and a few Egyptian Arab songs (by Layla Mourad). Later, into the 1960s, the vast majority of Israeli music was produced by this company. The most successful, prominent, and influential performers of Israeli popular music, including most of the lehaqot tzvayiot (army ensembles), singer Shoshana Damari, the singing group Ha-Tarnegolim (The Roosters), and many others, recorded with Hed Artzi. A few smaller companies that sprang up in the 1960s, among them Ha-Taklit (with the Ofarim Duo, for example, on its roster) and Israphone (with the Gesher Ha-Yarkon Trio) produced the rest of the records sold. None of these companies owned a recording studio, and there were almost no independent recording studios at the time. Thus many of the recordings of Israeli music were made in the Kol Israel radio studios, or in small performing halls like Ohel Shem and Beit ha-Moreh in Tel Aviv. Some of the companies had their own manufacturing plants; others relied on plants that served both Israeli music firms and companies representing foreign firms.

The turning point in the history of the record industry occurred in 1966–67, when CBS established an Israeli branch that acted not only as the representative for the distribution of music by its parent company, but as a local entrepreneur of Israeli music as well, an initiative that led to the inclusion of CBS on the Arab League boycott list. CBS signed recording contracts with various emerging Israeli musicians of the period, the most notable being Yehoram Gaon and Chava Alberstein. Alberstein was the first contracted singer for CBS in Israel, and she continued to record for the company for several decades.

CBS introduced new marketing devices, in the form of collections of hits by different local and foreign musicians. Its first album in this format, *Mitz'ad ha-kokhavim* (lit., star parade, but given the English title "Star Festival"), included the unlikely juxtaposition of Hebrew songs in diverse styles such as "Na'ara mamash otzar" (sung by Aliza Azikri; composed by Aris San), "La-shir, yalda" (sung by pop singer Geula Gill), "Pirhey zahav" (sung by Hava Alberstein), and the Hebrew version of the Jewish-Sephardi song "Dos Amantes" (performed by the Parvarim Duo), together with songs performed by Barbra Streisand, the Cyrkle pop band (the hit "Red Rubber Ball"), Les Compagnon de la Chanson, and Ray Coniff. CBS-Israel soon became the second major producer of Israeli music. The concentration of both Israeli and foreign productions within one firm set a pattern that would be followed by other companies.

This change can be understood in light of the increasing costs of music production. Around 1970, Israeli musicians' growing acquaintance with Anglo-American pop/rock greatly influenced their aesthetic perceptions of instrumentation and studio production. The emerging artistic consciousness about sound and electric instrumentation created a demand for sophisticated studio productions. Around 1970, the first multitrack studios in the country, Kolinor and Triton, were established. The aesthetic change involved higher production costs: lengthy studio hours, sound engineers' fees, instrument rental, and so on. The small market could not guarantee profits for costly productions, and some of the smaller companies producing Israeli music found it increasingly difficult to remain in business. Joining forces with foreign companies was a perfect solution and also suited the expansionist tendencies of the global music industry. The economic logic was simple: distribution of foreign music required minimal investment, and profits were almost guaranteed given the global marketing strategies for international musicians. At least some of this ensured income served as a steady flow of capital for investment in local music production. By the 1980s, the structure implied by this logic was consolidated with the transition of Israeli music to pop/rock-oriented music and as mergers between European and American companies dictated the merging of their branches in Israel. The cultural implications of this structure are best expressed by the chief executive of one of these firms:

> A certain part of the profits I expect to make in the international department goes to the Hebrew department. If I did not have this capital, I would not invest in the Hebrew department. If I were to take the Hebrew department, put it on a street in Tel Aviv on its own, to build its own productions, marketing system, distribution and retail—it would not survive. It constantly needs the backing of the international labels. That is, in the State of Israel, because of its size, if you don't have at least one international label, you cannot make Hebrew music. Therefore, saying something like "Eric Clapton subsidizes Israeli artists" is true on a certain level—yes, its true. Because without this, I would not have enough money to invest in Hebrew. If I did not invest, there would be no Hebrew department. (Interview with the authors, March 1995)

Thus, by the 1980s, CBS-Israel became the exclusive distributor of all the labels and companies controlled by its parent company (which in the 1990s became Sony Music) and of EMI. Hed Artzi gained exclusivity for the distribution of all music associated with the Warner group and later also the BMG group (including MCA, distributed worldwide by BMG). Phonokol retained its longtime association with Polygram (formerly Philips). Two changes in this structure took place when in 1988, CBS-Israel ceased to be an official branch of the parent company and became an autonomous local firm called NMC, retaining all the exclusive rights (except for Virgin, an EMI company distributed by Helicon), and when Phonokol lost its Polygram franchise in 1994 to the relatively new company, Helicon, which was established in 1985. It should be noted that the imbrications of the Israeli music industry with the global music industry, and the implied dependence of local music production on foreign music imports, are not dissimilar to the situation in other small countries (Wallis and Malm 1984; Campbell Robinson et al. 1991).

Smaller Recording Companies

There are record companies that produce Israeli music and profit without being representatives of large international conglomerates. Companies such as MCI and BNE maintain their activity by distributing small foreign labels in Israel, producing music for niche markets, or retaining one or two stars in their catalogs. A good example of this is Phonokol. After losing its Polygram contract, the company remained profitable and active by retaining most of the classic 1970s catalog of singer Arik Einstein (and a number of other artists) and by managing the most successful acts in the niche market of the highly popular electro-dance substyle known as "trance" music, which proved profitable in international markets as well.

The small companies that are genuinely local are those that came into being with the genre of musiqa mizrahit and exclusively produce it. These companies emerged in the 1970s and 1980s, when the genre was rejected by the major record companies and was practically excluded from the media. Serving as a truly alternative and independent mode of dissemination, these companies initially concentrated their production around the cheapest of phonograms—the cassette. Foremost among them is the Reuveni Brothers firm, which started up in the 1970s and owns the classic catalog of musiqa mizrahit: Zohar Argov, Haim Moshe, Margalit Tsanani, and others. Other notable firms are Koliphone (the Azulay brothers), which was active in the 1970s, and Ben Mush Productions, who entered the market in the late 1980s. By the 1990s, as musiqa mizrahit gained recognition and legitimacy, these cassette companies shifted towards CDs, although their cassette sales remained proportionally higher than those of other companies. They also signed distribution agreements with the majors.

· · ·

One major consequence of the structure of the organizational field of popular music in Israel is the differentiation of its professional communities.

The institutional complex of popular-music production, distribution, and broadcasting in Israel is divided, roughly, into three occasionally overlapping, but for the most part separate, professional communities. One is associated mainly with educational and public organizations and consists of people working with Shirei Eretz Yisrael. A second community is associated with firms producing musiqa mizrahit. The third community is the network of professionals associated with the local majors and with Israeli pop/rock. In addition to musicians and record company people, the third professional community has, since the late 1970s, also included most of the key journalists, critics, and radio music editors in Israeli media. This indicates that the development of Israeli rock is tied to the growth of both Israeli media and record companies, turning it into the complex culture industry seen at the end of the 1990s (Regev 1997a).

This development had the consequences of relegating anything associated with Shirei Eretz Yisrael and prerock popular music to a position of anachronism and nostalgia and of distancing any activity associated with musiqa mizrahit from the power centers of the culture industry, because their products were perceived by the industry as unsuited to accepted professional conventions. Hence, it should be kept in mind that a crucial mediating factor in the rise of Israeli rock to the status of the dominant popular-music culture of Israel was its embeddedness in the culture industry.

PART II

Popular Music and Nationalist Ideology

3 Shirei Eretz Yisrael
(Songs of the Land of Israel)

SONG OF CAMARADERIE (GURI-ARGOV)

On the Negev the autumn night falls
And gently, gently lights up the stars
When the wind passes through
Clouds wander along the road.

Already a year has elapsed
We practically did not feel
how the time passed in our fields.
Already a year and few of us are left.
So many are no longer among us.

But we will remember them all,
The handsome ones with beautiful curls
Because camaraderie like this
will never allow our hearts to forget.

Love sanctified by blood
Will return to flourish among us.

Q: You are very Israeli, an Israeli princess. Is it difficult for you to
cope with the new, multicultural Israel?

A: No. It's true that when I toured the country, lectured, and
organized political meetings, I developed a kind of index which
I called the "Shir Ha-re'ut index" [after "Shir Ha-re'ut," or
"Song of Camaraderie," by Alexander "Sasha" Argov and Haim
Guri, above]. When I walked into the meeting halls, I asked
myself, "To how many people in this room does 'Shir Ha-re'ut'
say something?" Some people say that this is an elitist index. But

I say "No." It is just an index of social change. Because the number of Israelis who shiver when they hear "Shir Ha-re'ut" is
decreasing. [The song] does not move *ḥaredi* [ultraorthodox]
Jews, Russians [immigrants from the former Soviet Union],
Arabs, some of the Oriental Jews and a large number of youngsters. . . . When I hear "Shir Ha-re'ut" [on Memorial Day] . . .
my heart skips a beat. Because [this song] is me. So I am aware
that today my kind of Israeliness is only one kind within a more
general Israeliness, which we cannot yet define. And I know that
my Israeliness which once was a community experience is today
the private experience of a minority.

> (Interview with Yael [Yuli] Tamir, Minister of Absorption
> and former leader of the Peace Now movement,
> by Ari Shavit, *Haaretz*, August 13, 1999)

Tamir here addresses one of the most canonic songs of the repertory known
today as "Songs of the Land of Israel" (henceforth SLI), the "Song of Camaraderie" composed by Alexander "Sasha" Argov to a poem by Haim Guri.
The song dates back to the period of the War of Independence and addresses
the sad memories of the war that had just ended and the yearning for the
unique relations created on the battlefield. It became an index of Israeliness
because of its poignant content and the somber, lugubrious melody that
changes to a patriotic marchlike tune in the refrain that effectively expressed
the mixed feelings of pain and joy that Israelis felt in the aftermath of the
1948 war. However what established its canonic status as a symbol of the
ethos of an entire generation of Jewish Israelis was its frequent broadcast and
performance on state occasions and holidays, in schools, and by youth movements. This mechanism of canonization enabled Tamir to establish familiar-
ity with this song as a measure of Israeliness during a period when this
mainstream identity was seriously challenged by other options.

Measuring the sense of "belonging" to mainstream Israeliness, based on
identification with one of the most canonic songs of the SLI repertory,
unveils the major role of popular music in the demarcation of identities in
contemporary Israel. Identifying with this repertory, not only with its musical or literary content but also with its delineation of Hebrewism as the
embodiment of Israeliness, thus became a parameter within the ethos of
Israeli national identity.

Since the inception of the Zionist project, the idea of a national Hebrew culture was musically expressed in the creation of a Hebrew "folk song" repertory. This repertory has recently been dealt with in a number of in-depth studies that addressed a variety of social, literary, linguistic, and musical aspects (see, for example, Eliram 1995, 2000; Reshef 1999; Shahar 1989, 1993, 1994, 1997a, 1998). While some studies on SLI have stressed the nature of this repertory as an "invented tradition" (Hirshberg 1995: ch. 9; Bohlman in Nathan 1994: 39–55), few have addressed its status as a component of the field of Israeli popular music (Regev 1989, 1990; Eliram 1995, 2000).

The present chapter focuses on two major issues related to SLI as popular music: the creation of the Hebrew folk song; and the transformation of a selected repertory of these songs, deriving from different sources (traditional Jewish songs translated into Hebrew, originally composed folk songs, theater and cabaret songs, youth movement songs, and so on) and composed between about 1882 and the present, into the genre of contemporary Israeli popular music known as SLI. In the framework of our discussion, we treat aspects of the complex process of canonization of a limited number of Hebrew songs, of the literally thousands of titles created over a century, into SLI. These aspects include the influential role of music educators and media critics in the valorization of the songs, the perpetuation of this repertory through its performance at sing-alongs, the close relations between the songs and the invented Israeli "folk" dances (Kadman 1969), the impact of the revival of oldies by pop/rock performers since the 1960s, and the emergence of a nostalgia industry that focused on the heroic early days of the State of Israel, the period for which SLI stands in the eyes of most Israelis today.

HEBREW OR ISRAELI FOLK SONG?
AN ARCHAEOLOGY OF LABELS

Historical processes in popular music can be understood by focusing on the shift in the meanings of terms employed by different sectors of a society (artists, critics, scholars, listeners) to define categories of music at certain historical junctures (Middleton 1985: 9). An archaeology of the label Shirei Eretz Yisrael, which defines the repertory of Hebrew songs in the context of the contemporary popular-music industry, is therefore necessary to the understanding of its deep social and emotional meaning.

Eretz Yisrael (the Land of Israel) connotes the geographical area where the Jewish people have developed since antiquity. There is no agreement, even among Zionists, as to its precise boundaries. In modern geopolitical terms, Eretz Yisrael denotes the area of Zionist settlement during the

Ottoman Empire and the British Mandate of Palestine. While the Jewish state was eventually called Medinat Israel (the State of Israel), the prestate term Eretz Yisrael has survived in contemporary Israeli vocabulary, reflecting, for example, for ultranationalists of Israel's political right wing, the entire area of the original British Mandate of Palestine, including the West Bank. Conventionally, the widespread term Ha-aretz (the Land) signifies simply [the State of] Israel. Eretz Yisrael is therefore a concept with strong national, emotional, and, at the same time, nostalgic overtones (Eliram 2000).

This introduces us to the evolution of other labels used to designate SLI in different periods and contexts. Three terms, *Shirei Eretz Yisrael* (Songs of the Land of Israel), *Ha-zemer ha-'ivri* (Hebrew song), and *Ha-shir ha-yisraeli* (Israeli song) appear in academic writings, in the media, and in daily language to describe "the folk song of the new Jewish society that came into being in the Land of Israel from the 1880s onwards" (Bayer 1980). Although frequently interchanged, these apparent synonyms denote distinctive ways of perceiving the same musical repertory. For example, the use of the word *zemer* instead of the more general term *shir* to denote "song" has overtones of respectability and antiquity, for zemer is an old word rooted in the traditional Hebrew literature (for example, the traditional *zemirot shabbat*, or sabbath table songs).

The use of the adjective "Hebrew" in the concept "Hebrew song" to refer to the folk songs from the Yishuv period is noteworthy in that it is an expression of the early stage of Israeliness that we defined as "Hebrewism" (Shavit 1990). As Zerubavel remarks, "The pervasive use of the term 'Hebrew' during the prestate period . . . implied both symbolic continuity with the ancient national past and departure from Exile. The mere addition of this adjective was indicative of the national significance attributed to its referent" (1995: 26).

Among scholars, the term "Israeli song" refers to the corpus of composed songs kept in written form, mobilized by the establishment to serve the development of the new Hebrew culture, and having distinctive modal, melodic, and rhythmic patterns (Bayer 1968; Ravina 1968; Shmueli 1968). These characteristics were defined at a special symposium organized in 1968 (Smoira 1968) and described by musicologists (see especially the influential monograph of Shmueli 1971; for the persistence of these views, see Gluzman 1989).

The labels "Hebrew song" and "Israeli song," as synonymous with the (Israeli) folk song, therefore represented a corpus of songs in modern Hebrew that were canonized by their performance at specific social contexts and by their inclusion in songsters published by the major cultural institutions of the Yishuv. However, according to composer and arranger Gil Aldema, only the term SLI continued to be used after 1969 and survived in the vocabulary of the Israeli media (and later in that of the scholarly community) as a distinctive genre of Israeli popular music.

CHARACTERISTICS OF THE HEBREW/ISRAELI FOLK SONG

The invented Israeli "folk song" had peculiar characteristics that scholars have focused on since the 1960s. First, it was mainly created by identifiable composers and well-known poets who expressed their experiences and feelings about the establishment of a new Jewish society in song: "The Hebrew song is . . . the creation of composers who consciously or unconsciously sought a means of tonal organization that would reflect both the people's attachment to the land and the ingathering of the exiles" (Cohen and Katz 1977: 9).

Second, the process of creation, publication, and performance of the new songs was encouraged and supported by agencies within the establishment, such as the Histadrut or the Jewish National Fund (Shahar 1993, 1994); Cohen and Katz (1977), for example, selected the corpus for their research from "collections published by various Israeli agencies . . . as well as educators and composers whose aim was the promotion of the Hebrew song." Interestingly, Cohen and Katz found it necessary to emphasize that the corpus they selected does not include "hit tunes" because "popular songs are short-lived, and closely connected with international fashions" (Cohen and Katz 1977: 11–12). This dichotomy between folk and popular songs assumes that the repertory of SLI was originally conceived as folk songs. However, many songs that are considered to be folk songs by contemporary Israelis originated in popular tunes of past periods.

Until the 1970s, musicologists relating to the evolving song repertory in Hebrew used the labels "Hebrew song" and "Israeli song." The focus on these specific terms reflected the agendas of Israeli music scholars, who were members of the Western-oriented academic milieu or of the media establishment. Such is the case of Michal Smoira-Cohen, a dominant figure in Israel's musical establishment, who held various posts in the Council for Culture and the Arts of the Ministry of Education and Culture and also directed the Music Department of Kol Israel (Smoira-Cohen 1963). How deep labels such as "Hebrew song" penetrated discourse about local music can also be seen in the names given to radio programs dedicated to this repertory, for example, Mo'adon ha-zemer ha-'ivri (Hebrew song club).

The established view of Hebrew/Israeli (folk) song as a written repertory sanctioned by the establishment continued to dominate academia during the 1980s. Natan Shahar made substantial contributions to the field through various publications. His major work is entirely based on an analysis of songs published in printed songsters between the 1880s and 1949 (Shahar 1989). Yet the concept used by Shahar in his study, *shir eretz-yisraeli* (Eretz-Yisraeli song, a term employed as early as 1942 by composer Yitzhak Edel) points to new vistas: "For obvious reasons the '*Eretz Yisraeli* song' does not include anything and everything that was sung, or intended to be sung, among the population of the *Yishuv*," and "the song [is categorized] as having been created within the framework of the Zionist establishment, or at least with the intention of establishment acceptance" (Shahar 1989: v–vi). While recognizing the existence of "a complex relationship between written and oral transmission" in this repertory, Shahar is skeptical about including under the label "Eretz-Israeli Songs" those that fulfilled criteria other than a basic one: being recorded in musical notation (Shahar 1989: vii; 1998: 495).

The bias toward notated sources resulted in ignoring the oral tradition of Hebrew folk songs, with few exceptions (for example, Bayer 1980). Moreover, only a few songs from the first Zionist settlements of the late nineteenth century or those that originated in the incipient globalized popular-music scene of Tel Aviv after the late 1920s were included under the label SLI. Steps toward documenting songs in Hebrew free of the ideological agendas of early Israeli scholars were taken by authors such as Eliyahu Hacohen (in his history of Tel Aviv in songs; Hacohen 1985), Meir Noy (composer and collector whose vast collection of Israeli songs is now located in the Jewish National and University Library in Jerusalem), and Dan Almagor (scholar of literature, writer, translator, and critic, who in 1974 produced the seminal TV series *Sharti lakh artzi* [I sang to you, my country], a retrospective of the Israeli folk song). Such documentary enterprises included the overlooked oral repertory of Hebrew songs originating in diverse contexts outside the establishment (see also Netiva Ben Yehuda's "autobiography in song" of 1992). This documentation opened the door for a more sophisticated consideration of SLI as a dynamic genre defined by its functions and contexts of performance rather than by its contents, period of composition, or form of transmission.

Eliram (1995, 2000) added significantly to these new research directions. First, she localized the ever-evolving repertory of SLI within the framework of communal singing, shirah be-tzibbur. These socializing events in the major cities of Israel after the late 1970s grew to be a favorite form of leisure. Second, she stressed the close relations between SLI and the choreographic design of new folk dances set to the tunes of these songs and performed in both amateur and professional folk-dancing contexts, such as social clubs, recreation centers, and universities. Third, she defined the profile of the consumers of SLI as a stratum of Israelis of mostly European background who were born before the establishment of Israel or during the first years of statehood and comprise the first generation of Israelis educated in the State of Israel. Fourth, she focused on the social functions of this repertory, especially on its ritual use as a kind of secular Israeli prayer. Finally, Eliram attempted to describe the stylistic characteristics that define SLI as a musical genre. Thus the context of performance of SLI, its uses and functions, the profile of its consumers, and the meanings attached to it, particularly by the media, as a recollection in song of the mainstream Israeli collective memory are the social factors that made this repertory a unique musical phenomenon in Israel.

SLI as a Genre of Popular Music

The case of SLI demonstrates the inadequacy of established categories of music such as folk, art, popular, and pop and reinforces John Blacking's opening remarks in the first issue of the journal *Popular Music* where he proposed to focus on the dynamic processes of making music rather than on categories of musical products, while dissolving the distinction between art, folk, and popular music (Blacking 1981: 14).

In an early attempt to define the musical categories of popular music in Israel in the 1980s, Regev refers to SLI as one of the four main types of contemporary popular music, while another, Israeli pop, is "the meeting between the tradition of SLI songs and the western popular music industry" (Regev 1989: 143–44; 1990: 81–82). This definition views SLI as Israeli folk music whose origins are mostly "Russian ballads and East-European rhythms brought to Israel by the founders of Israeli society in the first half of this century" and whose lyrics "generally deal with national themes and agricultural topics." Its creators "are not, for the most part, anonymous," its arrangements "tend to be acoustic, based on accordion, guitar and piano," and it is performed on "ceremonial occasions" or in shirah be-tzibbur. The latter tends to "symbolize national consensus and patriotism."

This early attempt to characterize SLI as popular music combines elements inherited from musicological literature on the Israeli/Hebrew song with two new elements: a particular sound and a unique manner of transmission. It implicitly recognizes the transformation of a certain repertory from the folk category to popular then to Israeli pop. However, the repertory to which Regev refers is an amorphous mass of songs in different styles. Moreover, by stating that "real popular music starts after the mid-1960s,"

Regev seems to deny the existence of any form of "real" popular music prior to the beginning of Israeli rock (1990: 83).

Another author, Amitai Neeman (1980), writing from the perspective of the media, avoided using SLI as a category of popular music, preferring the concept of the "Palestinian song" (clearly referring to songs originating in the prestate period). Interestingly, he totally disregards the musicological category of the Israeli song or the Hebrew song as a basis for the Palestinian song. For him, these Palestinian songs "germinated in the satirical theaters that entertained the young [Jewish] community from the late 1920s until the year of statehood, 1948. The same composers who wrote for those the theaters also wrote for the army entertainment troupes that came into existence during the War of Independence (1948–49). We find, therefore, that the prestate [popular] song style persisted in the ditties and ballads of the army troupes" (Neeman 1980: 61). What was created and accepted by the Yishuv establishment (and thereafter by Israeli musicologists) as "folk" (the Hebrew/Israeli song) has a number of the characteristics of what became known in the West after the beginning of the twentieth century as popular music, particularly compositions by known composers, their distribution first in written form and afterward in commercial recordings, and the crystallization of a new style. There is, however, a paradox in the case of such music in Israel: although the printed songsters can be considered a kind of sheet music, parallel to the early stages of the Anglo-American popular-music industry, most of these composed folk songs were orally transmitted via shirah be-tzibbur. By contrast, "real" folk songs (by anonymous composers, orally transmitted with many variants, based on several sources and styles) were in many cases written down and printed by the publishers of songsters together with composed songs.

Thus, in this early period, the term SLI bridged composed and real folk songs and added other layers of light music, to constitute a particular category of contemporary popular music in Israel, once a formal recording industry began to operate in Israel in the late 1940s. This category is defined not only by its historical origins but also by its literary forms and contents.

Literary Aspects of SLI

One of the major characteristics of SLI is its literary content. Critics of modern Hebrew poetry paid special attention to the ambiguous status of SLI as a literary genre located between two opposed systems: the "light" song (termed *pizmon* [pl. *pizmonim*], lit., a song with refrain, an ancient term renewed in modern Hebrew) and the art or lyrical song (see studies in Ben-Porat 1989). The social source of this ambiguity is located in the identity and status of writers who contributed to the SLI repertory. Many texts of SLI were written by poets who also wrote high or canonic poetry. One significant example is Natan Alterman (1910–70), a prolific and influential author of what he himself defined as *shirei zemer* (lit., songs for singing, as opposed to poems). The two-word phrase is needed because in Hebrew, the word shir means both "song" and "poem" (Meron 1981). Other writers of pizmonim who became part of the SLI repertory were also outstanding authors of "high" poetry, for example, Yaacov Orland (1914–2002) and Nathan Yonathan. Moreover, patterns and contents of canonic modern Hebrew poetry influenced authors who specialized only in the writing of pizmonim, for example, Yehiel Mohar (1921–69, who also wrote poetry using the name Yehiel Mer), Haim Hefer, Yoram Tehar-Lev, Ehud Manor, and Dudu Barak.

However, what distinguishes SLI poetry is not its formal or poetic aspects, but rather its themes. Designed to celebrate the renewed Jewish national experience and the ideals of the Zionist settlement in Eretz Yisrael, SLI emphasizes specific topics. Among these are descriptions of the Land of Israel (especially such locations valued by the Zionist ethos as the Jezreel Valley or the Jordan River), cultivating the land, and the defense of the territory. In other words, these songs focus on the major themes of Hebrewism.

Another major literary aspect of SLI emphasized by the critics is the persona of the texts. Many of the songs from early periods are narrated from the perspective of the first-person plural, "we." Using the plural reflected the concern of Hebrew/Israeli folk songs with the Jewish community in Eretz Yisrael as a collective, rather than with the individual. The change from "we" to "I" in Hebrew/Israeli songs marks a major turning point in the gradual transformation of SLI from folk to popular song.

A classic example of SLI is the song "Shir moledet" (Song of the homeland; also known as "Shir boqer" [Morning song]) written by Natan Alterman and composed by Daniel Samburski in 1934. The song was featured in the propaganda film *Le-ḥayyim ḥadashim* (lit., To a new life; distributed in English as Land of promise) commissioned by the Keren Hayesod (Palestine Foundation Fund, the financial arm of the World Zionist Organization), produced by the Urim company headed by Leo Hermann, and directed by Yehudah Lehmann.

SHIR MOLEDET (ALTERMAN / SAMBURSKI)

On the mountains the sun already blazes
And in the valley the dew still shines
We love you, homeland,
With joy, with song and with hard work.
From the slopes of Lebanon to the Dead Sea

We shall crisscross you with ploughs
We shall yet cultivate and build you
We shall yet beautify you.

Latter-day SLI addresses more intimate subjects from an introspective perspective, such as the private grief over those who fell in war. Naomi Shemer's "Shneynu me-oto ha-kfar" (The two of us are from the same village) is an example of this new type of SLI.

SHNEYNU ME-OTO HA-KFAR (SHEMER)

The two of us are from the same village
The same height, the same hairstyle,
The same way of talking, what can be said
Yes, we are from the same village.

Refrain

And on Friday nights,
When a gentle breeze
Passes through the black tree-tops,
Then I remember you.
I remember in the battle that did not end
I suddenly saw you fall
And when dawn appeared beyond the mountain
Then I brought you to the village.
You see, we are here in the village
Almost everything is still the same
I walk through a green field
And you are beyond the fence [in the cemetery].

SLI: CANON AND OPEN SYSTEM

The repertory that the contemporary popular-music industry perpetuates as SLI is a body of song in very diverse musical styles accumulated through a complex process of selection carried out over one hundred years of Zionist history. This process continues into the present, as new popular songs are judged by the people who participate in communal singing (leaders and singers), radio editors, and critics as belonging to SLI thanks to their musical style, contents, and/or the identity of their authors and performers.

A periodization of the diachronic evolution of the SLI repertory is problematic, since the different styles of composition and the creative periods of composers and lyricists overlap. Nonetheless, three periods can be distinguished on the basis of both social and musical criteria: the "classic" period or the "golden age" of the Hebrew/Israeli song, which lasted for about six decades from the beginning of the century to the mid-1960s; the middle period, from the mid-1960s to the early 1980s; and the contemporary period, since the 1980s (Eliram 2000).

Songs of the classic period include the remnants of folk songs from the first and second 'aliyot (1880–1917), many of which were adaptations of Diaspora songs or Hebrew texts set to Russian melodies (Mahanaimi 1988; Miron 1967), and, more rarely, Arabic tunes. Songs from the golden age of the Israeli folk song, those composed between the 1920s and the 1960s, are the bulk of the repertory of this period. These include original compositions by amateur and professional composers, new immigrants and Israeli-born, and Hebrew translations of chiefly Russian songs. We may distinguish here between the kibbutz composers, most notably David Zehavi (1910–75) from Na'an, Matitiyahu Shelem (Weiner) from Ramat Yochanan (1904–75), and Yehudah Sharet (Shertok) from Yagur (1901–79); and urban composers, best represented by Joel Engel (1868–1927), Yedidiah Admon (Gorochov, 1894–1985), Nahum Nardi (1901–77), Mordechai Zeira (1905–68), Daniel Samburski (1909–75), and Emanuel Amiran (Pougatchov, 1909–93). To this period also belong songs written for the satirical cabarets and reviews in Tel Aviv from the 1930s on (such as Ha-matate, Ha-qumqum, and Li-la-lo). The most prolific of the composers of this genre was Moshe Vilensky (1910–97). The Zionist youth movements are another source of songs of this period (Eldan 1989; Margol 1989). Later, two important and unique layers were added: songs from the War of Independence (1947–49), many of which are of Russian origin (Mahanaimi 1988) and songs of the lehaqot tzvayiot (IDF entertainment ensembles) of the 1950s and 1960s. This uniquely Israeli context of popular-music performance included songs by established civilian composers of what was called in the 1950s musiqa qalah (light music), such as Moshe Vilensky and Sasha Argov (1914–95). To these can be added the songs of groups such as Batzal yaroq (Green Onion) and Ha-Tarnegolim, which consisted of graduates of the lehaqot tzvayiot and may be considered an organic continuation of the military context. Latter-day additions to the classic period are songs composed by Israeli-born and/or educated composers after the mid-1950s, such as Emmanuel Zamir (1925–62), Nahum Heiman, Yair Rosenblum (1944–96), Naomi Shemer, and Nurit Hirsh for both the army and civilian stages. The contents of the texts, for example, glorifying the landscape or themes related to the defense of the country, and in some cases the melodic style of their songs recall Israeli folk songs from earlier periods.

The songs of the middle period belong to a time when SLI became nostalgia. The major development of this period, and one that shaped the perception of SLI as an "old" repertory, was the rise of Israeli rock. This combined with the perception that the old SLI repertory was winding down. The establishment of the Israeli Song Festival was one of the mechanisms dedicated to revitalizing the repertory of original Hebrew songs. Despite the threat from Hebrew rock and middle-of-the-road (MOR) pop, the SLI repertory continued to grow during these years, mainly through the addition of new songs from festivals and from the repertories of the "chamber" ensembles (duos or trios) fashionable in the 1960s.

In the contemporary period, SLI becomes a well-established genre. The most recent acquisitions of the SLI repertory in this period are rock and pop ballads that comply with the musical and textual requisites of the genre. An example of such a new addition is the song "'Od lo tamu kol pela'aikh" (Your wonders are not yet exhausted; better known by its refrain, "Artzenu ha-qtantonet," or Our tiny country; not to be confused with the 1940s tango, whose refrain opens with the same words). The fate of this song is an example of the expansion of the SLI repertory. It was written in 1981 by lyricist Yoram Tehar-Lev and composed by Rami Kleinstein for the lehaqa tzvait of the Northern Command. However, it was forgotten until its successful revival as a ballad, sung in the 1990s by Kleinstein himself (by then a respected rock star). Since then this song has been adopted by leaders and singers of communal singing. The refrain, with its biblical overtones, and its meditative minor melody based on a single rhythmic motif show why it easily penetrated the SLI repertory:

> Our tiny country, our beautiful country,
> Homeland without a gown, barefoot homeland.
> Accept me into your songs, beautiful bride,
> Open your gates, I shall enter them and praise you.

SLI as an Eclectic Repertory

The SLI repertory is, stylistically speaking, very eclectic. This eclecticism is a result of the complex musical scene of the Jewish community in Eretz Yisrael before and after the establishment of the state (see Hirshberg 1995, 1998, who focuses on Western art music; see also Topelberg 2000). Although ethnically dominated by Eastern and Central European Jews, the growing oriental and Sephardi minorities of the Yishuv contributed to the stylistic diversification of music, especially by raising the predicament of the pervasive idea of the "Orient" in new Hebrew culture. This predicament became more complex due to the physical location of the Yishuv in the Middle East and its contacts and conflicts with local Palestinian Arab culture.

Small in number and ethnically varied, the Yishuv (1880–1948) consisted of diverse social strata differentiated by types of settlements. Each type of settlement—urban (which refers chiefly to Tel Aviv and Haifa), the *moshavot* (the early agricultural settlements), and the kibbutzim (collective farms)—developed distinctive folk and popular-musical activities (Shavit 1990: 260).

In the cities, we find European/American-oriented light music in coffee houses, satirical cabarets, and dancing halls (such as the Casino on the Tel Aviv beachfront that operated in the late 1920s and featured live dancing music). The light music of the cities was derogatorily referred to as *musiqa salonit* (salon music) by the socialist-oriented, militant Zionist establishment, particularly on the kibbutzim.

The moshavot, whose population still observed a traditional religious way of life, were a more conservative musical context where one could find authentic Russian and Yiddish folk songs sometimes set to new Hebrew words, along with small fanfare orchestras performing at communal occasions. On the kibbutzim, we find the songs of the Zionist youth movements from Europe together with newly composed Hebrew folk songs and occasional performances of classical music usually imported from the cities or played on a gramophone for collective listening.

Jewish settlements in the different parts of the Yishuv (the Upper Galilee, the Jezreel Valley, Judea [central Israel of today], and Jerusalem) developed their own repertories because of the physical distance that separated them and the lack of unifying media such as radio. One can even find a distinctive musical repertory by groups of different ethnic backgrounds within one city or settlement. A symptom of this geographical diversity is the setting of different, local texts to the same Russian or Yiddish folk tune.

During the prestate period, the creation and consumption of authentic SLI is found mainly in Zionist circles, such as the youth movements in the cities and on the kibbutzim. The musical style of these songs varied, although composers were guided by a vague ideal, that of combining the Russian folk song with oriental elements. The popular and folk songs created by other segments of the Yishuv population, such as the musiqa salonit of the cities or songs of the moshavot, contributed to the stylistic diversification of SLI. However, these were conceptualized as SLI only after the War of Independence.

The eclecticism of the SLI repertory increased with the establishment of the state. After 1948 Israeli society was characterized by accelerated urbanization, increased social mobility, and ethnic and cultural diversification following the absorption of massive waves of immigration from Eastern Europe and Islamic countries. By the late 1950s, centers of musical creativity of SLI shifted from the agricultural settlements to urban centers and from public institutional sponsorship (for example, the Zionist Funds, the army, or the Histadrut) to an open, media-oriented music industry managed by the private sector. Since the 1960s, the creation of new SLI has occurred within the popular-music industry. However, it is the active performance of these new SLI songs at communal singing (rather than merely hearing them on the radio or on records and CDs) that ultimately determined their acceptance into the canon, and not their rating in the media or their sales figures.

The song "Qor'im lanu la-lekhet" (We are called to walk) by Efi Netzer is a typical example of the new SLI from a literary, musical, and social viewpoint (Eliram 2000). The song celebrates one of the most institutionalized rituals of Israeli educational and leisure activities: touring the Land of Israel on foot in organized groups (for example, school trips, youth movements, army units, tours sponsored by the Nature Preservation Society) and organized trips during vacations. Sometimes known as *yedi'at ha-'aretz* (knowledge of the land), the ritual dates back to the 1920s and was (and still is) an essential part of Israelis' patriotic upbringing. Although in a minor key, the melody moves in a forceful marchlike pace enhanced by the syncopated rhythm, a well-known code of Israeliness due to its close association with the *hora*, Israel's national folk dance.

QOR´IM LANU LA-LEKHET (NETZER)

Again our footfalls resound on the roads
And the pack on our back moves around more.
Again the valley is spread at our side
And the mountain range rises above it.
But joyful are those who march with us
And can conquer both on foot!

Refrain

Because the laughter of wild flowers rolls down the slopes
And the rains and falling leaves are behind us
And a thousand songs of canteens and voices
Call us, call us to walk!

Again the armies of spring burst out
In the Negev and in Galilee
The innocent heavens are blue again
And the gang is on the roads
They sing the song, again and again
And they walk and they walk and they walk.

PERFORMANCE, BROADCASTING, AND PRINTING OF SLI

One of the most distinctive features of SLI is the context in which it is performed—shirah be-tzibbur (Eliram 1995, 2000; Hirshberg 1995: 153–56; Shahar 1997a: 15–16). Communal singing, as an aspect of musical socialization created during the Yishuv period, persists today in establishments such as the MOFET cultural centers of the workers' councils of the Histadrut, in private clubs where the singing is accompanied by wine (for example, the renowned *Mo'adon ha-yeqev* [Wine Cellar Club], in the town of Rishon le-Ziyon near Tel Aviv), at private homes on Independence Day, and even on TV programs (such as the televised "Sing-alongs with Sarale Sharon" of the 1980s). The performance of SLI in these public contexts is a crucial factor in determining the evolving content of the SLI canon.

Another major factor in the perpetuation and performance of SLI are the *havurot zemer* (singing ensembles). The havurot zemer consist, according to Shahar (1997a: 29), of a group of amateur singers (ranging in number from eight to thirty-five) who love Hebrew songs and meet regularly to learn and perform these songs accompanied by instruments (most commonly accordion, piano, guitar or synthesizer, and Arabic drum; sometimes backup tapes are used) under the leadership of a conductor. The arrangements are rather simple, usually for two parts in parallel thirds or sixths with call-and-response dialogues between the men's and the women's sections.

The distinction between havurot zemer and the shirah be-tzibbur is sometimes subtle. Many havurot zemer sprang from the clubs in which Hebrew songs were performed on a purely voluntary and extemporary basis, in the context of entertainment, by an amateur public guided by a professional leader. Sometimes the leaders of havurot zemer, themselves composers, would introduce and disseminate their new songs via the ensembles they conducted. This is yet another venue for expanding the repertory of SLI through a mechanism with the characteristics of an oral tradition.

Havurot zemer sprang up in the late 1950s as a result of various processes: the decline of the permanent amateur choirs of the kibbutzim and regional councils and the subsequent professionalization of choral singing in the agricultural settlements, which left many song enthusiasts outside the circle of performance; the emergence and popularity of the lehaqot tzvayiot (Shahar 1997b); and the impact of the model of the French ensemble, Les Compagnons de la Chanson, that appeared in Israel in the late 1950s under the Hebrew name *Havurat ha-zemer ha-tzarfati* (lit., the French song company).

Once a feature of musical life in the agricultural settlements, by the early 1960s havurot zemer were also forming in the cities under the auspices of public cultural institutions. Conductors of these city ensembles, such as Meir Harnik in Jerusalem and Efi Netzer in Haifa, were also well-known leaders of communal singing. The repertory of these groups included not only the well-established canon of folk songs composed before and during the War of Independence but also current songs and ballads of the lehaqot tzvayiot and of the popular-music industry in general. Most important, the performance model, that is, the sound of the havurot zemer, permeated radio folk-music programming.

In 1962, the Havurat Renanim ensemble was established by Gil Aldema, a prolific composer, arranger, and conductor of Israeli folk songs. The purpose of this ensemble was to record old songs as well as new ones that were missing from the radio archives and to supply the increasing public demand for such materials. Aldema's arrangements were relatively sophisticated, sometimes including splits of three or even four vocal parts and the accompaniment of woodwinds and bass guitar.

The most successful and lasting of these ensembles was the Gevatron, originating in Kibbutz Geva' in the Jezreel Valley. This ensemble's commercial recordings and its impressive appearances on the radio, and after 1969, on television boosted its popularity. The Gevatron established the performance parameters and repertory of a well-established havurat zemer, making use of studio techniques to improve the sound quality and balance, and appeared wearing specially designed, uniform costumes of a pseudofolk Israeli style (adopted from the Israeli folk-dance dress designers). Thus the havurot zemer, from ad hoc performing groups of amateurs, became a component of the music industry that specialized in the stylized performance of SLI.

Boosted by the growing demand for SLI, the 1980s witnessed a revival of the havurot zemer. This revival led to the establishment of the Arad Festival, originally designed as a national encounter of havurot zemer, first held in 1982 in a small city in the central Negev Desert. Soon, however, this festival lost its intended nature and became a rock festival. About 250 havurot zemer, differing in size and professional standards, were active in the early 1990s (Shahar 1997a: 31).

Since the 1960s, both contexts, the havurot zemer and the shirah be-tzibbur, have reflected and been inspired by performances of SLI in the media. The media played an important role in the creation, diffusion, and empowerment of the SLI repertory, contributing to the canonization of SLI as a repository of the Israeli national identity. Particularly effective was the broadcast of SLI by state radio and television on special occasions. The canon of SLI, conceived as a representation of a wide consensus of Israeliness, is traditionally heard on the airwaves on national holidays, particularly on Yom ha-zikaron le-halalei tzahal (Memorial Day for the Fallen Soldiers of the IDF, which immediately precedes Independence Day), on days of mourning, such as after major terrorist attacks, and, more recently, in the days immediately following the assassination of Prime Minister Yitzhak Rabin in 1995.

Media initiatives also resulted in the renewed performance of old SLI or the production of new songs. An example of such initiatives are the programs *Erev shirei meshorerim* (Evening of songs by poets) produced by Galei Tzahal between 1972 and 1980. For these programs, composers of popular music were commissioned to write and arrange new melodies for poems written by canonic Israeli poets. This was a conscious attempt to elevate the literary aspect of SLI by choosing texts by serious writers. Other initiatives, such as the 1974 television series *Sharti lakh artzi* (I sing to you my country) or the radio series *Netiv ha-zemer* (Path of song) produced by Netiva Ben Yehuda, Ehud Manor, and Gil Aldema, stimulated new performances of SLI.

The persistence of the SLI repertory in the media derives from public demand as much as from its manipulation by programmers as a symbol of the Israeli national consensus. Broadcasting this canonic repertory and its consensual connotations appealed to many Israeli popular musicians of diverse backgrounds, from middle-of-the-road and rock to oriental. These artists have recorded a diverse array of arrangements of SLI.

While the media played a role in the public exposure of SLI during the 1970s and later on in the 1990s, the sing-alongs remained the main venue for their performance. Yet there was one other major form of dissemination of SLI: printed songsters, known as *shironim*. The publication of Hebrew/Israeli songs in print is a phenomenon that dates back to the earliest period of the Jewish settlement in Eretz Yisrael. During this formative period, folk songs were mainly printed by agencies of the establishment, such as the Histadrut and the Jewish National Fund. Social networks that demanded new Hebrew songs, such as the educational system, the youth movements, and the kibbutzim were intricately connected to the Yishuv institutions. Within these contexts, mimeographed hand-written pages, as well as personal notebooks filled with song lyrics were an additional mode of disseminating songs. After the 1950s, the private sector entered the business of printing songs for sing-alongs (though some such private enterprises existed earlier), such as the comprehensive anthology *1000 zemer ve-'od zemer* (1,000 songs and one more song; edited by Talma Eliagon and Rafi Pesaḥson [6 vols., 1981–94]). Sometimes the songsters (accompanied by cassettes or CDs) were produced by the renowned leaders of communal singing themselves, such as the series *Lashir ʿim Efi Netzer* (To sing with Efi Netzer [3 vols., 1983–91]).

SLI and the Recording Industry

If pop music is considered "a continuation of both formal and substantive elements of the folk tradition" and the audiences treat the "initial gramophone recording as the original 'publication' of a song" (Hatch and Millward 1987: 2), a comprehensive study of the meaning of SLI cannot ignore its relation to the recording industry within and outside of Eretz Yisrael.

One of the first collection of songs recorded by Aḥvah, the pioneer record company established in Tel Aviv (ca. 1934), was titled *Mi-shirei Eretz Yisrael* (Among the songs of the Land of Israel). This collection truly mirrors the complexity of the musical scene of the Yishuv. It includes "composed folk songs" by renowned composers of the old generation such as Mordechai Zeira, Emanuel Amiran (Pougatchov), and Joel Engel; Hebrew translations of Yiddish folk songs; songs with religious content; and, significantly, songs from the city cabarets and reviews, such as "Doda hagidi lanu ken" (Auntie, say yes to us), composed by Moshe Vilensky, apparently on the basis of a Yiddish folk song. Stylistically, these songs draw on elements from varied sources, ranging from the Russian style of composed folk songs to international styles of the 1930s, such as the Argentinean tango, adapted to Hebrew texts. A similar variety of styles can be found among the early 78 rpm recordings of modern Hebrew songs produced outside Palestine. These include recordings by singer Yossef Goland, produced in London circa 1934, by His Master's Voice.

The role of the media, especially of radio, in the revival of SLI as popular music can be traced back to 1959 when the musical reviews *Tel Aviv ha-qtanah* (Little Tel Aviv) and *Hayo hayu zmanim* (Once upon a time) were staged. Later, songs from these two programs appeared on an LP. Another example of this revival was the release of the LP *Hayu leylot* (There were nights [1961]) by popular singer Esther Reichstadt (later Ofarim) and of LPs by Nehama Hendel, in performances whose aesthetics recalled that of American folksingers such as Joan Baez.

A major turning point in the transformation of SLI into a mainstream genre of popular music was the album series recorded during the 1970s by singer Arik Einstein. Significantly titled *Eretz Yisrael ha-yeshanah ve-ha-tovah* (Good Old Eretz Yisrael [vol. 1, 1973; vol. 2, 1976; vol. 3, 1977]), the series presented a large selection of SLI, arranged by young rock- and jazz-oriented musicians such as Shem Tov Levy, Avner Kener, and Yoni Rechter. By the early 1970s, Einstein was already a central figure on the budding Israeli rock scene. His return to the "old" repertory of SLI was part of a larger trend in the 1970s of digging into the past of Israeli popular music (as were the television series mentioned above).

Indeed, Einstein's recordings of SLI, as well as recordings of such songs by other singers (Yehoram Gaon, Ilanit, Shlomo Artzi, and, later, Ofra Haza), were part of a trend to write and record new songs in the vein of SLI during the 1970s. This was saliently exemplified in songs and albums by Chava Alberstein, especially *Kmo tzemaḥ bar* (Like a wildflower [1975]).

Two highly memorable recorded contributions to the SLI canon in this period came from Naomi Shemer. One was the song "'Al kol ele" (For all of this) originally recorded by Yossi Banai in 1980, and the other "Lu yehi" (Let it happen), originally recorded by the Ha-gashash ha-ḥiver Trio in 1973 (the songs can be found on *Asif Zahav* and *Asif Kaḥol*, two albums that collect recordings of Naomi Shemer's songs by various artists). The latter was initially commissioned as a Hebrew paraphrase of the Beatles' "Let it Be," and Shemer composed a new melody whose style and melodic contour (especially in the refrain) recalls the Beatles' song.

LU YEHI (SHEMER)

There is still a white sail on the horizon
Beneath a heavy black cloud,
All that we long for, let it be.

And if in the windows of the evening
The light of holiday candles trembles,
All that we long for, let it be.
Please, let it be, let it be,
All that we long for, let it be.

"Lu yehi" became an instant hit and gained the status of a secular prayer soon after its release, a status extended to many other SLI songs. In fact, the SLI sing-alongs are perceived (among others, by Naomi Shemer herself) as a kind of secular Israeli response to the public rituals of traditional orthodox Judaism.

One can attribute the wave of recording of old SLI songs and the composition of new ones during the 1970s to the aftermath of the Yom Kippur War of October 1973. The Yom Kippur War is considered by many as a "national trauma" (Lomsky-Feder 1998), due to the perceived undermining of Israel's military might. Consequently, the return to SLI in the years following the war may be interpreted as a reflection of the yearning for earlier periods of national strength and as a way of recuperating from the trauma.

It should be noted, however, that the 1970s were the years when Israeli rock and musiqa mizrahit emerged, reflecting, respectively, the rise of global Israeliness and of mizrahiyut as challenging cultural positions to dominant Hebrewism. This included a growing critical examination of Hebrewism and sabra culture, especially in the Israeli cinema (see Shohat 1989). In light of this, the invigoration of SLI in the 1970s should be seen as an attempt to rescue, or at least honor, its status as historical, quintessential "authentic" Israeli music. Indeed, with consumerism invading many facets of life in Israel, by the 1980s the distribution and consumption of SLI had become a nostalgia industry.

Nostalgia Industry

Already in the early 1960s, it was clear that SLI was being transformed into a new form of cultural expression in Israel. Its original function as folk, school, theater, or youth movement songs was being diluted and an additional function developed: the representation of nostalgia. Different aspects of the nostalgia phenomenon are found in three distinct social settings: the opening of new communal singing clubs in major cities; the rapid expansion of the activities of havurot zemer; and the role of communal singing in the growing Israeli community abroad.

A more potent demonstration of the role of listening to and performing SLI as a signifier of Israeli national identity through the development of the nostalgia industry in Israel can be found among expanding communities of Israelis living outside their country, chiefly in the United States. In a perceptive study of this phenomenon, Shokeid (1988: 104–25) examines the performance of SLI at sing-alongs organized by Israeli *yordim* (lit., "those who descend," a euphemism for Israeli emigrants, as opposed to 'olim, "those who ascend," used to refer to immigrants to Israel) in New York in the early 1980s. Shokeid rejects as rather simplistic the interpretation that perceives participation in these sing-alongs as a "collective experience of nostalgia in the purest sense" (1988: 121). The definition of nostalgia as an evocation of a positive past in the context of a negative present does not apply to the vast majority of Israelis in New York, most of whom do not consider their present as particularly disadvantaged. In fact, Shokeid argues, following Geertz's concept of "cultural performance" applied to nonreligious contexts (Geertz 1973: 113), that "participants [of the Israeli sing-alongs] were making a cultural claim and expressing an existential predicament" (Shokeid 1988: 122). "Singing together, the participants not only evoked their national ethos through familiar symbolic repertory, but also updated their stock of songs and incorporated new symbolic references to present-day Israel" (Shokeid 1988: 124). The sing-along actually has the power to "transform reality, a process pertinent to most rituals and cultural performances."

. . .

Literary critic Ariel Hirschfeld attempted to summarize succinctly all the characteristics of "the Hebrew/Israel song" in a series of three articles published in the weekend supplement of the daily *Haaretz* in 1997:

> The Israeli song is the most "Israeli" of all artistic phenomena and is the only [art] medium in which something unique was created, [a phenomenon] which differentiates [the Israeli song] on the level of the medium, from what was created in this century in other cultures. It is neither a "folk song" nor an "art" song (as, for example, in the tradition of the German *Lied*), nor is it a product of the mass entertainment culture. In its heroic period, between the 1930s and the 1960s, it grew as a medium that combines artistic musical and literary activity, sometimes on the highest level, with a popular, communal performance in which the experience of the individual is at the center. (Hirschfeld 1997)

Since the beginnings of both the recording and the music publication industries in Israel, and until around the 1970s, SLI was a descriptive label designating most of the secular (and, exceptionally, religious) songs sung by modern Jews in Eretz Yisrael, regardless of their mode of production, style, or original social function. In the framework of the popular-music industry of the last quarter of the twentieth century, the concept still preserved some of its original connotations. However, as time passed, a process of selection constantly reshaped and redefined this category. Its promoters (such as the leaders of communal singing) added new songs while removing older ones or reviving them through new arrangements.

SLI thus came to stand for the repertory of songs that survived this process of selection. This corpus has certain stylistic characteristics, particularly its manner of performance (solo singer, havurat zemer, or the entire audience accompanied by acoustic instruments: accordion, guitar, or piano) and channel of transmission (communal singing, either live or recorded via radio or TV). The social connotation of this genre is clear: it is a musical reflection of the ethos of the Jewish society in Eretz Yisrael, including elements from various historical periods, from both the agricultural and urban experience. SLI elevates the values venerated by the majority of Israeli Jewish society, such as the attachment to and praise of the Land of Israel, the defense of the land, and the experience of immigration and settlement.

SLI is not a static genre of popular music, but rather an ongoing dynamic process through which songs from radically different sources become a symbol of the Israeli collective. Rooted in the Yishuv period, passing through the War of Independence and the first, now idealized, days of statehood, and continuing into the present, this process created a distinctive component within contemporary Israeli popular music. The contest over appropriation of both the repertory of SLI and of the label itself by different sectors of Israeli society is further testimony to its central role as a musical representation of Israeliness.

4 "In Spite of It All, She Has Something"

Popular Songs in the Yishuv and Early Statehood

There is a folk song that still circulates among young Israelis, especially in youth movements like the *tzofim* (scouts) that begins, "In the summer it is cold, in the winter it is hot, the fox is dumb and the ass is wise." Few people today are aware that this text is a paraphrase of a song written by poet, actor, and producer Avigdor Hameiri. The song was originally conceived and performed as a popular song and set to the tune of a Yiddish folk song different from the melody used today. It is in the style of the "contrast" or "upside-down" songs that were fashionable in contemporary satirical theaters of Central Europe. The song premiered in Tel Aviv in 1927 by the satirical theater company Ha-qumqum (The Kettle) and was sung by young, Yemen-born singer Bracha Zefira (Hacohen 1985: 42–43; on Zefira, see Chapter 9, below). Exemplifying the fine line that separates the "popular" from the "folk" in urban settings at the turn of the twentieth century, this song introduces us to the early stages of the development of the Hebrew song that was conceptualized by its composers, performers, critics, and audiences as popular rather than folk.

The ethos of the Zionist enterprise was linked to the "return to the land" in its most practical sense: to agricultural work, "the blooming of the desert," as David Ben Gurion once put it. The Zionist narrative celebrated the agricultural settlement as its most tangible achievement. The culture created in these settlements, especially in the communal kibbutzim, became a model for incoming Jewish immigrants as well as supporters of the Zionist movement outside Palestine, though the majority of the Jewish population both in the Yishuv and abroad belonged to the urban bourgeoisie. Thus the Israeli folk song, that is, Shirei Eretz Yisrael (SLI) and particularly the songs of its golden age (the 1920s to the 1960s), composed in many cases by kibbutz members, became the musical paradigm of the new Hebrew culture.

These songs were spread through all Zionist venues, especially the youth movements whose role was to educate the younger generation in the ethos of the new culture.

The invention of the Israeli folk song is a topic that has dominated academic discourse about Israeli music since the 1960s. This discourse overshadowed the existence of an urban, proto-popular-music scene whose eventual impact on Israeli music culture was no less significant than the folk song. This popular music is linked to the first Hebrew metropolis, Tel Aviv.

While the Israeli folk song was socially sanctioned and supported by the Zionist institutions (for example, the Histadrut, the youth movements, the educational system), the popular music of Tel Aviv between the 1920s and 1950s was a type of Hebrew music whose survival depended on public demand and market forces. The contexts of its performance and its literary content were not mobilized in the service of any educational or other edifying purpose and its aesthetic dimension was not dictated by the search for national authenticity. On the contrary, the composers, performers, and consumers of this music had no specific ideological agenda (except the use of Hebrew texts in the songs) besides entertainment. Stylistically, this musical scene was related to the contemporary international styles of musical theater and dance music.

The fourth and fifth 'aliyot provided the social background for the emergence of an early form of urban popular music in Tel Aviv. These two waves of immigration from Eastern and Central Europe (mainly Poland and Germany) brought industrialization and a sizeable urban working class to the capital of the Yishuv. A growing sector of merchants, craftsmen, and liberal artisans developed in the new industrialized society. Although a protobourgeoisie had existed among the Jews of the "old Yishuv" in Palestine before the arrival of the waves of Zionist immigration, the novelty of the fourth and fifth 'aliyot lay in its large numbers, in the industrial background of many of its members, and in their direct involvement with early-twentieth-century European urban culture.

The fifth 'aliyah had a particularly dramatic impact on the musical culture of the emerging Israeli urban society. According to Gertz:

> This 'aliyah consisted of property owners, people from the middle class. Its character was essentially urban, and it contributed to the prosperity of the cities and to their development. This prosperity led to the massive movement of Jewish agricultural workers towards the cities in response to their natural drive to improve their conditions of life. This process of urbanization was accompanied by prosperity and growth in all the branches of the economy. However, in the eyes of the political elite and

the intelligentsia (writers, journalists, educators and others) they were perceived as harming settlement-oriented, pioneering Zionism, because the pioneering cause was linked to agriculture and the "rural" settlement. Many articles that appeared in the press of that period decried the fact that the new immigrants left for the city and that veteran workers moved from agriculture to the construction industry. These articles perceived the abandonment of the rural settlements (including the *moshavot*) as a sign of weakness of the pioneering spirit. (Gertz 1988: 19)

The role of this bourgeoisie in the study of Israeli society and culture has generally been underestimated (Ben Porat 1999). The historical and ideological narrative of the Zionist enterprise was typically written by the intelligentsia of the agricultural settlements and the labor movement in general. Consequently, the bourgeoisie remained in the shadow of the official discourse, in spite of the fact that it generated much of the material resources needed for the growth of the Yishuv.

The incipient bourgeoisie of Tel Aviv brought to the Yishuv all the components of leisure culture of modern cities, including the development of an internationally oriented popular-music scene. This implied the creation of performance stages where musicians found jobs, the development of a recording and broadcasting industry, and the emergence of consumption markets for popular culture, including films. By the early 1930s movies, and especially musical films, became a main venue for exposing the public of the Yishuv to contemporary trends of American and other cosmopolitan popular music. The Tel Aviv scene was populated by multifaceted and interdisciplinary figures on whose initiative many popular-music activities developed. One such figure was Baruch Kaushanski (nicknamed "Agadati"), a dancer, painter, producer, and filmmaker who was famous for the parties he organized, especially around Purim, the Jewish carnival, for which new songs were commissioned (Dunevitch 1959: 77). That the citizens of Tel Aviv took pride in the lively cosmopolitanism of their small city is best exemplified by one of the popular songs about the city, "Be-khol zot yesh ba mashehu" (In spite of it all, she has something), written by Natan Alterman and composed by Moshe Vilensky for the Li-la-lo review company in 1946.

International-style popular music was the antithesis of the Eretz-Yisraeli folk song. The lyrics usually focused on the pleasures of the moment and on the concerns of individuals, and the music was borrowed from standard Western forms and dance rhythms. Thus it was only the use of the Hebrew language that reflected the commitment of the social network that supported this music to the new Hebrew culture.

It should also be borne in mind that at the time Palestine was under the British Mandate. The social fabric of Tel Aviv (and other cities) included the personnel serving in the British administration. Thus many venues of recreation and leisure aimed at entertaining the British armed forces and civil servants stationed in Palestine (see Segev 1999). These venues, such as the cafés of Tel Aviv, which were frequented by the British, were owned by Jews who employed European-Jewish musicians conversant with the most recent styles of European light music. This colonial setting, which often also included members of the growing Arab middle class, and which during World War II expanded to include large international contingents of the Allied Forces, contributed to the exposure of the Jewish bourgeoisie, and of the entire Jewish population of the large cities (Tel Aviv, Haifa, and Jerusalem), to current European and American popular music. This exposure was rather limited, however, since the Jewish population at large avoided socializing with the colonial establishment as part of the growing resistance of the Yishuv to the British presence in Palestine.

The dichotomy between the rural folk music of SLI and urban popular music lasted only until the 1960s. After that time, many of the songs created for the Hebrew theater stage, cabarets, or dance halls during the Yishuv period and in the first two decades of statehood became an integral part of the Shirei Eretz Yisrael repertory and were incorporated into the body of national "folk songs" associated with Israel's early period.

REVUE THEATERS AND CAFÉS

In the rural settlements of the Yishuv, music performances took place in collective spaces such as the kibbutz dining room and were shared by most of the population. A rapidly growing urban center such as Tel Aviv was not able to establish such a collective pattern of music consumption; as a result, new forms of music consumption soon emerged in public spaces where an anonymous aggregate of listeners gathered to listen to music on the basis of a market system of supply and demand. The establishment of such venues of public music performance is the hallmark of the emergence of the local popular-music scene in Tel Aviv. Although communal singing, such as that conducted by composer Daniel Samburski in Beit Brenner, the cultural club of the Histadrut, in downtown Tel Aviv, continued until the 1950s, the ethos of togetherness found in the musical performances of the Yishuv was gradually replaced in Tel Aviv of the late 1920s by a new, vibrant music market. The repertories heard in the new performance venues, unlike those of the public sing-alongs, were determined by the demands of a large, anonymous public rather than by ideologists of culture.

Ha-qumqum

The revue theater was one of the main venues of popular musical creativity that developed in Tel Aviv in the early 1920s. The idea of establishing a revue theater was conceived by poet Artur Koestler, a young immigrant from Budapest who arrived in Israel in 1926. He joined forces with another Hungarian Jew, poet Avigdor Hameiri. Modeled on the Hungarian cabaret of Budapest, in 1927 they founded the satirical theater Ha-qumqum (Carmel 1980: 256–57). They were joined by Hungarian-Jewish actor and cartoonist Robert Donat, who acted as "conferencier" (anchor) of the theater and also sketched the political caricatures that became the trademark of the stage of Ha-qumqum.

Ha-qumqum's first show was performed at the Shulamit Conservatory in Tel Aviv. The public sat around tables in the small conservatory. The show did not catch the attention of a wide audience, nor did similar attempts in other venues. After the failure of the first show, Hameiri shifted from the intellectual approach to theater, characteristic of the Hungarian model, to the revue theater or variety show, that is, a loosely connected series of scenes including light sketches and popular songs. Hameiri hired experienced actors and singers such as Rafael Klatchkin and Tova Piron, and booked Beit Ha-'am (the House of the People, founded in 1925), the largest and most popular open stage in Tel Aviv, located on the sand dunes on the outskirts of the city. In its new format and venue, Ha-qumqum was a great success.

Many of the songs composed for Ha-qumqum theater were pizmonim, which in modern Hebrew means "refrain" and became synonymous with "light songs." Some songs criticized the British Mandate government while others took on the Zionist institutions and political parties, especially the elite leadership of the workers' parties. The refrain of the Ha-qumqum song "One More Hole" says:

> They [the Zionist leaders] solve [the economic problems], who knows?
> And the pioneer here slowly starves,
> everything is OK and continues on,
> and me, I tighten my belt one more hole.
>
> (From the personal notes of singer Tova Piron,
> quoted in Topelberg 2000: 36)

The harsh criticism of the Zionist workers' parties and their leaders caused tension and eventually led the artists to challenge Hameiri. Many of these artists, immigrants of the militant third 'aliyah, were committed to the workers' parties. In 1929, the exiled artists of Ha-qumqum established a new revue theater, Ha-matate (The Broom). The two coexisted for a while, but after about eighteen months, Ha-qumqum was shut down.

Ha-matate

Ha-matate became the most successful Hebrew revue theater and continued to function until 1952. The name Ha-matate was explained in the song that opened each program in its early years:

> Oi, there is so much dirt here,
> at home and in the street,
> Really, it's disgusting,
> Really, it's no good!
> The dirt even sticks to the sun and the moon,
> I cannot be happy and dance here in the dust.
> What is needed is a broom!
> What is wanted is a broom!
> A broom, a broom that will sweep everything away!
> The dirt will be swept away
> What's disgusting will be swept away
> A broom, a broom that will sweep everything away!

Ha-matate succeeded because of the high quality of the group of artists in its ranks throughout the more than two decades of its existence. In the early years, its texts were written by poet Emanuel Harusi, but after 1934 the writers included some of the towering figures of modern Hebrew poetry, such as Abraham Shlonsky and Lea Goldberg. However, celebrated poet Natan Alterman (1910–70) was the poet who became most identified with Ha-matate. Alterman arrived in Israel in 1925. He wrote most of the lyrics for the songs of Ha-matate until 1944, shaping the content and format of the modern Hebrew pizmon.

The musical production of Ha-matate in its early years was the responsibility of Polish-Jewish composer and pianist Nahum Nardi. After 1932, the musical direction passed to a new immigrant from Poland: Moshe Vilensky. For the original songs written by different poets, Vilensky composed new melodies or adapted existing Jewish folk tunes (for example, Yiddish folk songs and Hassidic tunes) or tunes in an imaginary "Yemenite" style. Vilensky also arranged the songs and accompanied them on the piano. Other well-known Yishuv composers who contributed music to this theater were Vardina Shlonski and Daniel Samburski.

Among the singers who appeared in Ha-matate during its first decade, the most prominent was Yossef Goland. A "crooner," his singing style was different from singers previously heard on the Hebrew stage, whose background was more operatic or cantorial. Goland is the singer featured in *Mishirei Eretz Yisrael*, the first series of commercial recordings of Hebrew songs produced in Palestine by Aḥva in 1933. The content of this series of records reflected certain aspects of the eclectic musical repertory of Ha-matate in the early 1930s. In addition to the new hora dances and other hard-core Hebrew folk songs, artistic songs, and translations of Yiddish songs, the series includes a tango ("Nagen li ha-kinor") and a foxtrot ("Doda hagidi lanu ken") arranged in swing style, the first such instance in the Hebrew repertory.

The repertory of Ha-matate therefore included songs in contemporary international styles such as the tango, as well as original compositions. Many of the tangos and foxtrots were Hebrew adaptations of existing songs. An example of this process of adaptation is the song "Rina" (or "Romance on the bench") by Natan Alterman, which premiered in the thirty-seventh program of Ha-matate on May 15, 1935. The melody of "Rina," written as a satiric duet by a couple, was adopted from the theme song "The Heart" in the Russian film "The Merry Gang," which was extremely popular in Tel Aviv at the time. The tune is a tango composed by Russian-Jewish composer Isaac Dunievski.

Li-la-lo

A revue theater that competed with Ha-matate was Li-la-lo, which was founded in 1944 by actor and impresario Moshe Wahlin (born in Lithuania in 1906; immigrated to Israel in 1926). Wahlin, like many other actors and singers, was originally a member of Ha-matate who moved to Li-la-lo when the former began its economic decline in the mid-1940s. Wahlin ran Li-la-lo as an incorporated cooperative, using a formula similar to that of Ha-matate. The programs consisted of a mix of sketches and songs that dealt with current issues. He recruited the best poets of the 1940s such as Yaacov Orland, Natan Alterman, and Haim Hefer, as well as Moshe Vilensky as musical director.

Li-la-lo continued the prolific collaboration between Moshe Vilensky and Natan Alterman, a partnership that began in the 1930s in Ha-matate. This collaboration yielded some of the most enduring Hebrew popular songs. One exemplary pizmon of the Alterman-Vilensky crop from the Li-la-lo period was the aforementioned song "Be-khol zot yesh ba mashehu" (In spite of it all, she has something). Composed for the eighth program of Li-la-lo, the song was performed for the first time on September 14, 1946, by singer Jenny Lubitsh, a new immigrant who arrived from Poland in 1944 and was considered by critics as the "Marlene Dietrich of Eretz Yisrael" (Hacohen 1985: 134–35). The song has four stanzas and each describes, in an ironic tone, the shortcomings of women, of love, of the city of Tel Aviv, and of the future Jewish state. The refrain, in a more positive vein, suggests that all of these have "something," in spite of all their shortcomings. The tune that Vilensky composed for this song was inspired by the style of contemporary Broadway musicals and, in its swinging refrain in minor scale, recalls the music of George Gershwin. The stanza about Tel Aviv says:

BE-KHOL ZOT YESH BA MASHEHU (ALTERMAN-VILENSKY)

The people of Jerusalem say:
Yes, Tel Aviv is just a wheel:
She has no professors
And not a single prophet.
Not even a little bit of history
No significance, no weight
It's true, ladies and gentlemen,
She has nothing to her, nothing,
But . . .

In spite of it all, she has something,
Yes, there is something,
There was never anything like it somehow
And it's all hers somehow
Because she does have a spark somehow
That does no harm somehow
And she does have some charm somehow
That others do not have somehow.

Moshe Wahlin recruited the best performers for his theater. He contracted experienced singers and actors from Ha-matate, such as singers Yossef Goland and Shimshon Bar Noy, as well as new immigrants, including Romanian-Jewish comedienne Jetta Lucca. But the greatest Li-la-lo performer at its peak (1945–47) was Shoshana Damari, a singer of Yemenite origin. Her deep alto voice, her strong guttural Hebrew pronunciation, and her daring stage presence made her a symbol of the new Israeliness spiced with a dose of orientalism. For her, Vilensky wrote some of his most memorable songs, such as "Kalaniyot" (Anemones), "Ani mi-Tzfat" (I am from Safed), "Be-ḥeder ha-bubot" (In the dolls' room), "Zeh ya'avor" (This will pass), and many more. Some of the songs Vilensky wrote for Damari at Li-la-lo are orientalist in approach. Many other songs composed by Vilensky and Alterman relate to the Yemenite Jews whom Vilensky cherished. The songs treat diverse figures and scenes from the Yemenite neighborhood in Tel Aviv, Qerem ha-teymanim. "Miriam bat Nissim" (Miriam, daughter of Nissim), from Li-la-lo's tenth program, which premiered on March 18, 1947, belongs to this category. In addition to its treatment of Yemenite Jews, this song had clearly subversive overtones in that it described the illegal Jewish immigration to Palestine at a time when the British Mandate government imposed an embargo on immigration (some of these songs can be found on Shoshana Damari's three-CD compilation, issued in 1994).

MIRIAM BAT NISSIM (VILENSKY-ALTERMAN)

It happened in Aden a month ago
The wind of Yemen wept in the night
We recited the prayer of the traveler
And left—the whole family.
We put the pita in our bag
And drew water from the well
We lined up
And counted ourselves on the road to see
If we are all [here] and who is missing.

Li-la-lo had to stop operating during the War of Independence in 1948, when many of its artists were recruited into the army. For the artists, returning from the war was not easy. The cooperative organization that supported the theater had been disbanded. Shoshana Damari and Moshe Vilensky left for the United States to pursue new career horizons. By the end of 1950, Wahlin hired George Val, an experienced Romanian-Jewish operetta director to direct Li-la-lo. After a short time, Wahlin stopped directing and producing and became a full-time impresario, for the first time bringing major American popular-music and jazz artists such as Lionel Hampton to Israel (in 1955).

In 1951–52, Val hired many new artists, most of whom were new immigrants from Romania such as famous actress, singer, and dancer Dorotea Livio. He substantially expanded the theater's personnel. A big band was established under the direction of Paul Kosla, who emigrated in 1949 from Romania. Besides the revue programs, Li-la-lo produced operettas by Jacques Offenbach and Franz Lehar to expand its operations in order to survive. Yet, in spite of all the efforts to save it from bankruptcy, Li-la-lo discontinued operations in 1952.

Do-re-mi

Li-la-lo was succeeded by yet another revue theater, Do-re-mi, also directed by George Val, that was active between 1952 and 1962. Even more ambitious than its predecessors Ha-matate and Li-la-lo, the company staged operettas, including a full-stage production of the popular American musical *Pajama Game* (by Richard Adler and Jerry Ross). Renowned poet Abraham Shlonsky translated songs from operettas and taught Hebrew to new immigrant actors. Among the other writers who contributed to the revue theater was a young Hungarian Jew, Efraim Kishon, who later became one of Israel's most revered humorists and screenwriters before attaining international fame. Most of the songs for Do-re-mi were composed by Amos Yuster and Sando Perero Barzilay.

Cafés and Public Spaces

Another venue of popular-music performance in the Yishuv period were cafés, which offered live music. The model was the Central European café, a public space that served food and drinks and was the site of intellectual discussions, chess games, musical performances, and dancing. Many unemployed artists, "bohemians," gathered in the cafés, to exchange political views and current gossip but also to interact with their fellow intellectuals.

The first famous café of Tel Aviv to offer live music was Sheleg Ha-levanon (The Snow of Lebanon). It was established in the early 1920s on Allenby Street, one of the main arteries of the city, at its starting point on the seashore. Many of the poets who wrote in the pizmon genre, including Natan Alterman, Lea Goldberg, Emanuel Harusi, and Abraham Shlonsky, frequented this café, as did composer Mordechai Zeira. Another famous café of this early period was Kineret, also located near the beach. It gained a reputation as the place where, on Fridays, poet Alexander Penn and his friends used to drink and sing popular Russian songs.

By the 1940s, the number of cafés that offered live music in Tel Aviv expanded significantly. A famous one was the Café Piltz, which had a live dance orchestra conducted by accordionist and composer Menashe Beharav. Singer, lyricist, and actor Rafael Klatchkin regularly performed in this café, together with two immigrant cabaret singers from Poland, Jenny Lubitsh and Mina Bern.

Of special importance during Tel Aviv's formative years as an urban center was the Casino, a café that opened its doors with great fanfare in 1923. The Casino was a very special café. Built on the beachfront in eclectic architectural style, it was three stories high with an indoor café for winter and an outdoor café for summer. The upper floor was used as a dance floor. During its relatively short existence, the Casino was the "in" place in Tel Aviv for any type of socializing activity, from a romantic rendezvous to a meeting of intellectuals. Two orchestras played at the Casino every evening. One was a string ensemble that played background music at the cafés. The second was an orchestra that played for the dancers on the upper level. This orchestra's repertory included the three main genres of popular dance music at the time: tango, foxtrot, and the Charleston. Although the Casino went bankrupt after only two years and was eventually torn down to allow for the construction of Tel Aviv's beachfront promenade, it had an extraordinary impact as a model for the new cafés in Tel Aviv.

Besides the Casino and the cafés, other venues existed that provided dance music for the incipient bourgeoisie of Tel Aviv of the 1920s and 1930s. Orchestras played in the patios and gardens of several hotels in the city, such as the Bella Vista, a resort in the style of the French Riviera, the Palatin on Naḥalat Binyamin street (which was characterized by performances of popular songs and dances from Poland for the benefit of well-to-do Polish-Jewish immigrants) and, after the 1940s, the San Remo, which hosted a popular revue theater (Wahlin 1998: 117–19).

As the city of Tel Aviv expanded northward, more and more cafés with live music opened on the beach promenade and on nearby Allenby, Ben Yehuda, and Dizengoff Streets, thus creating a "leisure district" where live popular music was performed. This area remained the hub of Tel Aviv's night life until the end of the 1970s.

Throughout the Yishuv period and into the early years of statehood, the musical cafés and the dance venues, like the revue theaters, provided a commercial and cosmopolitan alternative to the SLI context and its "folk" attitude. The two popular-music cultures shared some major writers and composers such as Alterman and Vilensky. In addition, the commercial scene often incorporated the ideological and folk themes of SLI as a way to demonstrate its commitment to the national cause. There was no clear division between SLI and commercial popular music, which is well exemplified in the careers of some of the performers.

EARLY STARS AND A SLI TANGO

This notion of "stars," so central to the culture industries and to popular music, did not fit the socialist orientation of the Jewish Yishuv. Yet, as early as the 1930s, a few artists were greatly admired by large audiences, and their names and stage presence served as a magnet for the public. Their careers are the early manifestations of a quasi-star system in the Israeli popular-music industry.

Some of these early popular-music stars were Tova Piron in the 1930s; Freddie Dura and Alexander Yahalomi in the early 1940s; Yaffa Yarkoni,

Shoshana Damari, Israel Yitzhaki, and Buby Pinhasi Ariel in the late 1940s; and Dorotea Livio, Jetta Lucca, Paul Kosla, and Randy Rein in the early 1950s. With the exception of Yaffa Yarkoni and Shoshana Damari, who continued to sing Shirei Eretz Yisrael and children's songs, all these artists disappeared from the collective memory of Israeli audiences soon after their heyday. They represented a generation of "foreign" popular artists, that is, born and educated in Central and Eastern Europe (most from Poland, Hungary, Germany, and Romania), whose bourgeois art lacked local authenticity. Moreover, many of them, such as Mina Bern and Jenny Lubitsh, came from the European Yiddish theater and had almost no command of Hebrew. They were therefore the antithesis to the Hebrewist ideology, at its zenith during the 1930s and 1940s. After the early 1950s, these artists were gradually replaced by a new generation of Israeli-born artists who emerged from the lehaqot tzvayiot (army ensembles). Yet these professional immigrant artists set the foundation for the modern Hebrew-language popular-music industry. Moreover, despite the antagonism of the cultural establishment of the Yishuv, their music had a great influence on the more authentic forms of Israeli popular music, such as those represented by the lehaqot tzvayiot.

A review of the careers of some of these early artists reveals the unique features that characterized the development of the Hebrew popular song. These are stories of uprooted immigrants forced to adapt to a multicultural Jewish enclave in the Middle East striving to define its national culture through struggles with both the colonial power and the Arab national movement. This unique social context gave recent immigrant popular-music artists very few opportunities to develop their careers.

Freddie Dura

The long-lasting career of Freddie Dura is representative of the path of many of his contemporaries. Born in 1922 in Breslau (then Germany, today Poland), he immigrated to Israel in 1939 and settled on a kibbutz before moving to Tel Aviv. With no formal musical education but with a natural gift for acting and singing, he purchased a guitar and learned how to play after joining the British army during World War II. When he was released from military duty, he purchased a record player and opened a dancing school in Tel Aviv. At the same time he began to appear with his guitar, either as a soloist or as part of a duet, at private parties. His appearances on the small stage of Café Lilit in the entertainment district of Tel Aviv opened new opportunities to appear before British soldiers in nightclubs such as Noah's Ark and Maxim. During the War of Independence, Dura appeared at Café Piltz in Tel Aviv as a drummer with the band of composer and accordionist Menashe Beharav, who was well known for his adaptations of Hebrew texts to popular Russian tunes. In the early 1950s, Dura joined the Li-la-lo theater. In 1950, he began to record his songs at the Radio Doctor studio in Tel Aviv. His repertory included many sentimental ballads and tangos, some foreign and translated into Hebrew, others original Hebrew ballads. Significantly, he also sang and recorded in English, though he was not proficient in this language. In the absence of printed sources and LPs, Dura used to transcribe the songs in English from foreign radio stations that broadcast in Israel. With an eclectic repertory that also included Hebrew versions of German and Austrian popular songs, Dura toured Israel. Accompanied by a pianist and occasionally by a drummer as well, he appeared mainly before audiences of German Jews. The beach resort of Naharia in the Western Galilee, a town heavily populated by German-speaking Jews, was one of his favorite performance venues. In 1956 he moved there from Tel Aviv and opened Freddie's Bar, a legendary local institution.

Yaffa Yarkoni

The most successful popular artist during this period was undoubtedly Yaffa Yarkoni, sometimes called the "singer of the three wars" because she recorded songs that related to the War of Independence (1948), the Sinai Campaign (1956), and the Six-Day War (1967). In addition, Yarkoni was herself young war widow, having lost her first husband in World War II just two weeks after their marriage.

Yarkoni was born in 1926 to a family of Caucasian Jews. She began her singing career as a teenager in Gymnasium Herzelia, one of the Tel Aviv's prestigious high schools, and she also studied piano and ballet. Her family owned a café-restaurant called Tzlil (Sound) in one of Tel Aviv's new suburbs, where she launched her career as a singer.

During the War of Independence Yarkoni was recruited by one of the earliest military entertainment troupes, the Hishtron. The leaders of this ensemble, composer/lyricists Tuli Raviv and Buby Pinhasi, were influential in forming Yarkoni's artistic persona. The Hishtron, whose repertory consisted of rather sentimental ballads that dealt with individual love and longing for home, was not prominent among the military entertainment groups, partly because it did not emphasize songs dedicated to lifting the national spirit in times of struggle. Yarkoni's style suited this ensemble well. Her delivery was intimate and subdued in contrast to the assertive singing style of Hebrew songs predominant at the time. In an interview, Yaffa Yarkoni explained, "People did not understand that this was not singing, this was not a voice but a way to 'transmit' a song, to 'talk' a song! I never posed as a singer. The change I brought to the light popular song [*ha-zemer ha-qal*] was that I started to whisper the songs, people started to listen and love my songs. Those opposed to me had no alternative but to agree and accept me" (Topelberg 2000: 78).

During one of her leaves from military service, she recorded the song "Eynayim yeruqot" (Green eyes), a Hebrew cover of a Romanian hit, at the Radio Doctor studio for the Makolit record company. The success of this recording led to a contract with Hed Artzi in 1949 (just as the firm started operations), at the end of the war.

In three short years, between 1949 and 1952, Yarkoni recorded an astonishing total of 400 records (78 rpm's) for Hed Artzi, including many historical recordings of the heroic songs of the War of Independence, such as "Bab el-wad" (Gate of the valley, about the battle for the road to Jerusalem; lyrics, Haim Guri; music, Shmuel Fisher) and "Be-'arvot ha-negev" (On the Negev Steppes; after a Russian song, paraphrased in Hebrew by Rafael Klatchkin). However, she mainly recorded cosmopolitan songs, such as tangos (see the discussion of "Artzenu ha-qtantonet" below), ballads, foxtrots, boogie-woogies, and rumbas. She was also the first popular singer to record children's songs like "'Agala 'im susa" (A cart with a mare; music and lyrics, Avshalom Cohen [1949]) on a commercial basis. Hed Artzi's 1952 catalog includes sixty Hebrew songs by Yarkoni, by far the largest number by a single artist. As a result, hers was the voice most often heard on Kol Israel, the new state radio station.

Parallel to her recording career, Yarkoni continued to appear in cafés and nightclubs. At the end of the 1950s, she moved to the United States where she studied pop singing professionally. She recorded several LPs in different languages, including Hebrew and Yiddish, for CBS (America). When she returned to Israel in the late 1960s she was a different singer, not the young soldier who whispered her songs to the accompaniment of an accordion or a small band, but a full-fledged MOR pop singer capable of singing with a symphonic orchestra in the largest halls. During her stay in the United States and in the years thereafter, she remained one of the most prominent Israeli popular artists in the Jewish Diaspora.

Yet the debate about the quality of Yarkoni's voice and the crucial role of amplification in her appearances did not fade with the years. Even in the late 1990s, when she was more than seventy years old, she continued to appear as a guest singer on TV programs and talk shows, still competing with her contemporary, Shoshana Damari, for the title of "Great Lady of Israeli song" (see the 5-CD box set of her recordings, issued in 1998).

The eclectic, multilingual repertory performed by Yarkoni during her fifty-year career was a feature shared by many other, less well known contemporary artists. The content of a 1951 LP by singer Israel Yitzhaki, who was second in popularity to Yaffa Yarkoni, provides a glimpse into the diversified repertories of the singers of this generation. This album includes Hebrew translations or paraphrases of foreign hits, such as tangos ("Al hof Eilat," by Avshalom Cohen; and "Layla bahir," lyrics by Sh. Fisher, set to a Russian melody) and waltzes ("Tkhol hamitpahat," a song made famous by Tova Piron, lyrics by Natan Alterman, set to a Russian melody composed by Petersborsky), the Hebrew version of "Old McDonald Had a Farm" ("Ladod Moshe haytah havah"), Nat King Cole's hit "Mona Lisa," "Tea for Two" (originally written in 1925 for the musical "No, No Nanette" by Vincent Youmans and Caesar Irving, and later a standard of the popular-song tradition), "El Cumbanchero" (a rumba by Puerto Rican writer Rafael Hernández and widely performed in the late 1950s by many artists), as well as a guaracha, a bolero, a slow-fox, a swing, a beguine, a samba, a Romanian doina, a Yiddish song, and more. This range reflects the artist's need to serve audiences with diverse tastes in different contexts.

A Hebrew Tango Story

The early repertory of Hebrew popular songs that stemmed from the diverse musical stages reviewed in this chapter includes three broad categories of songs: Hebrew covers or imitations of foreign styles, especially foxtrot and tango; Hebrew versions of Jewish ethnic songs (for example, Russian, Yiddish, or Yemenite); and original songs. Although the music was extremely eclectic and cosmopolitan, the Hebrew lyrics sometimes treated topics of local concern, such as current political events.

The origin and evolution of songs from this early period provide an indication of the unique development of popular music in Hebrew. One illuminating case is the tango "Artzenu ha-qtantonet" (Our little homeland) by Shmuel Fisher and H. Gold Zehavi.

The tango as a popular Hebrew genre has its roots in the mid-1930s (see Hacohen 1985: 106–7) and should be considered one more instance of the spread of this Argentinean musical genre throughout the Eastern Mediterranean (Pelinski 1995). The first documented song of this genre was "Tango Tel Aviv," composed in the late 1930s by Vardina Shlonsky, then a new immigrant from Paris, with Hebrew lyrics by Natan Alterman.

"Artzenu ha-qtantonet" was composed in 1946–47 for Polish-born Yiddish singer Mina Bern, a member of the Tzimuqim u-shqedim (the Raisins and Almonds Trio, after the famous Yiddish song of that name) that also included Jenny Lubitsh and famous "conferencier" and songwriter

Alexander Yahalomi (b. 1912 in Vilnius, immigrated to Israel in 1943). The trio performed in Yiddish in the style of the Central European cabaret with connecting texts between the songs in Hebrew. It appeared in venues such as the garden of the San Remo Hotel and the Smadar nightclub located above the famous Café Piltz on Hayarkon Street.

"Artzenu ha-qtantonet" marked the "Hebrew-ization" of this Yiddish band and its acceptance by the Israeli public at large. However, it was not only the language that made this tango meaningful from the point of view of the Jewish national agenda. On the surface, its lyrical content shares with other tangos the theme of the return to an abandoned beloved. However, in this case, the relationship is of a very special kind, since the object of love is not a woman, but the Land of Israel itself. Thus, from the literary point of view, this tango is linked to one of the most common themes of the Israeli folk song.

ARTZENU HA-QTANTONET (FISHER-ZEHAVI)

Refrain
Our tiny country, our tiny country,
My land, my land, my soul so yearns for you,
Our little homeland, our little homeland
My mother, my little mother, you so love your child.

After two thousand years of dispersion, I returned to you
I returned to you, the only one.
Our little homeland, our little homeland,
Forever will I hand you down,
You will remain forever, our country.

This Hebrew tango became an instant hit in Tel Aviv. Young singer Israel Yitzhaki, who could only listen to the Tzimuqim u-shqedim Trio from beyond the walls of the garden of the San Remo Hotel, learned this tango and began to sing it at his amateur café appearances. Yet the canonization of "Artzenu ha-qtantonet" came about thanks to the legendary recording by Yaffa Yarkoni in one of her earliest Hed Artzi releases in 1949. Since then the song has enjoyed periodical revivals on nostalgic radio and TV programs.

"Artzenu ha-qtantonet" is an example of a song in the repertories of the revue theaters and cafés of the 1920s to the early 1950s that remained in the Israeli musical memory as part of the canonic corpus of Shirei Eretz Yisrael. The preservation of these popular songs was guaranteed when they were recorded by the most popular Israeli singers, such as Yaffa Yarkoni.

LEGACY

The popular-music scene of Tel Aviv and other cities declined after the 1950s. An interesting link between the cabaret theaters and the music that emerged in the 1950s and 1960s from the lehaqot tzvayiot was provided by Revi'iyat Mo'adon Ha-Teatron (the Theater Club Quartet). The members of this successful group, which was active from 1957 to 1965, were Gideon Zinger, Yaakov Ben-Sira, Shmuel Bar, and Reuven Sheffer. Modeled on the French trio Les Freres Jacques (an important influence on early lehaqot tzvayiot as well), the quartet had two successful shows of biting satirical sketches and songs (many of which simply took the French melodies and gave them Hebrew lyrics). However, though its general format directly continued the revue theaters of the 1940s, the content and general tone of its satire, especially in its second show in 1963, bore the strong mark of sabra culture. This was because the materials for this show were written by Haim Hefer and Dan Ben-Amotz, two renowned exponents of sabra humor. In addition, some of their most famous songs were later recorded by either lehaqot tzvayiot or by their civilian equivalent, Ha-Tarnegolim (the Roosters). The line between satirical cabaret and ideologically mobilized music of SLI was thus somewhat blurred. Other offshoots of the revue theaters that totally surrendered their satirical bite to nationalist tones were the musicals of the 1960s and later.

Musicals

The decline of the revue theater marked the beginning of a new era in the history of the Hebrew musical theater (Almagor 1996). In 1962, an experimental theater group in Haifa, shaped in the style of basement theaters of Greenwich Village in New York, produced a Hebrew adaptation of Harvey Schmidt and Tom Jones's musical, *The Fantasticks*. It was directed by the young Menahem Golan, who later became one of Israel's foremost film directors and the founder of the Golan-Globus production group. The success of *The Fantasticks* prompted Habimah, Israel's national theater, to produce Hebrew versions of some of the most famous Broadway musicals including *Irma la Douce* and *My Fair Lady*. The latter was produced in Israel using the original Broadway staging.

The appeal of the large-scale Broadway musical format generated an urge for original Israeli works in this genre and even led to the development of a Hebrew neologism: *mahazemer (mahaze*, theater play; *zemer*, song). The first all-Hebrew mahazemer was *Shlomo Hamelekh ve-Shalmai ha-sandlar*

(King Solomon and Shalmai the cobbler), with lyrics by Natan Alterman and music by Sasha Argov (Almagor 1996: 29–30). The tremendous success of this musical prompted the production of even more ambitious works. One of these was *Qazablan*, written by Dan Almagor on the basis of a book and theater play by writer Yigal Mossinsohn and set to music by Dov Seltzer. What distinguished *Qazablan* was its treatment of ethnic tension between the Ashkenazi establishment and the mizraḥim. The plot told of an exceptional Moroccan-born soldier who was discriminated against by society because of his origin, with a happy ending where the protagonist gets the Ashkenazi girl, thus symbolizing national unity and integration. The role of *Qazablan* was played by Yehoram Gaon, then a young and very successful "all-Israeli" singer of Sephardi origin. Six hundred twenty performances of *Qazablan* made it the most successful original Hebrew musical ever. Songs from the show became part of the Shirei Eretz Yisrael repertory and are still performed live and on radio today. Another successful musical of the late 1960s was *I Like Mike*, whose song "Le-ḥayyei ha-ʿam ha-zeh" (Let's raise a toast to this nation) also became a standard of the Shirei Eretz Yisrael repertory.

The musical format also provided the opportunity to bring the ethnic musical styles of different Jewish communities to public attention. A salient example of this phenomenon was the musical *Bustan Sfaradi* (The Sephardi garden, by Yitzhak Navon). The maḥazemer takes place on the patio of a house in an old Sephardi neighborhood in Jerusalem. The songs are lavish MOR arrangements of traditional Sephardi songs in Ladino (Judeo-Spanish) composed by Shimon Cohen. The original tunes were adapted from the collection of folklorist and singer Isaac Levy. Many of these songs became standards of the modern international repertory of Ladino popular songs after their release on an LP by Yehoram Gaon in the late 1960s (Seroussi 1995).

One impresario, Giora Godik, was responsible for most of the musical theater productions in the 1960s. When Godik's empire of more than two hundred employees collapsed in 1970, the pace of production of large-scale Hebrew musicals slowed considerably (Almagor 1996: 31). Since then, Hebrew versions of big Broadway and Hollywood hits such as *Cabaret, The Sound of Music, The King and I, West Side Story,* and *Evita* have been produced by the large theater companies while original Hebrew musicals became more infrequent. The late 1980s witnessed the success of the musical version of *Salah Shabbati,* a classic Israeli film of the 1950s about the clash between the sabra Hebrew culture and the mizraḥi Jews based on a play by Efraim Kishon. The music for *Salah Shabbati* was composed by Nurit Hirsh. The theme song, "Aḥ ya rab" (Oh my God; lyrics by Haim

Hefer), with its title in Arabic, is a celebration of the arrival of the mizraḥim in Israel. It became a standard of the Shirei Eretz Yisrael repertory soon after its release in 1989.

· · ·

In 1948, upon statehood, Tel Aviv already had an established infrastructure of professional artists, stages, and production companies from which a popular-music industry could be developed. The performance contexts of early popular music in Israel were mainly live: the revue theater stage and the cafés. Most of the new songs answered the needs of the shows and were geared to the available artists.

The incipient urban popular music in Hebrew relied primarily on the immigration, usually forced, of Jewish artists from Central Europe who were proficient in contemporary international music styles. These artists had to negotiate their survival in their profession by adapting their works to the context of a community in the process of imagining itself as a new nation and in the midst of a quest for a national culture. Hebrew, the revived language, was one of the powerful means to forge this new identity. In addition, the lyrical content of some songs, which dealt with the Land of Israel and its virtues or with current political events, linked the songs to the ethos of the new society.

Yet, at the same time, powerful undercurrents connected this new scene to European and American models of popular song. The cosmopolitan orientation of the Tel Aviv middle class in the 1930s, as well as the presence of a large number of British civil servants and officers, created a market for trendy popular music. Indeed, as Shamir (2000, 2001) pointed out, the relationship between Central European middle-class Jews and the British colonial presence in Palestine was a key element, often overlooked by historians and sociologists, in the formation of the civil institutions of the future State of Israel. In the case of popular music, this relationship forged the roots of the cosmopolitan-oriented styles that remained a constant feature of the dominant culture after statehood. Although marginalized in the 1950s and early 1960s, these cosmopolitan tendencies reemerged in the late 1960s and in the 1970s, when Israeli rock became the dominant variant of Israeli popular music. In other words, by laying the foundation for cosmopolitan popular music, the early popular music discussed in this chapter anticipated the emergence of rock in Israel as a major force in the 1970s and beyond.

5   The Lehaqot Tzvayiot (Army Ensembles)

The song "Praḥim ba-qaneh" (Flowers in the barrel of the rifle) was a hit song on Israeli radio in 1971. Describing a time in the future when soldiers would return home to town and a young girl would hand them a flower (a ragwort, to be precise), the lyrics expressed longing for the end of war, for a time when there would be "flowers in the barrel of the rifle (or cannon)" and "girls on the turret" (of the tank). The text was probably inspired by the famous press photograph from the anti–Vietnam War demonstrations of the period, of a young hippie girl putting a flower in an American soldier's rifle. The song is a midtempo ballad, sung with much emotional conviction and seriousness by a female vocalist. Its sound is dominated by few simple riffs of a Farfisa electric organ and drumming that loads it with a slight feeling of rhythmic energy. In other words, it is a simple and catchy pop song.

The lyrics were written by Dudu Barak and the music by Efi Netzer. The performance is credited to Yehudit Schwartz and the Artillery Ensemble—an army pop band of soldiers during their obligatory military service: young men and women aged eighteen to twenty-one. It was recorded at the peak of Israel's "empire days," between 1967 (the Six-Day War) and 1973 (the Yom Kippur War), when euphoria about the country's military might and its superiority dominated the public sphere.

The gap between the nature of the song, "Praḥim ba-qaneh," as a cultural artifact on one hand, and the social and cultural context of its production and reception on the other, reflects the paradox that underlies one of most important phenomena in Israeli popular music: the lehaqot tzvayiot (military or army ensembles). This is a paradox because these were soldiers in full uniform, serving in ensembles that bore the names of and represented combat units, who often sang about peace and an end to war. It was music that fit the ideological requirements of a nation-state and its army, yet it enjoyed enormous success in the civilian pop market.

The lehaqot tzvayiot exemplified, in this regard, the intense ideological mobilization that characterized much of Israeli cultural practice during this period. To a great extent, for approximately twenty years, between the mid-1950s and the mid-1970s, the repertory of the lehaqot tzvayiot dominated the field of Israeli popular music. It was only with the weakening of Hebrewism and the emergence of global Israeliness during the 1970s that the cultural tensions at the heart of the lehaqot tzvayiot came to the surface, eventually leading to their decline.

SOME GENERAL FEATURES

The lehaqot tzvayiot were entertainment units put together by different army units. Their self-declared purpose was to provide light entertainment for soldiers, to raise morale, and to express the specificity of the particular unit or command to which they belonged. The following text, found on the sleeve notes of the album of the seventh program of the lehaqat piqud ha-merkaz (Central Command Ensemble), is a typical portrayal of their aims:

> The Central Command's Variety Ensemble came into being in 1954. Its goal was to provide the men and women in uniform with entertainment which would add some chuckles and light music to a somewhat somber army existence. It also aimed to teach Israeli songs to those in uniform. All the members of the Ensemble are soldiers in compulsory military service. As such, they bring with them natural talent, youthful zest and lively Israeli originality. To date the Ensemble has presented six different shows [that] enjoyed a long and exceptionally successful run on the professional stage. This illustrates the natural way in which Israeli art developed—from the tents of *Tzahal* to the halls of art and entertainment. (1957)

Between the lines, it is clear that an additional function of the lehaqot was ideological. Indeed during the 1950s and the 1960s, because the majority of youth aged eighteen to twenty-one who were doing obligatory military service were sons and daughters of recently arrived immigrants, the lehaqot were, in effect, the cultural tool that introduced these young immigrants to the essence of Israeliness in its Hebrewist variant. Their repertory was constructed as a prime exponent of the meanings and spirit of the sabra and aimed to present the core themes of the dominant variants of Zionist ideology.

The very first lehaqot tzvayiot were established as early as 1948, during

Israel's War of Independence. They were modeled after similar ensembles that existed in the British army during World War II (among them the ensemble of the Jewish Brigade, whose soldiers were mostly from Palestine). The most famous of these early lehaqot was the Chizbatron. This ensemble provided the prototypical format of the lehaqot to come: a group of young soldiers, men and women, who performed skits and songs that alternated in mood between the heroic and the joyful (see Shahar 1997b).

In the mid-1950s, after attempts to establish lehaqot as full theater units failed, the model set by the Chizbatron was recreated and the typical format of the lehaqah took shape. It should be stressed that although the same word—*lehaqah*—is used to designate a rock band, the lehaqah tzvait was a larger ensemble, typically consisting of ten to fifteen members. Most were recruited after singing and (usually comic) acting auditions, and a few were chosen for their ability to play musical instruments. Their membership period was limited to the length of their obligatory military service. This resulted in massive turnover every two or three years. In other words, hundreds of soldiers passed through the ranks of the lehaqot tzvayiot during the twenty years of their heyday. Each lehaqah, at any given time, included new and veteran members. The history of each lehaqah therefore is a series of incarnations.

The history of the lehaqot tzvayiot can be divided more or less into two periods. The first period, from the mid-1950s until 1966–67, was marked by the simplicity of the musical and stage production. This was most clearly evident in the typical instrumentation of the ensembles: an accordion and a *darabuka* (an Arabic tambourine) were usually the only instruments that accompanied the singing. The second period, from 1966–67 to 1975, was marked by much more elaborate productions and accompaniment that consisted of basic "rock" instrumentation: drum kit and electric guitar, organ and bass. The two epochs can also be contrasted in their stylistic sources of inspiration and influence. The key influence on the lehaqot in the early period were two French ensembles: Les Compagnons de la Chanson, and Les Freres Jacques. The second period was inspired by American musicals and, by the early 1970s, by rock musicals such as *Hair*.

Four major lehaqot were the most successful during the early period. They were lehaqat ha-nahal (the Nahal Ensemble), lehaqat piqud ha-tzafon (Northern Command Ensemble), lehaqat piqud ha-merkaz (Central Command Ensemble), and lehaqat geisot ha-shiryon (Armored Forces Ensemble). The first three continued their success into the second period when they were joined by lehaqat heil ha-yam (Navy Ensemble) and lehaqat piqud darom (Southern Command Ensemble). Other lehaqot (the Parachute

Troops Ensemble, the Artillery Ensemble), as well as smaller units known as "*tzivtei havai*" (entertainment crews) also functioned occasionally, with limited success. The presence of the lehaqot tzvayiot in the field of popular music declined after 1975. In 1979 they were officially dissolved. In 1982–83 the lehaqot were formed again, but this time they mainly performed well-known songs. Only occasionally were new songs written especially for them.

On discharge from service, many members of the lehaqot became successful singers or theater actors. Their training and experience in the lehaqot, and the fact that some of them had already gained star status during their military service, made them highly attractive to entrepreneurs in the civilian popular-music market. In fact, by the late 1960s, entrepreneurs were known to sign contracts with notable soloists of the lehaqot when they were still in uniform. The lehaqot tzvayiot functioned, in other words, as a state-supported training framework for pop stars.

Indeed, for more than twenty years, Israel's most successful popular-music singers were graduates of lehaqot tzvayiot. Lehaqot graduates were also saliently present among the ranks of theater actors and in other fields of entertainment. Highly prominent names in the 1960s and 1970s included singers Arik Einstein, Yehoram Gaon, Yigal Bashan, Avi Toledano, Shula Chen, Yardena Arazi, and Shlomo Artzi; actors Oded Kotler, Haim Topol, and Moni Moshonov; entertainers and film personalities including members of the Ha-gashash ha-ḥiver Trio, Uri Zohar, and Dudu Dotan; these are only some of the famous names in Israeli culture who were graduates of lehaqot tzvayiot.

Another element in the structure and work of the lehaqot was the notion of a program (or show). Each program was a set of songs and skits, usually written especially for the lehaqah. The writing, performing, and recording of a new program roughly corresponded to the recruitment of new soldier-members. Thus every year or two (and in the early years more frequently) each lehaqah introduced a new program. The programs formed a rich repertory on which each ensuing incarnation of a given lehaqah could rely, in addition to its own new program. The programs were regularly performed for soldiers all over the country, as well as for ticket-purchasing general audiences. Starting in 1956, most of the songs of each new program regularly appeared on record albums.

For writing and staging new materials, the army units usually enlisted professionals in the popular-music industry. Unlike the lehaqot members, these were civilians who worked for the army on salary or by special contract and included composers, lyricists, arrangers, and directors. They represented one key connection among many that blurred the difference between army and civilian cultural practices, and in fact between the army and civilian society in Israel in general (on this, see Ben-Eliezer 1998). In addition to acquiring the services of established writers and composers, the lehaqot also served as an outlet for emerging talents in the area of popular-music writing. In addition to being the major source of young performers and actors who would dominate Israeli culture, the lehaqot also advanced the careers of writers and composers. Thus composers Sasha Argov and Moshe Vilensky, as well as lyricist Haim Hefer (a founding member of the Chizbatron), although already known for their early work in the 1940s, considerably expanded their impact on Israeli music as a result of their connection with the lehaqot during the 1950s. The lehaqot also provided a platform, and often a major outlet, for composers and lyricists such as Yehiel Mohar, Dov Seltzer, Naomi Shemer, Yohanan Zarai, Dan Almagor, Nurit Hirsh, and Yair Rosenblum.

The advent of Israeli rock and pop and the decline of Hebrewism as the dominant variant of Israeliness relegated the lehaqot tzvayiot to the status of a cultural relic, cherished by some and detested by others. It is, however, indisputable that the lehaqot played a crucial role in the history of popular music in Israel. This role is often attributed to the rich repertory of songs recorded by the lehaqot and the number of graduates who went on to long-lasting careers in Israeli culture.

But the impact of the lehaqot tzvayiot on Israeli popular music was not just a matter of numbers. In strictly sociological terms, the lehaqot tzvayiot were the setting that produced for their members, and the musicians associated with them, the social and cultural capital that propelled them to dominant positions in the field of Israeli culture. Put differently, the success of the lehaqot gave many of its members instant access to and close connections with professionals in the music industry and media, which enabled their successful careers. It was a fruitful relationship for both sides because the industry often received ready-made stars, singers who had already gained a reputation during their military service. The network of ties and relations that emerged over the years, to a great extent, dominated the field of popular music in Israel.

Closely related to this, and perhaps even more important, was the issue of cultural capital and habitus associated with the lehaqot. The lehaqot tzvayiot served as a laboratory in which a unique formula of Israeli popular music was invented that was ideologically mobilized for national causes while at the same time expressing genuine pop sensibilities. Service in the lehaqot meant learning and mastering this formula. It was then carried over to the rest of the field of popular music in Israel by the many singers and musicians who graduated from the lehaqot. It thus became the dominant habitus, the standard cultural capital for entrance to the field, or at least for gaining an initial legitimate presence in it. It remained a reference point for popular-music practices in Israel for many years, either as a blueprint for making music, or as a model to break away from, a formula to be challenged.

Needless to say, the central role played by the lehaqot made it extremely difficult for musicians not working within the stylistic framework or the social network associated with them to begin a career. This state of affairs mainly affected the early rock bands known as *lehaqot ha-qetzev* (beat bands) and musiqa mizrahit musicians.

ARMY-MADE POP

Taken together, between the early 1950s and the late 1970s, the lehaqot tzvayiot performed approximately 1,300 songs (Tessler 2000). Most of them were written especially for the lehaqot, and a large proportion of them were recorded and distributed on album records. While these historic albums are gradually being reissued on CDs, several CD compilations issued during the 1990s best capture the essence of the lehaqot tzvayiot repertory: *Ha-lehaqot ha-tzvayiot: Ha-shanim ha-rishonot* (The army ensembles: The early years [1988]), *Lehaqat ha-nahal: Ha-lahitim ha-gdolim 1963–72* (The greatest hits of the Nahal Ensemble [1989]), *Lehaqat piqud ha-tzafon ve-lehaqat piqud ha-merkaz: Ha-lahitim ha-gdolim 1963–72* (The greatest hits of the Northern and Central Command Ensembles [1990]), *Lehaqat geisot ha-shiryion, lehaqat piqud darom, lehaqat heil ha-yam: Ha-lahitim ha-gdolim 1962–72* (The greatest hits of the Armored Forces, Southern Command, and Navy Ensembles [1992]).

Several elements merged to produce the specific cultural aura of the lehaqot. One was the fact that many of their members and the musicians working with them found themselves caught between conflicting percep-tions of their work. On the one hand, there was the general demand, or requirement, to make music that served the ideological needs of the unit and the army in general, as well as those of state and country. It should be stressed that rarely was this requirement translated into direct demands or censorship (some notable exceptions are discussed below). The ideological themes were implied in the very existence of the lehaqot as army units and in the commitment of their members to the dominant national themes. Yair Rosenblum, the manager of lehaqat ha-nahal in the late 1960s says it all: "There was no repertoire committee. Just the director and me. Occasionally, there were requests from the General, or education officers, but there was no coercion. We were captured by the national consensus, and easily persuaded. We were part of a mobilized culture. . . . [I]t was not difficult to mobilize us, because we had already been voluntarily mobilized" (Yair Rosenblum, interview with the authors, June 1995).

On the other hand, the young people involved in the making of the lehaqot were very well aware of trendy styles, fashionable genres, and innovative practices in Western popular music. In the 1950s these were mostly Latin rhythms (cha-cha, rumba, and so on) and jazzy French chansons (of the type associated with Serge Gainsbourg, Georges Brassens, and Les Freres Jacques); in the 1960s it was first rock'n'roll and its offshoots (like the twist), and later rock music. Consequently, many of the members and musicians involved wanted to implement components of this music into the repertory and sound of the lehaqot. But this often conflicted with the ideological setting, which viewed importing foreign music as "inauthentic" and harmful to the general context of inventing a Hebrew national culture. Members of the lehaqot were thus caught between their ideological role, which they respected but also often found trite, and the wish to open up to global trends.

One song that exemplifies this nicely is "Twist moledet" (Homeland twist, after the twist dance craze of the early 1960s), words and music by Drora Havkin, recorded by lehaqat piqud ha-merkaz in 1963.

> A new song, "Twist moledet" is the hit of the new program of lehaqat piqud merkaz—the director recounts that he faced the eternal problem of lehaqot tzvayiot directors: how to bridge the demands of the soldiers and the demands of the education officers. There is no doubt that the soldiers in the field like the twist, but what will the pedantic education officer say to that? A lehaqah tzvait—and the twist? A solution was found: patriotic lyrics that educate to love of the homeland and its scenery. It begins slowly—and then slides into a sweeping twist. In fact, this is the way other foreign melodies and dance rhythms were smuggled into lehaqot tzvayiot programs in the past. The camouflage was usually "parody," and that is how the educational role was fulfilled, and the soldiers were also satisfied. (Dan Almagor, *Maariv La-No'ar*, January 1963)

Indeed, this song, that opens with a musical phrase reminiscent of the Eretz-Yisraeli song "Kineret sheli" (My Kineret, or the Sea of Galilee), followed by the sudden transition to the trendy twist, dominated by a saxophone (an instrument rarely heard in lehaqot at that time), took the audiences by surprise. But it was a pleasant surprise, as another reviewer notes:

"Initially, the audience is shocked. They are not accustomed to such sparkling beats in a lehaqah tzvait. But slowly they were won over and began to roar their approval and applaud vigorously" (Moshe Natan, *Ba-Mahane*, January 1963).

If "Twist moledet" was indeed a parody, it remains unclear what the parody aimed at: the love-of-the-land pathos of Eretz-Yisraeli songs, or the twist craze. Probably both. The main point was to express light humor, unconnected to anything serious. The song, like many others, was a sort of inoffensive, nonsarcastic mockery of both the ideological zest and the enthusiasm for foreign pop.

The solution to the tension between trendy pop and ideology was a kind of gentle satire, inspired by the work of Israeli writer Ephraim Kishon (who also wrote skits for the early lehaqot). The songs conveyed the ideological messages expected from the lehaqot as army units, in a way that could be interpreted as parodying those messages. At the same time, trendy pop was introduced in ways that could be seen to serve nationalistic concerns. It was ideology as entertainment and entertainment as ideology. The lehaqot used foreign pop to create a humorous stance that radiated a sense of youth, innocence, and fun—but never actually rebellion or harsh criticism. Playfulness was the key feature in the presentation of much of the lehaqot repertory.

The double meaning of the songs was expressed not only in the lyrics, vocal techniques, and arrangements but also through the performances. Inspired by Les Freres Jacques, the lehaqot developed a form of presentation known as *ha'amadah*. Literally, the word means setting up or placement. In the context of the lehaqot, it referred to the choreography of the songs, the acting out of the lyrics. A special director was typically enlisted for the ha'amadah of the songs. Mime and simple body movements of individual members were orchestrated to correspond to the lyrics in a way that supported the light humor by overstating the emotions and meanings of the song. Naomi Polani, a member of the Chizbatron and later the first director of lehaqat ha-shiryion, is usually credited with being a major figure in the creation of the practice of ha'amadah.

It would be inaccurate, however, to view the lehaqot tzvayiot repertory as exclusively consisting of light pop tunes in the mode described here. On many occasions, the ideological aspect was fully manifested, without a hint of parody. This was particularly true in the case of soft ballads that eulogized soldiers who died in war. The pain caused by the death of soldiers was too sacred to be treated lightly. In such cases, both the music and the ha'amadah were dramatic and filled with pathos. One salient example is the song "Mah avarekh" (What shall I bless), lyrics by Rachel Shapira and music by Yair Rosenblum, performed by lehaqat ḥeil ha-yam (the Navy Ensemble) in 1968–69. The high-pitched and emotional vocal delivery of Rivkah Zohar dominates the song. It was a huge radio hit when it first came out, and its performance evoked a great deal of excitement, and not only in the audience, as singer Rivkah Zohar herself testifies: "When I first sang the song in rehearsal, the members of the lehaqah were very moved . . . and when I performed for soldiers during the day and I could see their eyes, it was something special. I saw them all and became terribly emotional. I felt I was blessing each one of them" (Rivka Zohar, quoted in *Ba-Maḥane*, February 1969).

There was a problem with such songs regarding their status as pop, as songs played on the radio together with ordinary hits, Hebrew or foreign. The quasi sacredness of these songs was clearly at odds with their pop and entertainment context. An incident surrounding the song "Givʿat ha-taḥmoshet" (Ammunition hill) sung by lehaqat piqud merkaz, best exemplifies this. The song, lyrics by Yoram Tehar-Lev and music by Yair Rosenblum, tells the story of a fierce battle that took place during the Six-Day War (June 1967) in Jerusalem. The heavy face-to-face fighting between Israeli and Jordanian soldiers remains in Israel's collective memory as one of the difficult and dramatic moments of the battle in Jerusalem.

The lyrics depict the battle through first-person monologues performed by male members of the lehaqah. Alternating between straightforward recounting of episodes from the battle and dramatic harmony singing, and accompanied by monotonic organ riffs and hypnotic drumming, the song successfully creates a sense of tension, horror, fear, and heroism. Needless to say, "Givʿat ha-taḥmoshet" became a huge hit and reached the top of the Hebrew hit-parade during 1968. At this point, however, radio music editors felt uneasy about the song going down the chart. They felt it would be disrespectful for such a song to be treated like an ordinary pop song. The solution they found was to "honorably" remove the song from the chart, without letting it decline from the number-one slot.

Peculiar as this incident is, it epitomizes the growing discrepancy between the cultural tasks of the lehaqot tzvayiot and the changing nature of Israeli popular music during the 1970s. As the field turned toward rock-inspired practices, the effort of the lehaqot to adjust became more and more problematic. Not only were the basic messages associated with rock in sharp contradiction with the ideological role of the lehaqot, but the rising costs of studio and stage production awakened growing opposition to the lehaqot among various high-ranking officers.

The simple beginnings, cultural success, transformation to pop/rock, and the eventual decline of the lehaqot are best traced through the career of lehaqat ha-naḥal, the most famous and successful lehaqah tzvait.

LEHAQAT HA-NAHAL

The word *naḥal* means "small river," but in army vocabulary it is an acronym for *No'ar Ḥaluzi Loḥem:* Combating Pioneer Youth. This is the name given to combat units in which military service was combined with agricultural work on kibbutzim and new settlements. On lehaqat ha-naḥal albums, it is described thus: "The Naḥal is one of the fighting units of the Israel Defense Army. Its soldiers are trained as paratroopers, yet at the same time, the Naḥal is involved in the development of new agricultural settlements on Israel's borders and in the Negev."

The Naḥal unit was established immediately after independence, an almost direct continuation of the prestate Palmaḥ units. The combination of two activities—"working the land" and "fighting the enemy"—that had always been at the heart of the sabra myth, and the fact that most of the youth recruited for this service came from the dominant sectors of Israeli society, gave the Naḥal unit a special aura of exclusivity. Lehaqat ha-naḥal was the first lehaqah tzvait, established as the ensemble of the Naḥal unit in 1950, on the initiative of actor Giora Manor.

It took several years before the lehaqah emerged in its final format. Under Manor's guidance, the first four lehaqat ha-naḥal programs were full plays, written for the lehaqah by Manor himself or others, with songs inserted into their plots. Only in the sixth and seventh programs, in 1954, was the pattern changed to include mainly songs interspersed with humorous skits. Among its members at this point were future actors Yossi Banai and Haim Topol, future singing star Nehama Hendel, and future film directors Uri Zohar and Avraham Hefner. The skits were written by up-and-coming satirist Ephraim Kishon. Its songs were written by well-established authors: Moshe Vilensky, Sasha Argov, Haim Hefer, and Yehiel Mohar. It was at this point that the aura of the Naḥal unit as the embodiment of the genuine Zionist pioneering spirit merged with the lehaqah formula of fun and naiveté, to create the specific habitus that proved so influential on the other lehaqot tzvayiot, and on Israeli popular music in general.

Three different moments in the history of lehaqat ha-naḥal stand out as highly notable expressions of this unique creation combining a concentration of future famous names and a remarkable string of classic songs. These three moments—1957–58, 1966–67, and 1971–72—represent the three stages that characterized all the lehaqot in Israeli popular music: the simple, almost naïve, early stage of the 1950s; the vibrant and enthusiastic pop of the mid-1960s; and the extravagant showmanship of the early 1970s.

Early Simplicity

The sixth program of lehaqat ha-naḥal, held in 1954, was the first made into a record. By the tenth program in 1957, recording the songs had become routine. The songs on these early records were marked by directness and simplicity, both in terms of arrangements and of sound production, as well as the fulfillment of the official role of the lehaqah. With the exception of one or two songs accompanied by a piano, the instrumental backing was solely accordion and darabuka. The songs were typically performed in unison harmony, with only occasional short vocal solos. The singing, especially the phrasing of words and sentences, was clear, trained, and disciplined. A certain flatness in the quality of the sound and the constant presence of a light echo are evidence of the fact that these recordings were made with the simplest equipment, with no postrecording treatment, and with all participants playing and singing directly into a few microphones.

The technical simplicity is well suited to the lyrics and the obvious conviction of the performers. It has become customary to refer to these early days in terms such as "innocence," like, for example, in this passage from a review of lehaqat ha-naḥal's 1970 program by Yoram Kaniuk. Comparing that program to the early years of the lehaqah, back in the 1950s, he writes, "In the past, the performers were less pretentious and more naive, but they had the grace of amateurism that examines its own environment, discovers its deficiencies, and produces poetry from it" (*Davar*, June 1970).

Indeed, lehaqat ha-naḥal of 1957–58 was not directed by notions of pop or popular music in general. Its songs were inner-directed, humorously and lovingly expressed themes from the Naḥal life on kibbutzim and in the army. One of the most memorable songs of the period is "Hora Heaḥzut" (Hora [dance] of the Naḥal settlement), music by Dov Seltzer, lyrics by Yehiel Mohar. It is a cheerful description of the way vegetables are "ordered" to grow in straight lines and to "obey orders." Another famous agricultural song is "Shneim-esre ton" (Twelve tons), music by Sasha Argov, lyrics by Yehiel Mohar. A swinging foxtrot, the song is highly reminiscent of the 1950s American hit by Tennessee Ernie Ford, "Sixteen Tons." It, too, joyfully comments on the "orders" to grow fixed amounts of vegetables and fruits, while adopting foreign influences.

Another concern of the songs was army life itself. "Ya mishlati" (Oh, my army post), music by Moshe Vilensky, lyrics by Yehiel Mohar, is a love song dedicated to the "home without walls" where soldiers have to reside for long periods, and where the only heating is that of "body warmth" and "combat fire." Another famous hit of the period is "Dina Barzilai," a love song to a female soldier, sung by a group of male soldiers. It expresses the collective adoration of the young soldiers for a girl who is a clerk in the lieutenant's office. During their lunch break, they look through her file and sing about the color of her eyes, her height, and other details noted there. The song stands out as a light, male-chauvinist look at the presence of women in the military.

National ideological issues were also included in the repertory. A particularly salient example is "Mul har Sinai" (Facing Mount Sinai). Written by Yehiel Mohar (lyrics) and Moshe Vilensky (music) during the short Sinai campaign against Egypt in late 1956, this song depicts the excitement of young sabras facing this historically significant mountain. Reminiscing on singing the song at the foot of the mountain during that war, Haim Topol remarked a few years later, "You will be surprised, but all the generals stood and cried. It was a sublime moment—maybe the greatest moment the lehaqat ha-nahal has ever had" (quoted in *Ba-Mahane*, December 1964).

Finally, the lehaqah of this early period also experienced a few exceptional moments of sheer romanticism. Most remarkable is the song "Ruah Stav" (Autumn wind), music by Yohanan Zarai, lyrics by Yehiel Mohar, which became one of the lasting standards of lehaqat ha-nahal. The song is remembered not only for its rare expression of male gentleness, but also because it was, for the most part, a solo by Arik Einstein, who would become a prominent rock singer. Accompanied by tender male harmony in the refrain, he was joined by Yehoram Gaon in a performance that anticipated their future collaboration in the Gesher Ha-Yarkon Trio. This makes the song an early reference point for Israeli popular music of later years.

Among the members of lehaqat ha-nahal of this period were future actors and singers Aliza Rosen, Gavri Banai, Israel Poliakov, and Hanan Goldblat. The innocence attributed to their early performances was probably one of the elements that made the songs so successful among the general public. However, the popularity of lehaqat ha-nahal in the civilian market put pressure on its directors and managers to seek contents with more general appeal. By the mid-1960s, this meant reorientation toward a general pop sound.

Enthusiastic Pop

The success with the general public, as well as the growing market for foreign contemporary pop, led the lehaqot tzvayiot to adjust their repertories. The transition to a more general pop attitude did not mean that the ideological and other commitments of lehaqat ha-nahal were abandoned. Rather, it meant that the directors and managers of the lehaqah sought to blend the two. In the programs of the mid-1960s, this formula resulted in some very successful moments of joyful pop for the lehaqah.

The first hints at the new direction were already evident in 1963 in the program *Shemesh ba-midbar* (Sun in the desert). Most of its songs were written, both words and music, by Naomi Shemer. While a song like "'Od lo akhalnu" (We haven't eaten yet) dealt humorously, in the traditional lehaqah tzvait manner, with the issue of food and meals in the army, other songs displayed much more general concerns. "Mahar" (Tomorrow), for example, was a utopian hymn to peace, to a time when "battleships will carry oranges," not relating specifically to Israel; and "Mitriyah bi-shnaim" (An umbrella for two) was a tap-dance song à la "Singing in the Rain." The accordion and darabuka, however, still dominated the sound.

The great leap into pop came in 1966, with the twentieth program. For this program, the Nahal unit recruited the services of Yair Rosenblum as musical director and arranger. Rosenblum was accordionist for the lehaqah from 1961 to 1964. He was born and raised in Tel Aviv and studied composition and orchestration before his army service. Thus Rosenblum had both the professional skills and the firsthand acquaintance with lehaqat ha-nahal's internal culture that no other musical director had before him. This combination can explain his phenomenal success with lehaqat ha-nahal from 1966 to 1972. At the same time, in charge of ha'amadah was Danny Litay. After their initial success with lehaqat ha-nahal, they were recruited to work with other lehaqot tzvayiot; consequently, as a team, they dominated the sound and stage not only of lehaqat ha-nahal but of other lehaqot tzvayiot for several years:

> A style of singing and ha'amada crystallized in the lehaqah tzvait through the unique cooperation between Yair Rosenblum and Danny Litay. It presents a varied show that expresses the unity of the lehaqah but also allows more and more room for solo singing. Rosenblum took advantage of all the musical possibilities he had at his disposal. He diversified his composition, the vocal and instrumental arrangements, so that the lehaqah sang in various modes. . . . With his talent, Rosenblum placed new challenges for the instruments, for their rhythmic and melodic diversity. . . . Danny Litay and Yair Rosenblum became names equivalent with the lehaqah tzvait. (Tessler 2000)

Rosenblum combined his vision of the cultural role of the lehaqot and his perception of Israeliness, with his knowledge of the social and organizational dynamics of lehaqat ha-nahal. He was thus able to create a musical formula that upgraded the traditional elements of the lehaqah tzvait. Under his direction, lehaqat ha-nahal sound became fuller, richer, and less constrained.

Decades later, in an interview Rosenblum was very clear about all these points. Thus his reflections on himself and Israeli culture are completely within the framework of the "melting pot" approach of Zionist ideology:

> Just as Naomi Polani was oriented to the French, there were different orientations. . . . Sasha [Argov] was naturally Russian, but they were all searching for a way, and in this search there were very unique styles. . . . Israeli music means being native of the country, getting your education here, absorbing the culture and then letting it out through your own filters. . . . What comes out is a symbiotic process of many cultures. . . . All these attempts were fruitful because people listened to them and eliminated some aspects, so that only the positive cores remained. And then the people who were born here heard all these things. . . . So I come from a different place [than earlier composers]. All of this goes through my filters, and it turns out that I never thought of being "Israeli," or of the relation between my music and Israeliness. Because I am Israeli and I have no other pretensions. Even if I wanted not to be Israeli, it would be impossible for me. (Yair Rosenblum, interview with the authors, June 1995)

Describing his and Litay's pattern of work, he explained how the military organizational framework facilitated the execution of their musical and cultural ideas:

> There was me and Danny Litay, we were like generals; we had all the authority in the world. Today, I think that maybe we often overused our power. But it was never for personal aims. It was always for advancing the artistic aspect. We were obsessive in this regard. . . . Only totalitarian regimes can allow a person to be engaged only in dancing and singing for three years. So the lehaqot were a sort of totalitarian microcosm. You take talented people, give them three years, let them sing and receive instruction from the best musicians, and then some experience of performing for soldiers. (Yair Rosenblum, interview with the authors, June 1995)

The first lehaqat ha-nahal program directed by Rosenblum was the twentieth program. It included songs by veteran composers Argov, Vilensky, Zarai, and Shemer, three compositions by Rosenblum himself, and one composition by a lehaqah member, a future Israeli rocker, Shalom Hanoch. In addition to Hanoch, the lehaqah members at this point included future pop singers Shula Chen, Sassi Keshet, and Motti Fleisher, as well as future entertainers Menachem Zilberman and Meir Suissa.

Two songs stand out as heralds of the new pop sensibilities explored by

Rosenblum. The first is "Geshem bo" (Come rain), music by Alona Turel, lyrics by Tirza Atar. The song begins slowly with the short phrase, "geshem geshem, bo," sung several times by different singers, building up tension. About thirty seconds into the song, the tension erupts into a rhythmic pattern, strongly underlined by a beat supplied by drums. The harmony singing that follows, as well as the rest of the solo singing, radiates a sense of spontaneity and looseness. The rhythmic drive and the vocals thus create a sonic presence clearly indebted to the trendy Anglo-American pop/rock of the period.

A second song is "Yeshnan banot" (There are girls), music by Yair Rosenblum, lyrics by Yoram Tehar-Lev. A catchy rhythmic song with salient presence of Latin percussion, it has solo vocal performances by female members of the lehaqah. The lyrics compare two types of girls. On the one hand, there are those who read only women's magazines, whose clothing is inspired by the fashion columns of such magazines, whose blouses have "holes in holes" so that "everyone can choose," whose skirts go "up and up" (referring to the miniskirts of the 1960s), and who think only about boys. On the other hand, there are girls, presented in the first person by the singers, who are "not like that"—they are serious and modest. The merry melody and the vocal performance load the lyrics with obvious self-parody, mocking the extreme righteousness of the "good" girls. "Bad" girls are actually what everyone eventually becomes, as the punch line at the end of the song admits. Thus playfully dealing (again) with the growing cultural threat of consumerism and Westernization that preoccupied many educators of the time, lehaqat ha-nahal produced a local version of a "girl group" pop song. The perceived contradiction between Israeliness and foreign influences that underlined the work of the lehaqot tzvayiot received clever treatment in this song and did not concede to either position. More than thirty years later, the song was given an extra twist of meaning when Dana International, the male-turned-female singer, made an electro-dance cover of it.

The twenty-first program, held in 1967, marked a complete transition to pop. The orchestration was now that of a rock band. Electric guitar and bass, drums, and especially the sound of an electric organ not only supported the often complex vocal harmonies but also in an unprecedented way enhanced the total sound. Of the twelve new songs in this program, eight were composed by Rosenblum. "Shalvah" (Tranquility), lyrics by Avi Koren; "Besimlah adumah" (In a red dress), lyrics by Ruthi Sifroni; and "Qarnaval ba-nahal" (Carnival in the Nahal), lyrics by Leah Naor, are lasting hits from this program.

This program is also the last one in which a sort of equilibrium could be sustained between official cultural roles and growing pop/rock tendencies. Later in the decade and into the 1970s, lehaqat ha-naḥal, as well as other lehaqot tzvayiot, faced the emergence of Israeli rock. Keeping pace with that development meant further "rockization" of sound and content and ultimately a breach in the balance in a way that either contradicted the national ideological aspect of the lehaqah, or produced heavily nationally mobilized rock that sounded ridiculous.

Extravagant Showmanship

The most fitting word to describe the lehaqot tzvayiot around 1970 is "big," in the sense that the work of the lehaqot came to be associated with elaborate stage shows, rich sound production, stardom of individual members, and the prestige that they were supposed to bring to their parent military units (and especially to the commanders of those units).

Thus, for example, the navy invested greater resources in its lehaqah, a small and low-key ensemble up to 1968, by enlisting Rosenblum and Litay and giving them a free hand to produce a spectacular show for this invigorated lehaqah in that year. A year later, with Benny Nagari as musical director, another program was produced. A string of hits and media attention made stars of Rivkah Zohar and Shlomo Artzi (while still in uniform), and the navy lehaqah was selected as "band of the year" for 1970, in the traditional end-of-year polls conducted by Kol Israel's pop radio station. In a similar vein, Avi Toledano of the armored forces lehaqah and Yigal Bashan of the Northern Command lehaqah became pop stars as soloists thanks to the lavish programs of their lehaqot.

Indeed, the Rosenblum and Litay formula for pop at this point was inspired by the notion of the rock musical exemplified by *Hair*. They were able to make the traditional format of the lehaqah tzvait more elaborate thanks to the adoration of the Israeli Defense Forces following the Six-Day War of 1967, which was a salient phenomenon of public culture at the time. Generals especially became society figures and celebrities. One result of this was the emergence of a quasi competition among army units for cultural prestige. Cultural prestige came to be perceived as supposedly reflecting the unit's contribution to the country's security. Consequently, the commanders of various units allocated resources to their "own" lehaqah tzvait, believing that greater success of the lehaqah would enhance the unit's prestige in the eyes of the public.

This meant that Rosenblum and Litay were able to recruit a larger ensemble, including a larger instrumental section, for lehaqat ha-naḥal. They could also afford better instruments and technical equipment for sound and stage production. When Rosenblum's musical direction came to be inspired by rock, he clearly had at his disposal much more than what a typical rock band needed. At the same time, he was confined by the lehaqah tzvait tradition of choreography and ha'amadah and by national ideological roles. The rock musical therefore seemed a perfect arrangement.

For its twenty-second program in 1969, lehaqat ha-naḥal produced a stage show that included elaborate sets and sophisticated lighting; on the whole, it was a grand spectacle of sound and color. Among its members were future pop singers Yuval Dor and Leah Lupatin; the core of the future rock band Kaveret—Danny Sanderson, Gidi Gov, Alon Olearchik, Ephraim Shamir, and Meir Fenigstein; and two female stars, Miri Aloni and Yardena Arazi. Almost all the songs were composed by Rosenblum.

Evidence that the marriage between a pop/rock spectacle and the lehaqah tzvait was a highly problematic one could be seen in this program in the controversy surrounding "Shir la-shalom" (Song for peace). The song was written, almost by accident, by Rosenblum and lyricist Yaakov Rothblit when they met on a ship en route to London. Rothblit, who had been severely injured as a soldier in the 1967 fighting in Jerusalem, was one of the younger rock-inspired lyricists who brought the influence of Bob Dylan, John Lennon, and other rock auteurs into Israeli music (Sheffi 1989). This particular song was inspired by the "flower-power" ideology of "make love, not war" and included some unmistakably antiwar sentences:

Tnu lashemesh la'alot,	Let the sun rise
laboker leha-ir	and give the morning light,
Hazakah shebatfilot,	the purest prayer
otanu lo tachzir	will not bring us back.
Mi asher kavah nero,	He whose candle was snuffed out
uve'afar nitman,	and was buried in the dust,
bekhi mar lo ye'iro,	a bitter cry won't wake him,
lo yakhziro lekhan.	won't bring him back
Ish otanu lo yashiv,	Nobody will return us
mibor takhtit afel,	from the dead dark pit.
Kan lo yo'ilu,	Here, neither the joy of victory
lo simkhat hanitzakhon,	nor songs of praise
velo shirei halell!	will help.
Lakhen, rak shiru shiru lashalom,	So sing only for peace,
al tilkhashu tefillah!	don't whisper a prayer,
mutav tashiru shir lashlalom,	it's better to sing a song for peace
bitze'akah g'dolah!	with a giant shout!
Tnu lashemesh lakhador,	Let the sun penetrate
miba'ad laprakhim.	through the flowers,

Al tabitu le-akhor,	don't look backward,
hanikhu laholkhim.	leave those who have departed.
Se-u einayim betikvah,	Lift your eyes with hope
lo derekh kavanot	not through the rifle sights
shiru shir la-ahavah,	sing a song for love
velo lamilkhamot	and not for wars.
Al tagidu yom yavo,	Don't say the day will come,
havi-u et hayom!!	bring the day,
Ki lo khalom hu	because it is not a dream.
Uvekhol hakikarot	And within all the city's squares,
hari'u lashalom!	cheer for peace.
Veshiru, shiru shir lashalom,	And sing, sing a song for peace,
al telkhashu tefillah!	don't whisper a prayer,
mutav tashiru shir lashalom,	it's better to sing a song for peace
bitze'akah g'dolah	with a giant shout!

(Translation as it appears on the official Web site
of the Israel Ministry of Foreign Affairs; translator not cited)

In addition to the song's opening line, Rosenblum's melody and arrangement and Litay's ha'amadah of the song were clearly inspired by songs from the rock musical *Hair*, especially "Let the Sun Shine." The song "intro" is a long electric guitar solo (played by Danny Sanderson), followed by solo singing by Miri Aloni, building up tension that grows steadily until the enthusiastic group singing of the final refrain.

Given the stylistic inclination of lehaqat ha-nahal, the song was nothing exceptional for its members. After all, rock was equivalent to protest and certainly to antiwar attitudes. But in Israel, in 1969, when the Hatashah (the War of Attrition) on the Suez Canal between Egypt and Israel was taking a toll in lives of soldiers almost daily, the song was unacceptable to the cultural establishment and certainly not when it was being performed by a lehaqah tzvait, an ensemble whose role was to raise soldiers' morale. The lehaqah was consequently pressured to drop the song from its repertory. The controversy reached a peak when the commander of the Central Command banned the lehaqah from performing in bases and posts under his jurisdiction. Although the lehaqah continued to perform the song, the incident symbolized the contradictory forces acting on it. In later years, "Shir la-shalom" became the anthem of the peace movement in Israel, acquiring almost legendary status when Prime Minister Yitzhak Rabin sang it with other participants at a peace rally in November 1995, minutes before his assassination. The blood-stained lyrics of the song were later found in his pocket.

The irony of the situation in 1969–70 was that some of its prominent members were also critical of the style of the lehaqah, although from a completely different point of view. If in earlier years, members had been willing to accept the ideologically informed adjustment of trendy foreign pop, this was no longer the case. At least not for some key members whose commitment to rock as art and ideology caused them to resent the type of singing and playing they had to do within the lehaqah. This was not rock as they understood it. Serving in a lehaqah tzvait was just a way of doing their obligatory military service without having to abandon music for several years. Ephraim Shamir, for example, who as a teenager was active in rock bands in Poland, was recruited to the lehaqah almost immediately after arriving in Israel. He recollects, "For me, lehaqat ha-nahal was the pure Israeli incarnate, which I could never understand. . . . The lehaqah was divided into two camps. One consisted of those who were on front stage, acting and singing. And then there were the musicians in the band, who were only interested in jamming all the time, in playing rock'n' roll" (quote from the television series *Sof ʿonat ha-tapuzim,* pt. 3).

For its next program, in 1972, perhaps in response to the criticism of "Shir la-shalom," lehaqat ha-nahal came up with a back-to-roots program. Many of the songs dealt with the spirit and way of life of the prestate Palmah units. Benny Nagari was now in charge of musical direction, and the rock tendencies still dominated. The lehaqah enlisted Haim Hefer and Sasha Argov, who had written some of the classic songs associated with the Palmah in 1946–48, to write some new songs. The lehaqah also recorded a new version of "Shir Ha-reʿut" (Camaraderie), by Sasha Argov and Haim Guri, one of the most famous songs of the Palmah and the 1948 War of Independence. Argov and Guri wrote a new song, "Balada le-Yitzhak Sade" (A ballad to Yitzhak Sade), about the much-admired commander of the Palmah. The song glorified his life and contribution to the nation. It was given a cheerful rock treatment by Nagari, thus becoming an exponent of what one might awkwardly call "Zionist rock."

Indeed, lehaqat ha-nahal was not the only group to produce such songs in the early 1970s. Other lehaqot tzvayiot did the same. The Armored Forces Ensemble recorded "Herzl" (music by Rosenblum; lyrics by Tehar-Lev), which listed early-twentieth-century Zionist leaders (Theodor Herzl, Menachem Usishkin, Max Nordau) and praised some of the deeds they performed for the nation. By this time, the adaptation of trendy foreign sounds to the style and roles of the lehaqot had lost the double edge it had ten years earlier. The lyrics were totally mobilized this time, with barely any sense of parody. At a time when rock musicians were beginning to create Israeli rock as a critical stance toward Hebrewism, such use of the rock sound idiom to convey national ideological messages was a practice that met with much criticism. "I have the feeling that those who work with the lehaqot tzvayiot and write their material live in a fools' paradise. The lehaqot tzvayiot are stuck today in one place. They do inauthentic things. How is it possible to sing about tanks through a sound inspired by the Beatles?" (Shalom Hanoch, *Haaretz*, September 1970).

But criticism of the lehaqot was not confined only to issues of content and style. The rising costs of their stage productions and the extravagant nature of their shows also met growing resentment by army officers. The criticism was aimed not only at the budgetary aspect, but also at the fact that with such elaborate shows, the ability of the lehaqot tzvayiot to perform for soldiers at faraway posts became very limited. While the earlier lehaqot, with only accordion and darabuka and hardly any sets, could move and perform easily almost everywhere, the complex shows of the lehaqot of the early 1970s made them, in effect, immobile. What the soldiers in small bases and posts received were bits of the lehaqot, performing unplugged versions of parts of their programs. In other words, there was a growing feeling in the army that the lehaqot had become an exaggerated phenomenon, and that perhaps they were no longer needed.

Thus, in the aftermath of the October 1973 War, the lehaqot seem to have lost their place. Yair Rosenblum, in an article published in 1988, describes the situation: "The massive support gradually stopped. They remained an aimless framework, that continued only by inertia. . . . At this point the process of their dissolution accelerated without incurring any effective objection" (Rosenblum 1988).

After an extended period of decline and finally disappearance from the public eye and ear, the lehaqot tzvayiot were officially disbanded in 1979. A few years later they were reassembled, mainly as "cover" ensembles of songs of past glory. Attempts to reinvigorate them in the vein of earlier periods failed.

THE IMPACT OF THE LEHAQOT

Assessments of the contribution of the lehaqot tzvayiot to the history of popular music in Israel conventionally point to the abundance of stars that sprang from them to achieve short or long-lasting careers. Another major point is the body of recorded songs of the lehaqot, which in itself is a significant section of what is typically called zemer ʻivri (Hebrew song). However, the lehaqot also had a strong impact on the field by creating the blueprint for group singing and haʻamadah. This particular pattern of performance inspired various early attempts to create civilian ensembles and remained for decades the quintessential mode for making music by many public-supported youth ensembles. It also had some impact on Israeli rock, most notably on the work of the seminal band Kaveret.

The success of the lehaqot tzvayiot in the 1950s and 1960s, as well as the perception of their sound and style of performance as expressing "authentic Israeliness," ushered in several commercially driven initiatives to create similar ensembles. The idea was to produce authentic Israeli entertainment that would address issues of daily life, perform love songs, and express the emerging local culture. Needless to say, the members of such ensembles were all graduates of lehaqot tzvayiot.

Not all of these attempts were successful. Two ensembles that had some success were Batzal Yarok (Green Onion) in 1957 and lehaqat piqud dizengoff (the Dizengoff Command Ensemble) in 1969, a name that refers to Dizengoff Street in Tel Aviv, whose cafés and shops made it, for many years, the symbol of artistic bohemian life and elite consumer culture of Israel. The most memorable and canonized civilian lehaqah was Ha-Tarnegolim (the Roosters).

Ha-Tarnegolim

Tarnegolim was formed in 1960 by Naomi Polani, who was responsible for musical and acting direction, choreography, and ha'amada. The first program contained mostly covers of songs already known to the public from lehaqot tzvayiot and other performers. But the ensemble is best remembered for its second program, produced in 1963, with all-new material. The songs were composed especially for the ensemble by Sasha Argov, with lyrics by Haim Hefer and Hillel Omer (known as "Ayn" Hillel). The entire repertory has been available since 1989 on one CD album. Tarnegolim ardently retained the joyful spirit of the lehaqot tzvayiot, including the simple accordion and darabuka accompaniment (occasionally adding a clarinet), harmony singing, and the ha'amadah of the songs. However, Argov supplied the ensemble with some intricate melodies, and Polani's work on the ha'amada and vocal performance was demanding. The members' enthusiastic cooperation with her vision created a stage show and a record that many commentators regard as one of the most authentic Israeli creations of all time.

This is attributed to the successful integration of Argov's sophisticated compositions and the depiction, in the lyrics and ha'amada, of themes from the spirit and daily life of young urban sabra culture. In their lyrics, Heffer and Hillel portrayed a prevailing atmosphere of "cute naughtiness" among teenagers in Israel's growing towns of the 1950s and 1960s—especially in mixed neighborhoods where veteran Israelis predominated over recently arrived immigrants. Tarnegolim's songs lovingly evoked the joy of harmless pranks against teachers or older citizens, the light sexual tension, and the type of straight-talking language (called *dugri*) used by these teenagers (Katriel 1986). These elements were notable in songs like "Kakha stam" (Just like that; lyrics, "Ayn" Hillel), "Ha-kol zahav" (Everything's gold; lyrics, Hefer), and especially in the more than six-minute-long "Shir ha-shkhunah" (The neighborhood song; lyrics, Heffer).

"Shir ha-shkhunah" opens with the line: "*hevre, hevre, rega', rega'*" (Guys, guys, just a minute). "*Hevre*" is a slang word referring to a bunch of friends, a small company of chums, whose centrality to sabra culture has often been noted (Almog 2000; Katriel 1991). Indeed, Tarnegolim's songs expressed the conspicuous value of togetherness that dominated youth life and sabra culture, not only by evoking the theme in the lyrics but also in the work patterns created by Polani:

> I truly don't know why Tarnegolim is called "the most 'Israeli' thing ever created in the country." Maybe it is because they were born in the country and breathed it. . . . Maybe there was something in it that was simply created in a society that lived for many years in the country and was attached to it. . . . With singers you have to invest in vocal arrangement, and we worked on that a lot. . . . We felt that something that we respect is coming out of us. There was much "togetherness" in it, and I love the human quality of the "together." Like the military parades of Independence Day, I'm crazy about it; it gives expression to human might. I found it to be exactly the opposite of a machine, unlike what many people think. (Polani, *Musica* 12, March 1988)

Using the patterns created by the lehaqot tzvayiot, and somewhat improving on them, Tarnegolim left a body of song, to which later performers like Arik Einstein and Shlomo Artzi have repeatedly returned. Although the type of Israeliness that these songs represent has declined and become demystified, they are still the object of nostalgia and yearning for a lost innocence—as became evident in 1999 when a new group of young singers recreated Tarnegolim, once again under the direction of Naomi Polani.

.   .   .

The decline and, in fact, disappearance of the lehaqot tzvayiot from their major position in Israeli popular music and the rise to dominance of Israeli rock do not mean that the lehaqot heritage has vanished. Their spirit has been kept alive in the work and performance of publicly supported youth ensembles throughout the country. Ensembles created by municipalities and regional councils, ensembles of youth movements, as well as high-school graduation shows are the frameworks in which the pattern of singing and performance associated with the lehaqot tzvayiot continue to exist. This indicates that in some parts of the educational system and the national-ideological work the heritage of the lehaqot is perceived as a representation of deep-rooted elements of early Israeliness. That teenagers are willing to participate in such projects, side-by-side with their routine personal interest in current foreign and local pop trends, is evidence of the commitment to national culture that still prevails in the age of globalized Israeliness.

This phenomenon also hints at the fact that the transition from Hebrewism and the lehaqot tzvayiot to globalized Israeliness and Israeli rock was not necessarily in the nature of a split. Rather, it took the form of smooth replacement, of adjustment. This change is nicely captured in a film, *Ha-lehaqah* (The ensemble, also known as The troupe), directed in 1978 by Avi Nesher. The film depicts the atmosphere of a lehaqah tzvait sometime in the late 1960s and explores the tensions among its members. The plot focuses on the way two new recruits are treated by the older members of the lehaqah. According to Talmon (2001), the new recruits symbolize, in both behavior and character, emerging cultural change. Eventually, they are integrated into the togetherness of the lehaqah. However, says Talmon, here the typical Hebrewist process of integration is inverted. Instead of the new ones being incorporated into the existing sabra culture, the veteran members and the lehaqah as a whole accept the style and conduct introduced by the younger, new members. Togetherness is preserved, but the cultural contents change. One of the two protagonists in the film is played by Gidi Gov, himself a graduate of lehaqat ha-nahal of the early 1970s and someone who in 1978 had already been the highly successful lead singer of the rock band Kaveret. His role heightened the mixture of fondness for and criticism of the lehaqot tzvayiot that the film expresses.

Indeed, criticism of ideologically mobilized music and a fondness for the typical formula of pop are combined in the attitude toward the lehaqot tzvayiot at a time when Israeli popular music is dominated by rock and musiqa mizrahit. This reflects the ambivalence toward the naiveté of the belief in the possibility of constructing one Israeliness that the lehaqot tzvayiot epitomized.

6 "And the Winner Is . . ."
Popular Song Festivals

In 1960, the Israeli Broadcasting Authority (IBA), then still known as Kol Israel, inaugurated a song contest. Its aim was to provide a framework for encouraging the writing of new, high-quality Hebrew songs. As an annual event, the contest survived in various permutations and under various names (see Ben-Porat 1989: 73–74) for four decades. Originally called by its initiators Festival ha-zemer ha-yisraeli (the Israeli Song Festival), the contest is remembered in collective memory as Festival ha-zemer (the Song Festival). By the early 1970s, it had become a blueprint for many other song contests, also called "festivals," whose impact on the local field of popular music was enormous, especially during the 1970s and 1980s. By commissioning new songs, drawing media attention to new performers and authors, and creating the aura of winners around particular songs, these song contests have been a major feature of the field of popular music in Israel.

Popular song contests were conceived and produced by state radio stations in Europe in the early 1950s and became routine by the 1960s. Most prominent among them was the San Remo Festival of the Italian Song, first held in 1951. The idea of a contest in Israel drew on the model set by this and other European festivals.

According to Fürst (1999), no fewer than 1,500 new songs were accepted and produced in twenty-seven different festivals held in Israel between roughly 1960 and 1990. Ten of these festivals survived for only one year, others endured for more than twenty years. These extraordinary numbers do not take into account several thousand songs submitted to the festivals and rejected at the preliminary stages of selection, some of which later found their way to the public via alternative routes of production.

Festivals in Israel take place once a year around the same date (usually connected to Jewish or national holidays) and usually consist of a single event, one and a half to three hours in length, held in the evening in a concert hall or sports arena. The festival is presented as an organic performance that includes, in addition to the songs, connecting texts read by the anchor(s) of the evening, additional artistic presentations outside the contest, and rich staging throughout the evening.

The proliferation of popular song festivals was closely related to the general quest for Israeliness that underlies the field of popular music. The original Festival ha-zemer, initially committed to SLI traditions and to Hebrewism, gradually changed during the 1970s into a middle-of-the-road pop contest, thus reflecting some of the cultural tendencies of global Israeliness. The IBA, responding to pressure from various interest groups, inaugurated two additional festivals in the 1970s, supposedly reflecting mizrahiyut and religious Israeliness. Also salient were the various children's song festivals, initiated by entrepreneurs, which enjoyed enormous success for many years.

In addition to the major festivals, a large number of smaller-scale festivals take place around the country, organized by municipalities, regional councils, various unions associated with the Histadrut, and ethnic organizations (typically, Jews from a specific country). These are publicly sponsored events, modeled after the large festivals organized by the IBA. Their aim is to voice additional claims about Israeliness and the authenticity of various groups and factions.

The major festivals, however, have always been those organized by the IBA and those dedicated to children's songs. One important difference between the IBA festivals and the children's song festivals was the selection of the songs to participate in the contest. The IBA, as a public body, attempted to maintain selection procedures that ensured wide participation. With some exceptions, a general "call for songs" was usually announced to the public at large, and a professional committee then selected the most suitable songs of those submitted. The children's song festivals, by contrast, were initiated and produced by bodies within the music industry and selected songs and performers in line with current pop trends.

The dominant position of IBA and children's song festivals is primarily reflected in their status as national media events, often broadcast live on radio and television. In addition, the participating songs, especially the contest winners, became hits, and albums of the songs of a particular festival often sold well.

FROM HEBREWISM TO GLOBAL ISRAELINESS:
THE ISRAEL SONG FESTIVAL

The Early Years

The Israel Song Festival was the most prominent song contest in Israel. Established in 1960, it was held almost every year, under different names, for about four decades. The original name of the festival, Festival ha-zemer ha-yisraeli, is not arbitrary. We have already discussed the special significance of the term zemer as a symbol of Hebrewist authenticity, in the context of the SLI tradition. When the IBA decided to establish its song contest, it was this term, rather than other synonyms like shir or pizmon, that was chosen.

The main goal of the Israeli festival was to promote the writing of original Hebrew songs, with emphasis on both music and lyrics. For the occasion, the IBA published a document called "Festival Rules" (vaguely inspired by the San Remo Festival rules) from which one can learn about the aims of the festival in the eyes of its promoters: "The festival will be competitive and its goal is to promote the writing of Israeli songs 'in the spirit of the Land [of Israel]'" *[be-ruah ha-aretz]*. Apparently in the late 1950s, there was, among the decision makers of state radio, a sense of decline in the creation of authentic Israeli songs. Hanoch Hasson, director of the entertainment division of the IBA in the 1970s and producer of several song festivals, states:

> In the 1950s there were singers who sang good songs, some of them even
> artistic, side-by-side with "trash" songs, i.e., [songs] from abroad . . .
> [like the songs of Shimshon Bar Noy and Israel Yitzhaki]. We [the IBA
> establishment] decided to clean the noxious weeds, to expel the tango,
> to establish frameworks that would provide room for Israeli singers who
> shared our feelings, [singers] that you would feel a spiritual link to them,
> not an operatic connection. . . . One of these activities was the [Israel
> Song] Festival.

In reaction to growing exposure of the field of popular music in Israel to foreign styles in the 1950s, the Israel Song Festival was designed to promote a popular song that differed not only from the tango, as Hasson expressed it, but also from Hebrew songs inspired by French chansons, Russian songs, Italian ballads, and Greek songs. These were genres that emerged in the 1950s on the live musical stages (cabarets, cafés, musical theaters, dance halls, and so on), in commercial recordings, and even on state-owned radio.

The Israel Song Festival underwent several metamorphoses. During the first period of its existence (1960–69), the festival crystallized its format. Building up the festival as a space for the celebration of Israeli national culture, two of its most salient features were the fact that it took place on Independence Day and that it usually involved representatives of the entire Israeli population in the judging procedure. After the performance of the songs, the audience present in the concert hall and selected audiences scattered throughout the country (in large urban centers, peripheral cities, and rural settlements) cast their votes. The judging audience across the country created a feeling of togetherness, of the Israeli "tribe" sitting around the radio and listening to its new songs.

Three features of the event reflect the festival promoters' will to generate high-level and original authentic Hebrew songs: the composition of the committee that screened all the songs submitted by the public and selected the finalists; the double performance of each song; and the assiduous use of biblical texts.

Although the festival was nominally dedicated to popular music, the screening committee in the early years included distinguished figures from the art-music establishment, such as composers Paul Ben Haim, Haim Alexander, Noam Sheriff, and Yehezkel Braun. They were joined by musicians who held powerful positions within the entertainment department of the IBA, such as Moshe Vilensky and Gil Aldema. Even a government minister sat on these juries. The composition of the screening committee was thus designed to provide an aura of respectability (without being entirely elitist) and a certain prestige to the judging process.

The double performance of each song aimed at detaching the song from its performer(s). It was clear that the popularity of a performer could bias the judging public. To avoid this link, two different performers, one male and one female, sang each song. This idea failed, as songs were identified with the most popular performers anyway, and it was dropped in 1967.

The use of biblical text or Bible-inspired lyrics aimed at detaching the literary content of the songs from the mundane atmosphere of current popular songs. One should also bear in mind that in the 1950s the Bible enjoyed high status among the secular Zionists, chief among them, Prime Minister David Ben Gurion. The Bible was the source of inspiration for the renaissance of modern Hebrew as well as the basic document underlying the Jewish claim to the Land of Israel after two thousand years of dispersion. Setting biblical verses to music strengthened Hebrewist Israeliness and its link to the entire Jewish people.

The idea of a homogeneous national culture implied by the ideology of the Israel Song Festival designers did not appeal to many critics and musicians. Soon after its inception, it came under attack on several fronts. Well-established composers of Israeli songs voiced their opposition to the very idea of a competitive song festival. In 1969, Sasha Argov argued that the general public had no tools to judge the songs and added that the festival "does not contribute to authentic creativity in this field." Naomi Shemer, already recognized as one of the most prolific Israeli songwriters by the late 1960s, maintained that the festival did not aim at established musicians but rather at beginners. Composer Yohanan Zarai stated his position succinctly: "I refuse to participate in the song contest. I am a composer, not a sportsman."

Yet the entire production of the 1960 festival tells something about the high expectations of the organizers in terms of its musical level. The 9 songs that reached the final stage, selected from more than 450 songs sent by the public, were accompanied by the IBA Symphony Orchestra conducted by maestro Gari Bertini, one of Israel's leading classical-music conductors.

Two memorable festivals that encapsulate the essence of the early years were the ones held in 1967 and 1969. The 1967 festival took place amid the growing tension on Israel's borders that led, three weeks later, to the Six-Day War in June of that year. The winning song was a sentimental love song, performed by Mike Burstyn, which was soon forgotten. The event, however, entered collective memory because of one of five new songs especially commissioned by the major of Jerusalem, Teddy Kolek. The song was "Yerushalaim shel zahav" (Jerusalem of gold), written by Naomi Shemer. Performed (outside of the competition) by Shuli Natan, who accompanied herself on acoustic guitar, the song "that changed the country forever" in Dan Almagor's words, expressed almost prayerlike longing for the city, as though anticipating the eruption of national sentiment few weeks later, when the Old City of Jerusalem was brought under Israeli control. Interestingly enough, this was one of the first modern Israeli songs about Jerusalem written from a national, rather than a traditional religious, perspective.

Another pinnacle of the festival's early years was singer Yehoram Gaon's taking the first two places in 1969. This firmly established his position as an "all-Israeli" singer. One of the songs was "Balada la-ḥovesh" (A ballad to the combat paramedic; lyrics, Dan Almagor; music, Efi Netzer), depicting an incident of heroic sacrifice during battle. The other was a pastoral "nature" song, "Etz ha-alon" (The oak tree; lyrics, Yoram Tehar-Lev; music, Moni Amarilio). The two songs, with Gaon's dramatic delivery and rich orchestration, stood in sharp contrast to the emergent sounds of Israeli pop and rock that appeared in that year and exemplified the typical combination of national-ideological themes and the general-popular song traditions of the festival.

"Eurovisionization" of the Israel Song Festival

The social currents that eventually undermined the respectful, national aura of the Israel Song Festival originated in the popular-music industry. Israel in the 1950s and 1960s was still a very centralized society in which the government fully sponsored and controlled most cultural activities and products. In a sense, the privately owned popular-music industry in Israel in the 1950s can be interpreted as a "counterculture."

Thus, under pressure of developments in the growing private music industry, especially the rise of Israeli rock, the Israel Song Festival began to change its character. The seeds of this change were noticeable as early as 1964, when the name of the festival was changed to Festival ha-zemer veha-pizmon ha-yisraeli. The addition of the word pizmon ("light" song) to the name of the festival along with the venerable label "zemer" signaled the acceptance into the festival of the very same international music genres that its founders had wished to avoid. The following comments express this point well:

> The Israel Song Festival was "on vacation" last year [1963]. . . . Those "in the know" spread rumors and gossip that were intended to vilify the festival and to present it to the public as a kind of institution of *"politruks"* [culture inspectors in the Soviet system] of the art of song, that dictated an official line of development for the Israeli song. Public opinion bashed [the festival] unmercifully and disseminated the view that only songs that were written in a "biblical spirit," or songs whose style was "Zionist" and "official" were selected. There are those who maintained that songs were rejected because they were too "light" and did not suit the national holy of holies—called "Independence Day." . . . For this reason, when it was decided to renew the tradition of the festival and a competition was announced, they introduced a small amendment. They called it Festival ha-zemer veha-pizmon ha-yisraeli. . . . [T]his expansion [of the name] was not intended to encourage the writing of Israeli twist, but rather of "lighter" songs. . . . The rules according to which the judges worked did not reject every "light song" . . . but only open imitations of cha-cha-cha. (Tzvi Lavi, "'Asara mi-tokh hamesh me'ot" [Ten out of five hundred], *Maariv,* June 10, 1964)

In 1969, the screening committee did not find any of the 685 songs submitted by the public worthy of participation in the festival and decided to commission songs from well-established composers. Some of the composers approached, such as Sasha Argov, Yohanan Zarai, and Naomi Shemer, turned down the offer. By 1972, following the decline of the idea of a general "call for songs," only songs commissioned by the IBA participated in the festival. The festival of that year offered additional significant changes. The anchors were Rivkah Michaeli and Yossi Banai, two of Israel's most popular comedians. They replaced the former presenter, Yitzhak Shim'oni, a member of the IBA old guard. The transformation of the festival into pure entertainment devoid of deep national significance thus became clear. Finally, the winning song of that year, "Tov li lashir" (I feel good singing) by Shmulik Kraus (a member of the High Windows Trio), performed by the Duda'im and Jozi Katz (an ensemble also known as Ha-tov, ha-ra' veha-ne'ara [The Good, the Bad, and the Girl]), departed from the soft and symphonic approach of previous festivals in the use of a stressed beat. By 1977, the festival was no longer held on Independence Day, its original and meaningful date.

The "coup de grâce" of the Israel Song Festival as it was conceived in 1960 occurred in 1978. By then, the annual Eurovision song contest, produced by the European Broadcasting Union, had become a major focus of attention for Israelis. As a member of the EBU, the IBA has participated in the Eurovision contest since 1973, when Israel was the first non-European country to be accepted into the competition (see Gambaccini et al. 1998). At that time, a professional committee selected the Israeli song for the Eurovision contest. In 1978, however, the IBA decided to transform the Israel Song Festival into a competition whose goal was to choose the song that would represent Israel in the Eurovision contest. In 1981, the festival was renamed again, this time called the Taḥarut ha-qdam-Eurovision (the Pre-Eurovision Competition).

Needless to say, the "Eurovisionization" of the Israel Song Festival dramatically changed the contents of the songs, their arrangement and performance, and the judging parameters. As one journalist wrote in 1979, "The Song Festival of 1979 is a little Eurovision, because many of the participants think of themselves as having one foot in the European market. Many of the songs actually became 'productions.' Once, when the [Israel Song] Festival ended, daily life continued. Today there is Eurovision, and profits are expected; this is a commercial business and for this reason a production effort greater than ever before is invested" (Yossi Harsonski, *Maariv,* January 29, 1979).

The pre-Eurovision experiment of the IBA succeeded beyond anyone's expectations. The winning song of the 1978 festival, "Abanibi" (The word "me" or "I" expressed in a children's word game; lyrics, Ehud Manor; music, Nurit Hirsh; sung by Izhar Cohen), a song that could easily have been submitted to one of the children's song festivals, won first prize in the

Eurovision contest that year. The win brought prestige and national pride, and the right to host the 1979 Eurovision contest. The extravagant production of the event in 1979, broadcast live from Jerusalem to tens of millions throughout Europe, and the first-place win achieved again by the Israeli entry—"Halleluyah" (lyrics, Shimrit Or; music, Kobi Oshrat; performed by the vocal ensemble Ḥalav u-devash [Milk and Honey], with soloist Gali Atari)—swept the Israeli public with national pride.

"Halleluyah," perhaps one of the most "Eurovisionic" songs ever composed, was chosen by a clear margin. The song had all the elements of the Eurovision formula: a catchy, "international" word *(halleluyah* is a biblical Hebrew word known to every Christian) repeated in almost every line (the song has no refrain); a short symmetric melody of sixteen bars that builds up to a climax through constant changes in texture; and successive modulations of a minor second upward in each repetition of the chorus, an effect that creates the illusion of increasing tension in the song and a movement toward a peak.

National pride in winning and successfully hosting the Eurovision contest replaced, in a sense, the original national goal of the festival, to create authentic Hebrew songs. Indeed, public interest and the relative success in the Eurovision song contest continued well into the mid-1980s (on the interesting analysis of countries' votes for each other in the Eurovision contest, see Yair 1995; Yair and Maman 1996). Israeli songs twice won second prize: in 1982, with the song "Hora" (a pop take of the national folk dance; lyrics, Yoram Tehar-Lev; music and performance, Avi Toledano); and in 1983, with the song "Ḥay" (Alive; lyrics, Ehud Manor; music, Toledano; performed by Ofra Haza). During the 1990s, diminishing success and interest led to the occasional replacement of the pre-Eurovision contest with an IBA-nominated committee of music professionals that selected the Israeli entry. This meant, in effect, the disappearance of whatever remained of Festival ha-zemer.

Still, in 1991, the Israeli song "Kan" (Here, by Uzi Hitmann; performed by the Datz Duo)—a song about love of the country, full of patriotic vigor—came in third at the Eurovision contest. And, in 1998, Israel again won first prize, this time with "Diva" (lyrics, Yoav Ginai; music, Tzvika Pick). Extravagantly performed by the popular transvestite electro-dance singer Dana International (accompanied by loud protests from religious members of the IBA directorate and Knesset members), "Diva" became a European hit, embraced by gay and lesbian communities across the continent (on Dana International, see Swedenburg 1997). The song lyrics include almost no Hebrew words, an indication of the profound change that the IBA entertainment establishment has undergone since the early days of the Israel Song Festival, when even single words in foreign languages were not acceptable.

It was not only the winning Israeli hits of the Eurovision contests, such as "Kan," that remained in the canonic Israeli repertory of popular songs. Throughout the years, the Israel Song Festival contributed many songs to the repertory. The songs that survived the test of time were not always the ones that were awarded prizes. Examples of this phenomenon are "Al kapav yavi" (He will bring on his palms, by Yoram Tehar-Lev and Yair Rosenblum) performed by Rivkah Zohar at the 1969 festival that became the song of the year on the Hebrew charts, and "Selihot" (Forgiveness), by Lea Goldberg, one of Israel's most prestigious poets, and Oded Lerer. A very personal song first heard at the 1977 festival, "Selihot" became a major hit of Yehudit Ravitz, then an anonymous young singer and today one of Israel's leading female rockers.

The evolution of the Israel Song Festival reflects the gradual transformation of Hebrewism into global Israeliness. A testament to this transformation was unhappily foreseen in the following citation by art music composer Alexander Boskovich, one of the judges of the third Israel Song Festival in 1964. Boskovich, a pivotal figure in the attempt to create a national style of Israeli art music in the 1950s, says:

> Around 400 songs . . . came before the jury of the Third Israeli Song Festival. . . . It is hard to believe that all 200 composers and 400 songs and melodies could really be beautiful. Even among the ten songs presented for the judgment of "the people" . . . there were some that in my opinion were far from being an Israeli pizmon ["light" song], not to mention Israeli zemer ["authentic" folk song]. The unique pastoral landscape of the Israeli zemer has disappeared behind the urban singing and folklore and in most cases the only authentic Israeli feature left is the language; and then the only statement you can make is that you can hear a French chanson or a Hollywood "song" [in English in the original] in fluent Hebrew. . . . Any Israeli who has experienced the tremendous historical event of the revival of the State [of Israel] . . . cannot but be sorry for the loss of the values that molded the style of the Israeli song in the past. Those [old] melodies are really witnesses of the wonderful spiritual drive of a great historical period. . . . And now the pizmon threatens the very existence of the authentic zemer. . . . The folkloric Israeli zemer tends to be entertainment—I would say individualistic and somewhat egocentric entertainment, "urban art" without character; . . . the commercial industry and technology govern everything. (Boskovich 1964)

One year later, Moshe Vilensky (1965) offered a different, more pragmatic evaluation of the role of Hebrewism in the Israeli popular song, when he argued, "The local character [of a song] cannot be imposed by an order, and generally the 'light song' speaks in an international language, except for the local sound . . . and such a sound exists in our song because of the Hebrew language. . . . It is also worth mentioning that what is considered among us as a folk song is not a real folk song; it was also invented in an artificial manner."

REDEEMING MIZRAḤIYUT: THE ORIENTAL SONG FESTIVAL

Opposition to the idea of an officially sanctioned song festival produced by the IBA existed throughout the years it was held. Music critics, musicians, producers, politicians, educators, and individuals representing practically every public sector had something to say against the form, content, or judging procedures of the festival in its various metamorphoses. Yet the festival somehow survived all this public criticism because its producers constantly adapted themselves to changing cultural circumstances. Moreover, in terms of its musical direction, the festival always remained faithful to its original purpose: to serve as a stage for the representation of Israeliness as perceived by Hebrewism and global Israeliness.

For this reason, one crucial social issue remained beyond the boundaries marking the territory of the festival: the expression of the multicultural composition of Israeli society. Some measure of pseudo-Mediterraneanism was found in songs that participated in the festival throughout the years (especially in the early festivals). This was expressed in the use of compound meters (7/8 for example) or of modes instead of major/minor scales. There was, however, never room in the festival for the music of the mizraḥi Jews or other forms of traditional Jewish music, and certainly not for Arabic music. These musical traditions had no chance of entering even the preliminary stages of the competition.

The flagrant exclusion of the Israeli "other" from the Israel Song Festival generated social pressure on IBA authorities. Eventually, public lobbying by diverse groups led to the establishment of sectarian festivals dedicated to specific musical styles associated with well-defined social sectors. The most prominent of these festivals was Festival ha-zemer ha-mizraḥi (the Oriental Song Festival).

Once again the word zemer appears in the name of an Israeli festival, in this case conveying the yearning of the promoters of the new festival to belong to mainstream Israeliness in spite of the stylistic difference of the music. This kind of affirmative action was explicitly expressed by Yosef Ben Israel, former director of the Folklore Department of the IBA and the promoter and producer of the Festival ha-zemer ha-mizraḥi in its formative years:

> In 1970, several festivals were aired and supported by the IBA in Israel. I came to the board of directors [of the IBA] and told them, "There is an Israel Song Festival but I do not hear anyone there who sings a mizraḥi melody." . . . I had to fight hard. They told me, "We will let you [organize a mizraḥi song festival] on condition that you find the money." I asked, "What about the [Israel] Song Festival, why don't you lay down conditions there?" They said, "[The festival] is on the [regular IBA] budget." I proposed that using my entire annual budget [that is, the budget of the Folklore Department], I would hold the [mizraḥi] song festival. Because in my opinion this is what unifies the *'edot* [Jewish ethnic groups]. (Interview with Yosef Ben Israel by Shifra Fürst, 1998)

Using the Israel Song Festival as its model, the Oriental Song Festival reproduced most of the procedures of the original including the use of the largest halls in the country, live broadcasts on radio and TV, a public call for songs, the judging system, arrangements of songs by musicians commissioned by the IBA, and so on. However, many social issues were raised regarding the production of the Oriental Song Festival as a copy of the Israel Song Festival. One of these issues was the symbolic meaning of space. According to Ben Israel, through the festival, he wanted to bring mizraḥi Jews, in the most physical sense, to the two main halls where IBA festivals took place:

> I always said, you have Heikhal ha-tarbut [Shrine of Culture—the hall of the Israel Philharmonic Orchestra] in Tel Aviv and no one from Shekhunat ha-tiqvah [a south Tel Aviv working-class neighborhood] has any reason to go there. You have Binyanei ha-uma [House of the Nation—a hall in which many state events take place] in Jerusalem, and no one from Musrara [a poor Jerusalem neighborhood inhabited mostly by working-class Moroccan Jews] has anything to do there. (Interview with Yosef Ben Israel by Shifra Fürst, 1998)

Another issue that Ben Israel raised was that the Oriental Song Festival had a dual educational goal: one, to open the Ashkenazi ear to the musical world of mizraḥi Jews in order to close the cultural gap and the lack of understanding between Western and Eastern Jews; and two, to "domesticate" the music of mizraḥi Jews and to raise its standards to the level of the rest of Israeli popular music (that is, Western-style pop music in Hebrew). The songs of the festival did not reproduce folkloric materials. Rather, the mizraḥi melodies selected were arranged by Ashkenazi arrangers using Western techniques like harmonization. The songs were performed by the best singers available, some, but not all, mizraḥi, accompanied by the Oriental Orchestra of the IBA, a prestigious ensemble led by professional Iraqi Jewish instrumentalists. Thus the main goal was not to focus on difference, but rather to bring all mizraḥi Israelis separated by different cultural traditions under one musical umbrella.

This bringing down of cultural fences resulted in a semantically vague type of musical "Orient." One reason for this vagueness was that composers, judges, arrangers, and performers of the Oriental Song Festival came from diverse cultural strata and ethnic origins, including many Ashkenazi Jews. For example, in the 1975 Oriental Song Festival, seven of the ten competing songs were composed by Ashkenazi Jews, in a vaguely oriental style.

The first festival was in held 1970. It was named Lamnatzeaḥ shir mizmor—Festival ha-zemer ha-mizraḥi. The name means "For the Leader a Song" and is a paraphrase of a recurring theme in the Book of Psalms. This biblical reference made it immediately clear that the festival was traditional—not in the strictly religious sense, but in terms of having some link to the cultural past of non-Western Jews. By default, this attitude also implied that the "official" Israeli Song Festival was not "authentic" but rather "invented."

Notice that the name of the Oriental Song Festival did not include the word "Israeli." According to Ben Israel, the board of directors of the IBA refused to authorize the use of the adjective "Israeli" in the name of the Oriental Song Festival because it was already in use by the "official" festival. Thus, in a very symbolic way, mizraḥi music remained outside the fold of Israeliness.

Moreover, state television, a relatively new institution with few hours on the air in 1970, initially refused to broadcast the first Oriental Song Festival in prime time. The main reason given by the IBA authorities was that the musical style of the songs was more appropriate to Arab-language programming of Israeli TV (in the early evening). It was finally decided to broadcast the festival as part of the Arabic program on a Friday afternoon, right before the sabbath, but vociferous public protest challenged this decision. Eventually, the festival was transferred to the Hebrew program, but broadcast in installments of twenty minutes each, for a span of several days, right after the main 9 p.m. evening news.

Beginning with the second Oriental Song Festival (1971), in the middle of the evening while the songs were being judged, "authentic" folk ensembles of Jewish ethnic groups (from India, Bukhara, and so on) and a Druze ensemble appeared. This was followed by the mainstream female pop trio Shoqolad, menta, mastik (Chocolate, Mint, Chewing Gum), one of the most popular ensembles of that time. The programming of this part of the Oriental Song Festival reflected an ambivalent position. It signaled, on the one hand, a return to mizraḥi Jewish musical roots and, on the other, a yearning to be accepted as part of global Israeliness without overlooking diverse ethnic Jewish identities.

The ambivalence shown in the 1971 program grew over the years. The Oriental Song Festival of 1979, which was not a competitive one, included songs from previous festivals and arrangements of mizraḥi melodies with new Hebrew lyrics. More than at any time in the past, the 1979 festival was eclectic in nature. It included variations on a Yemenite Jewish melody sung by Izhar Cohen (then at the peak of his career after winning first prize in the Eurovision contest) accompanied by modern jazz dancers in the background, followed by Shagririm (the Ambassadors), singing Bukharan Jewish tunes with a disco beat. Moreover, at this festival, there were many crossovers between the ethnic origins of the singers and the materials they sang. There was also a crossover in orchestral sound; it combined the IBA Symphony with several Eastern musicians playing santur, qanun, tar, and so on. In some items, the orchestra was joined by the Chamber Choir of the Rubin Academy of Music in Jerusalem. And, at the same event, a Kurdish Jewish female folksinger performed a capella traditional songs from her heritage together with this large symphonic ensemble.

This undefined array is exemplified by the song that won first prize at one of the most successful Oriental Song Festivals, in 1974: "Liqrat Shabbat" (Toward the sabbath), by Avi Koren, Avner Tzadok, and Avihu Medina, sung by Yigal Bashan. The text strongly recalls a traditional sabbath eve scene, a topic off-limits to the Israel Song Festival. The first two lines of the opening stanza are an exact quotation from "Lekha dodi," the sixteenth-century mystic poem that opens the sabbath eve service at the synagogue, called "Welcoming the Sabbath." The fourth line of this stanza is the opening line of another famous sabbath poem, "Deror yiqrah," by Dunash ben Labrat (Spain, tenth century). There is, therefore, only one original line in this stanza, the third one, in which the head of the family (an allusion to the patriarchal hierarchy of the mizraḥi family) sings with *silsulim* (vocal inflections of long pitches), a clear reference to the singing style of oriental Jews.

The music has no other reference to mizraḥiyut other than the modality of the final cadence in A minor natural, yet even this mild index of mizraḥiyut is watered down by the lavish orchestration, harmonization, and singing style. The "subversive" subtext of this song, that is, the attempt of its writers, composers, and performers to preserve elements of mizraḥiyut despite pressure to dilute them, is found in the lyrics rather than in the tune.

LIQRAT SHABBAT (KOREN, TZADOK, AND MEDINA)

"Come, beloved Israel, greet your bride,
welcome the coming of the sabbath tide."
And father waves his voice
with sabbath songs.
"Freedom will call
to the son with the daughter."

Other songs of the 1974 festival that became classics of this type of watered down mizraḥiyut (for example, "Yerushalaim ha-aheret," by Yossi Gamzu and Amos Meller; "Agadat Shalom Shabbazi," by Uri Barzilay and Yehuda Badihi; and "Qiriya le-melekh ram," by Barak Amrani), especially those composed by Avihu Medina who took the first three places in 1974, share the characteristics of "Liqrat Shabbat." From a musical point of view, some of them could be easily accepted by the general Israel Song Festival. Their success in winning over the general public and their survival in the Israeli repertory many years after the festival itself was only a memory were functions of successful musical manipulation by the producers, all of them connected to the IBA. For this reason, musiqa mizraḥit, the grassroots popular music of the mizraḥi sector of the Israeli society, was not found at the Oriental Song Festivals of the 1970s. Only in the early 1980s did the festival make contact with the world of musiqa mizraḥit. In 1982 the festival opened its stage to the all-time greatest star of musiqa mizraḥit, Zohar Argov. However, the need for an Oriental Song Festival was by then obsolete. In 1985, after the Israel Song Festival officially became the Pre-Eurovision Contest, Yosef Ben Israel tried to transform the Oriental Song Festival into a more general "Israeli" festival (called *Dror*, lit., freedom, in honor of Drora Ben Avi of the IBA, who contributed to advancing the oriental song on Israeli radio) by opening the contest to all musical styles. This was an illusion since the stylistic differences between the two festivals were minimal from the start. With the meteoric rise of musiqa mizraḥit, the Oriental Song Festival became obsolete and in 1986 was no longer produced.

THE HASSIDIC SONG FESTIVAL

The third large festival, Festival ha-zemer ha-ḥasidi (the Hassidic Song Festival) was produced for the first time in 1969. Like the Oriental Song

Festival, this festival was also modeled on the Israel Song Festival and even the key word, zemer, was retained. Unlike the Oriental Song Festival, the Hassidic Song Festival was a product of private initiative, since the chances of producing such an event from within the IBA were null at that time.

The main question here is why the festival was called "Hassidic" rather than "religious." Hassidism is a mystical movement that arose within Ashkenazi Jewry in Eastern Europe in the mid-eighteenth century. It stressed the use of textless vocal music *(niggun)* as a means of attaining a deep religious experience (Hajdu and Mazor 1971). The view of Hassids as "musical Jews" was certainly one of the main reasons underlying the name selected for this festival.

However, a deeper explanation is warranted here. While the Israel Song Festival was a celebration of Israeliness, the Hassidic Song Festival was a reaction by the national religious sector, which was struggling to find its path into mainstream Israeliness. Yet, by selecting the term Hassidic for the name of their festival, the producers were influenced by the secular Zionist perception of the traditional Eastern European Jew. This perception was generally negative because Zionism regarded the religious Jew of the *shteytl* (the rural town in Eastern Europe where most Ashkenazi Jews lived) as an antithesis to the main ethos of Zionism: the "new" Jew. The mystical Hassids, by contrast, enjoyed a more favorable status. They were "happy" religious Jews, with singing and dancing as their main activities. This stereotypical, albeit banal, view of Hassidic Jews was celebrated in Israeli literature and was the topic of two very influential musicals, the American *Fiddler on the Roof* (presented in Israel in Hebrew as *Kanar ʻal ha-gag,* shortly after its successful release on Broadway) and the Israeli *Ish Ḥassid haya* (Once there was a Hassid, by Dan Almagor).

Antecedents of the Hassidic festival can be also found in the light religious music, also called "Hassidic," that developed in Britain and in the United States in the 1960s. One style is associated with children's choirs called the Pirḥe (Cadets). These choirs sang to the accompaniment of a pronounced beat played on bass guitar. The second influential style was that of Rabbi Shlomo Carlebach, known as the "singing" or the "dancing" rabbi. A Lubavitcher Hassid of very unusual character, Carlebach developed a unique style of composition and performance, inspired by the folk rock of Bob Dylan. Indeed, he even shared a stage with Dylan and Joan Baez at a 1963 event held in San Francisco (Brandwine 1997: 29).

Armed with a guitar, dressed like an "orthodox hippie," and using the most basic harmonies and short, repetitive melodies, Carlebach appeared at concerts that became a kind of unorthodox prayer that recalled the tradi-

tional Hassidic *tish* (lit., table), an assembly of Hassidim around the table of
the Rebbe (leader of the Hassidic sect), held on special dates, and characterized by singing and dancing.

When Carlebach finally settled in Israel in 1970 (after appearing sporad-
ically during the 1960s), he was adopted by the young generation of
national religious Israelis who aspired to a deeper religious experience than
regular orthodoxy could provide. His community in Israel, called the
"House of Love and Prayer," became a focus for many members of this
young generation. This community became a framework for patterns of
music consumption that recalled the secular pop-music scene, even from the
sphere of rock, without necessarily crossing the lines into the dominant
Israeli secular society. Carlebach's influence on the Hassidic Song Festival
was decisive. Many of his best-known hits were first heard at these festivals.

As in the Oriental Song Festival, the distinctive message of the Hassidic
Song Festival resided in the text rather than the music. For example, the festival included a song entitled "The Besht Superstar" (acronym for the Baal
Shem Tov, founder of the Hassidic movement), an obvious reference to
"Jesus Christ Superstar." Lyrics often consisted of biblical verses (with
emphasis on Psalms) or quotations from the prayer book. However, while
the texts expressed the "religiosity" of this event, other aspects of the performance were entirely secular. For one, many performers, composers, and
arrangers of the Hassidic Song Festival were not observant Jews. Even more
significant, female singers participated in the festival, in spite of the religious Jewish ordinance that forbids men from listening to a woman's
singing voice. Moreover, the attire of the singers departed considerably from
the religious code of modesty.

As such, the Hassidic Song Festival did not appeal solely to the religious
community. It apparently struck a chord with some secular Israelis, who
found in it an expression of their sentimental longing for the stereotypical
traditional Jewish past. The following review exemplifies this point:

> The Hassidic renaissance emerging in Israel is a paradox. Who hates
> *qapotot* and *streymels* [the long black jackets and large hats characteris-
> tic of the ultraorthodox Jews], or *ay, ay, ay* and *ya, ba, bam* [nonsense
> syllables associated with the Hassidic niggun] more than we do? In the
> 1920s, we replaced the Hassidic dance with a Torah Scroll for the hora
> [dance] around the campfire. The Hassidic songs in our mouths became,
> actually, anti-Hassidic ("When the Rabbi Sneezes" [an Israeli parody of
> a traditional Yiddish song "When the Rabbi Laughs"]). After the estab-
> lishment of the state, the rabbis, the lazy, and the *talmidei hakhamim*
> [students of religious academies] disappeared from our stages. The

actors of [the musical] *Ish Ḥassid haya* were hippies in jeans who gave up the violin, clarinet, and contrabass, the traditional Hassidic instruments, and played the guitar. (Michael Ohad, *Haaretz*, August 29, 1975)

The success of the Hassidic Song Festival was not immediate. The first edition in 1969 was a failure. However two of the songs from this festival became instant hits on the general hit parade of the Israeli radio, thus exposing the new festival to a very large audience. The first of these songs was "'Ose shalom bimromav" (May He create harmony in the heavens, by Nurit Hirsh; performed in the festival by Yigal Bashan; the text sanctifying God's name, taken from the prayer *qaddish*), considered to this day one of the most successful Israeli popular songs, even by international standards. Part of the success of the song is in its ambiguity, for it conveys a general longing for peace far beyond the heavenly peace to which the text refers. The characteristic accelerando of the refrain may be associated with the evolving ecstasy characteristic of the Hassidic dance tunes.

The second song was "Ve-ha'er eyneynu be-toratekha" (Enlighten our eyes through thy Torah; from the sabbath morning prayers) by Rabbi Shlomo Carlebach, one of his most famous songs. This simple song, whose lyrics include just a few words from the prayer book, has all the ingredients of the Carlebach style: two contrasting sections of only eight bars each, with the second one in a higher register, melodic sequences, assiduous syncopation, and three-chord harmony (I, IV, V). The arrangement is in a clear pop style, performed by the Shlosharim Trio, far removed from traditional Hassidic music.

The 1977 Hassidic Song Festival was a turning point in the development of the festival, for it introduced meaningful novelties. First prize was given to the Diaspora Yeshiva Band, a band of amateur musicians that included "born-again" American Jews and Israelis (that is, secular Jews who became ultraorthodox). This band offered rare authenticity, because its members were and behaved on stage as true Hassids. Moreover, many of the songs were by American-Jewish composers. While the festival took place in Israel, the entire production was later exported to Jewish communities abroad. The rapid spread of these festival songs in the United States was remarkable. Tunes from the festival, especially those by Shlomo Carlebach, were even introduced into religious services. The Americanization and internationalization of the Hassidic Song Festival, inherent from its beginnings because of the dominant figure of Carlebach, had become manifest by 1977. The rapid de-Israelization of the Hassidic Song Festival and its transformation into a sectarian event led to its gradual disappearance.

CHILDREN'S SONGS FESTIVALS

One of the most original developments of the popular-music industry in Israel is the creation of a sizeable market of songs for children. Festivals of children's songs are the channels through which this type of song is created, produced, recorded, and distributed. This concern for Hebrew children's songs has its roots in the beginnings of Israeli culture.

Creating a new repertory of children's songs was an important aspect of the new Hebrew culture of the Zionist Yishuv. The songs were used, among other goals, as educational tools, for example, to introduce children to modern Hebrew and to strengthen their attachment to the Land of Israel. The pioneering work of prolific Ukrainian-born Jewish poet Levin Kipnis (1894–1970), who wrote hundreds of poems for children, led a gallery of distinguished Israeli composers including Nahum Nardi, Yedidiya Admon, Daniel Samburski, Paul Ben Haim, Nissan Cohen Melamed, Joel Walbe, Matitiyahu Shelem, and Emmanuel Amiran to set his poems to music. In later periods, composers associated with the Hebrew folk song, such as Mordechai Zeira and David Zehavi, and with popular music, such as Moshe Vilensky and Naomi Shemer, composed children's songs as well.

In the Yishuv period, Hebrew songs for children, though composed by well-known composers, were transmitted orally by kindergarten and elementary schoolteachers. Thus the songs were not identified with a specific performer. With the development of the popular-music industry after 1948, record companies began to invest in the profitable children's market. Traditional folk songs for children by Kipniss and other authors from the Yishuv period were commercially recorded by prestigious popular singers of the 1950s and 1960s, such as Yaffa Yarkoni and Nehama Hendel. Since then, certain songs have become associated with specific singers.

The Israel Festival of Children's Songs was first produced during the Hanukah holiday in 1970. The idea of a festival in which the songs are performed by children was conceived by several private entrepreneurs and modeled after an Italian TV show that starred children. The festival had two parts. In the first, the selected songs were sung by popular adult singers, and in the second part, the same songs were performed by children. The singers were accompanied by a large orchestra and the songs were staged in the style of the Israel Song Festival. The selection system was also adopted from the Israel Song Festival, that is, there was a public call for songs, followed by a screening procedure that led to the selection of ten songs for the final competition. Beginning with the fourth festival, the producers commissioned the songs and selected the performers.

Unlike the children's songs of the Yishuv period, which were composed according to specific requirements such as narrow range and simple, repetitive rhythmic patterns, festival songs were written as truly MOR popular songs. Thus the message of the song relied on the texts, most of which dealt with themes from the world of children, such as relations with parents, animals, and fictional lands.

Modeled on the Israel Song Festival, held in the large concert halls, and recorded and broadcast on national television, the Israel Festival of Children's Songs soon acquired official status. However, unlike the adult's song festival, the children's festival was an ongoing performance, held several times during the Hanukkah vacation in order to increase profits. This fact also made participation in the festival extremely appealing to popular singers who were attracted by the prospect of exposure on national television.

Concerns about mistreatment and exploitation of children were associated with various aspects of the children's song festival. Selection of the young singers became a public matter when thousands of parents, lured by the prospect of future stardom for their sons and daughters, pushed them into the screening process. An educational issue raised by the children's festival concerned the level of the songs: "There was denial of the children's level of intelligence . . . a campaign teaching poor and low taste. . . . We are witnesses to turning children into clowns and to their exploitation in order to buy their hearts" (Heda Boshes, *Haaretz*, February 10, 1972).

Despite all the criticism, the festival enjoyed sweeping commercial success; 27,000 copies of the LP containing the songs of the first Children's Song Festival were sold, a sizeable number for those days in local terms. Capitalizing on the success of the Children's Song Festival, in the early 1980s the music industry produced several successful LPs of children's songs. Noteworthy among these, was the LP *100 shirim rishonim* (First 100 songs) that included modern arrangements of the traditional canon of children's songs in Hebrew to the accompaniment of a band.

In 1982, a new festival of songs for children, the Haifa Festival of Children's Songs, also called the "Festigal" (Festi-wave), was established. Unlike the pioneer Israel Children's Song Festival, the Festigal took place in a large sports arena rather than in a concert hall. This setting called for sophisticated staging, including lavish lighting effects, turning the festival into a complex musical spectacle, a mixture of musical and rock concert. More important, the Festigal related to children as adults.

Technological developments affecting music consumption by young audiences called for songs in current pop styles, especially rock, with less childish texts and performed by the most popular artists and bands of the year. As a result of these changes, the Festigal was able to address a wider audience in terms of age, and its identity as a children's festival became a marketing gimmick rather than an essential feature of the event. As one journalist noted:

> All ten songs competing this year for a prize in the Festigal could easily participate in the Pre-Eurovision contest and the differences would not be noticed. The rhythms, lyrics, and style of performance of most of the songs are more akin to the parameters of the Eurovision than to a competition of children's songs. . . . [Rock star] Ricki Gal, a veteran of the children's events and a star of the Festigal this coming Hanukkah said that today the approach to children is different. There are not really children's songs, and most [songs of the festival] also suit adults. "The children," said Gal, "are exposed to things like music videos and therefore there is a different approach to them." (Yaakov Hacohen, *Maariv*, December 13, 1982)

The children's song festivals produced many popular hits that became a component of the Israeli canon of both children's and Shirei Eretz Yisrael repertories. These festivals promoted writing of songs for children by the most distinguished pop artists. Songs of the early children's song festivals like "Ratziti she-teda'" (I wanted you to know, by Uzi Hitmann), "Ima" (Mother, by Shaike Paikov), and "Barba-aba" (by Yoram Tehar-Lev and Nurit Hirsh) are still sung by Israeli children almost three decades after their composition. Songs of the Festigal, by contrast, composed in a less childish style, remain part of the SLI repertory, and include songs such as "'Od yihiye tov be-eretz yisrael" (Things will still be good in the Land of Israel, by Shaike Paikov).

By the 1990s, the marketing of children's songs underwent substantial change. In 1993, the Festigal became a production of the children's television channel, leading to the participation of the channel's most beloved actors. In this way, the transformation of this event into just another major musical production was completed. Musical videos, some composed by major popular composers such as Naomi Shemer and Nurit Hirsh, contributed to the gradual disappearance of the children's song festivals.

•　　•　　•

Twenty-seven song festivals were produced in Israel between 1960 and 1998. The IBA festivals set the parameters for the entire phenomenon that remained a major feature of popular music in Israel for several decades. Besides the major festivals discussed above, there were many other smaller events that focused on specific musical styles, ideological motives, or ethnic ties. These small festivals, mainly noncompetitive, survived for only a short time. Yet some of them produced memorable popular songs.

One of these events was Festival shirei meshorerim (Poets' Song Festival), organized by Galei Tzahal and held for several years during the 1970s. Another was the Festival shirei ha-yona (Songs of the Dove Festival), organized by peace movements and held three times: in 1980 in Hayarkon Park (Tel Aviv's Central Park) to celebrate the signing of the Peace Treaty between Israel and Egypt; in 1984 in a park in the Upper Galilee as a protest against Israeli intervention in Lebanon; and in 1993 to support the Israeli-Palestinian peace process. The Festival shirei yerushalaim (Festival of Songs of Jerusalem) held on Jerusalem Day, commemorating the battle for Jerusalem in the Six-Day War (1967), when, in the late 1970s, rumors spread that the partition of Jerusalem might be discussed during the Egyptian-Israeli peace negotiations. Still others included various festivals of Yemenite songs and also festivals of Arab songs organized in Arab towns.

A different event was the Arad Festival of zemer 'ivri. Although called a festival, it was not a song contest, nor was it a one-evening event. The Arad Festival took place for the first time in 1983 in several venues (some of them in the open air) in Arad, a town in the Negev Desert. Lasting for several days (and nights), the Arad Festival soon lost its original intention of hosting only havurot zemer and focusing only on the SLI repertory, and became a rock festival. For several years it was an annual summer event to which youth flocked; at its peak were midnight concerts, which lasted until dawn, at an open-air venue near the historical site of Massada. Following a tragic incident during a concert by rock band Mashina in 1995 in which several young spectators lost their lives, the festival lost much of its appeal. Since this incident, the Yemei zemer be-Holon (Days of Song in Holon; Holon is a city in the Tel Aviv metropolitan area) has fulfilled the role of the Arad Festival.

During the decades of their heyday, the song festivals, especially the competitive ones, were a major venue of creativity, performance, and promotion within the popular-music scene in Israel. Their gradual decline during the 1990s may be attributed to the diversification of Israel's media. Multichannel cable television has greatly reduced the likelihood that the festivals would attract "the whole of the nation" on any one evening. One may also speculate that the introduction of music videos and other new formats of music on television rendered the traditional concept and format of the song festival obsolete.

PART III

Israeli Rock

7 The Invention of Israeli Rock

Since the early 1980s, Israeli rock has been the dominant music culture in Israel. This is manifested in various ways. The "best" musicians of Israel according to the media and relevant professionals are those whose careers are closely associated with the sound idioms of rock, musicians such as Arik Einstein, Shalom Hanoch, Yehuda Poliker, Yehudit Ravitz, and Shlomo Artzi. Prominent on the playlists of all radio stations and in the sales figures of the major record companies are songs and albums by Israeli rock musicians and bands; even among "middle-of-the-road" musicians, the sound textures, musical production, and arrangements are saturated with typical rock instrumentation. This dominant position in popular music is a direct result of the success of various musicians and supporting professionals to "Israelize" rock—that is, to localize it and make it fit the specificity of Israeli culture and, in particular, the Israeli field of popular music.

"Israelizing" rock has meant two things: making rock music in Hebrew, and demonstrating that Israeli rock serves the general goal of constructing an "authentic" Israeli-Hebrew culture. As a result, Israeli rock has seldom had connotations typically associated with the term "rock": rage, anger, anxiety, hedonism, bliss, sexuality, and so on. The adoption and implementation of rock in Israeli music was mainly concerned with issues of musical and aesthetic form, creative practices, and artistic consciousness. This meant that electric and electronic instrumentation, studio craftsmanship, expressive vocal delivery, emphasis on musicians as authors and not only performers, and lyrics that dealt with personal issues and occasionally a critique of Israeli social reality, politics, and ideology—in short, the major elements of the rock aesthetic—became dominant practices when making the most artistically valued and commercially successful music in Israel (for more on the rock aesthetic, see Frith 1996; Gracyk 1996; Regev 1994).

According to the conventional narrative—as reflected, for example, in the television series *Sof 'onat ha-tapuzim: The Story of Israeli Rock*, edited by Yoav Kutner and broadcast on Israeli television between November 1998 and January 1999 (see also Regev 1992)—rock music was successfully "Israelized" and therefore "born" or "invented" during the 1970s by a specific group of musicians, all men, who created a network of musical collaboration. As participants in each other's solo efforts, in bands, in duos or trios, these musicians made the albums that were eventually consecrated as the early classics of Israeli rock. Core members of this network—henceforth the "elite" of Israeli rock—include Arik Einstein, Shmulik Kraus, Shalom Hanoch, members of Kaveret, Ariel Zilber, Shlomo Gronich, Shem Tov Levy, and Matti Caspi. Also notable are lyricists Yonatan Geffen, Yaakov Rothblit, and Meir Ariel (1942–99), who wrote the lyrics to many of these musicians' songs and whose writing was influenced by figures such as Bob Dylan and John Lennon. By 1980, with the body of musical work made by this elite group, Israeli rock as a cultural stance, as a genre, was established as a legitimate position in the field of popular music in Israel. It became a major component of the wider cultural stance of globalized Israeliness, which successfully opened Israeliness to, and adjusted it within, contemporary global culture.

Crediting the elite group of musicians with the birth of Israeli rock somewhat distorts the fact that its members were not the first to make rock music in Israel. Their contribution was the "Israelization" of rock music, the musical formulation of sound textures that incorporate elements of rock, yet retain a feeling of Israeliness. But the actual pioneers of rock music in Israel, who enthusiastically embraced rock music as it was, without Israelizing it, were the bands and members of lehaqot ha-qetzev (the beat bands).

LEHAQOT HA-QETZEV AND THE START OF ROCK IN ISRAEL

Rock music began in Israel sometime in the mid-1960s, when young aspiring musicians, fascinated by the sounds and images of Anglo-American rock of the period, purchased electric guitars and drum kits, formed bands, rehearsed, and began to perform in small clubs. Many were middle- to lower-middle-class mizrahi men who lived in Tel Aviv's southern suburbs or satellite towns. Their repertories consisted of imitations, in poor English, of hits by British and American bands: the Beatles, Rolling Stones, Kinks, Byrds, Beach Boys, and so on. The bands were known collectively as lehaqot ha-qetzev, as the beat groups. Performances at clubs in Tel Aviv's satellite towns, Ramla and Bat-Yam, of bands such as Ha-shmenim ve-ha-razim (the Fat Guys and the Thin Guys), Ha-kokhavim ha-kehulim (the Blue Stars), or the Goldfingers, were attended by thousands of enthusiastic youth. But it was not until several years later that a few of them had the chance to record a single, an EP, or a full album. Israeli record companies of the period did not believe in local rock. The attitude of the industry was symptomatic. With the exception of paid advertising for clubs and performances, there is barely a trace of the phenomenon in the press of the period, and not one of the bands was heard on the radio.

Given the fact that Israeli popular music of the period was dominated by the lehaqot tzvayiot, SLI, and songs in the style of Festival ha-zemer, the phenomenon of lehaqot ha-qetzev reflected two complementary messages: a rejection of, or at least disregard for the meanings, aesthetics, and contents of the dominant, ideologically mobilized nationalistic music culture; and a desire to participate in what was perceived as a new and exciting universal music culture, in which fun and sexuality played major roles. While the phenomenon of lehaqot ha-qetzev was ignored by the state-controlled media and culture industry, it was not actually oppressed, persecuted, or prohibited by state agencies. This signaled the ambivalence of the cultural establishment toward the phenomenon of rock music in general. Self-perceived as a "Western democracy," Israeli authorities were committed to dialogue, free import, and openness to change and innovations in global culture. But as leaders of an imagined national community in the formative phase of its self-invention, cultural authorities in Israel were highly suspicious of elements that could harm what was considered the "proper" ideological commitment of youth to the national collective. This ambivalence was reflected in attitudes and policies toward the existence of Anglo-American rock in Israeli public culture. Records by all leading musicians and bands were either imported or locally pressed and were generally available in the stores. Radio stations like Ha-gal ha-qal and Galei Tzahal played contemporary hits, and anyone interested could become well informed about pop/rock culture in the United States and the United Kingdom. At the same time, the education system, and especially the highly influential youth movements, denounced and stigmatized pop/rock fandom as inappropriate and vulgar. Israeli youth in the mid-1960s were divided between those who participated in youth movement activities, following the "proper" cultural path of the sabra stereotype; and those stigmatized as "salon" society (because of the private dance parties, held in the living room, known as the "salon" in vernacular Hebrew; see Adler and Peres 1968), who were viewed by teachers and youth movement leaders as egotistical and socially irresponsible.

A notable example of this ambivalence toward Anglo-American rock culture was the unbalanced policy toward performances of leading foreign musicians in Israel. A special government committee with the authority to allocate foreign currency to concert arrangers functioned as a "bureaucratic gatekeeper" in this context. In 1962, without hesitation, the committee approved a concert by U.K. rock idol Cliff Richard and his band, the Shadows, probably because this was perceived as innocent entertainment. The concert drew thousands of fans and several members of lehaqot ha-qetzev later recalled that this event, and especially the playing of Hank Marvin, lead guitarist of the Shadows, was what caused them to take up the electric guitar. Three years later, when a number of organizers teamed up to bring the Beatles to Israel, the committee rejected their request on the grounds that the band did not possess a sufficiently high cultural level. Although tickets were printed, the organizers did not receive the permit and the Beatles never came.

The initial problem concerning the introduction of rock music into Israeli culture was legitimacy. For rock music to become as dominant as it eventually became within Israeli culture, it had to gain legitimacy and recognition as "Israeli" music. The members and music of lehaqot ha-qetzev had little chance in this respect. Stigmatized as *pushtakim* or *chah-chahim*—derogatory terms designating mizrahi youth as vulgar, uneducated, quasi criminal, and cheap and conspicuous in terms of fashion and appearance—members of these bands had no chance to be considered serious musicians by the media and music professionals. Accordingly, their music was perceived as completely unrelated to the meaning and content of "authentic" Israeliness.

By 1968–69, the impact of the cultural upheaval of the 1960s on Israel had become much stronger as a result of two changes in the politics of culture, both related to the Six-Day War in June 1967. The economic growth following that war (on this point, see Shalev 1992) catalyzed consumer culture and, with it, Israelis' growing consciousness of anything new and trendy in fashion, style, design, or the arts. In addition, the outcomes of that war—the occupation of the West Bank and Gaza, and the adoration of the military in the media as well as in official and vernacular culture—provided a local cultural platform that allowed increased identification with major themes of the counterculture (for example, "make love, not war"). Rock music thus became a trendy consumer good, a noteworthy component of the modern lifestyle, and, at the same time, a signifier of cultural criticism, of popular avant-garde. Making rock music and listening to it became, in Grossberg's words, a "practice of empowerment" (Grossberg 1984).

Toward the end of the 1960s, bands and individual members of lehaqot ha-qetzev had achieved some degree of legitimate media presence and, consequently, a few gained some prominence in Israeli music. Perceived as local exponents of either the commercial or the artistic aspect of rock, some of the lehaqot ha-qetzev received media attention. At this point, record companies were prepared to produce a single, an EP, or even an album of several of these bands. This encouraged members of the bands to write original material, in English or Hebrew. It was at this time that musicians who possessed the cultural capital and habitus of "proper" Israeliness—most notably, singer Arik Einstein—began making rock music in Hebrew. Since musicians with new rock dispositions were scarce in the Israeli context, bands and individual members of lehaqot ha-qetzev were sought after for collaboration.

Thus, between 1968 and 1970, several of the lehaqot ha-qetzev had local hits with songs in English—originals and covers. Ha-arayiot (the Lions) topped the Israeli charts (of foreign pop) with "Our Love's a Growing Thing"; and Uzi ve-ha-signonot (Uzi and the Styles) were very successful with the singles "Friends," "Daytime," and "Morning Train" and with a full album as well. The most artistically and commercially successful musicians of lehaqot ha-qetzev, who eventually enjoyed long-lasting careers in the field, were members of the Churchills and pop singer-songwriter Tzvika Pick.

The Churchills

The Churchills were formed in Tel Aviv by guitarists Haim Romano and Yitzhak Klepter (a.k.a. "Churchill"), drummer Ami Triebich, and bassist Miki Gavrielov in 1965, when they were still teenagers. In late 1967 Klepter left the group for military service (he eventually played in a lehaqah tzvait—something rare for members of lehaqot ha-qetzev). The band was joined by foreigners Rob Huxley (a guitar player from the United Kingdom) and Stan Solomon (an American singer) who also provided the band with most of its original material. With this lineup, the Churchills had a hit in "Too Much in Love to Hear," before moving first into "psychedelic" and later "heavy" directions. They wrote the soundtrack for director Jacque Katmor's avant-garde film, *A Woman's Case*, which, together with additional songs, became their first and highly appreciated album, *Churchills* (1968), one of the most valued collector's items of Israeli music. Another artistic project was a concert with the Israeli Philharmonic Orchestra. With Zubin Mehta conducting, the band played two excerpts by Bach. In 1970, Stan Solomon left the band and Israel; he was replaced by Danny Shoshan. They recorded covers of the Beatles' "She's a Woman" and Led Zeppelin's "Living Lovin'," before traveling to Europe in search of international success. After changing the band's name to Jericho Jones (and later to Jericho), they recorded two albums of original material in England in 1972, toured Europe, and finally folded in 1973.

The most important mark that the Churchills made on Israeli rock resulted from their association with singer Arik Einstein. In 1969 they became his regular band, softening their "psychedelic" and "heavy" textures. They supported him on stage and in recordings of the seminal Israeli rock albums *Poozy* (1969) and *Shablool* (Snail, 1970). A third classic Einstein album, *Ba-deshe etzel Avigdor* (1972, lit., "on Avigdor's lawn," but given the English title "At Avigdor's Grass" on the record sleeve, hinting at incidents of marijuana use of which Einstein and his friends were accused) was credited equally to Einstein and Miki Gavrielov, as composer and musical producer. Other collaborations followed, and through this association, Gavrielov became one of the elite group credited with the "birth" of Israeli rock. Guitarist Haim Romano became highly in-demand as a session guitarist, leaving his mark on dozens of Israeli rock albums and occasionally also acting as musical producer.

In terms of strict standards and aesthetic values of rock music, the Churchills were a good rock band. Many rock music devotees in Israel have been proud of the fact that the Churchills were on the same artistic level as many other English or American bands. In spite of this, the important cultural fact about the band and its music is that they remained a marginal note in the history of Israeli popular music. Their music was not "Israeli" enough to be included in the canon of Israeli rock.

Tzvika Pick

The most commercially successful musician who emerged from the lehaqot ha-qetzev scene was Tzvika Pick. His career and musical output exemplifies the mechanism of exclusion that characterized the emergence of Israeli rock. During the 1970s, Tzvika Pick recorded extensively, his albums sold in tens of thousands copies, and he was idolized by his teenage fans like no other local musician. He was one of the first musicians to succeed with his own compositions of rock music in Hebrew, yet his work was never canonized or glorified like that of his contemporaries in the elite group. His rock music was perceived as too "imitative" and not Israeli enough.

During the later part of the 1960s, Tzvika Pick was a member of several lehaqot qetzev—Telstar, Ha-shmenin ve-ha-razim, and Shokolada. Unlike many of his peers, he had received formal classic musical education in his native Poland; therefore, his role was mainly that of keyboard player and arranger. In 1970, he was chosen to play Claude in the Israeli production of the musical *Hair* (in Hebrew). In 1972 he began a recording career with the album *Zohi ha-derekh sheli* (This is my way), singing his own compositions. By 1980 he had released about ten albums, most under the Azulay Brothers label (Koliphon), a company associated with musiqa mizrahit and not rock. Only in 1978, with the release of *Musiqa*, did Pick move to a major company, CBS.

Tzvika Pick's presence in the local field was characterized by emphasis on visual aspects and other elements of stardom. At concerts, dressed in shiny, flamboyant, and colorful outfits and wearing makeup, he attempted to produce a local version of "glam rock." In interviews, he declared himself the "Israeli David Bowie." One of his record sleeves carried a photo of his body covered in silver, clearly inspired by the cover of Bowie's *Aladdin Sane* album. But on other albums, he was pictured with seminude females kneeling at his feet—Pick as a sex idol. This was replicated in many publicity photos and other marketing devices.

His emphasis on "glam," sexuality, publicity, and gossip caused reviewers of the 1970s to sneer at what they perceived to be a vulgar and ridiculous imitation of rock and star practices. This attitude was exacerbated by his tendency to use the synthesizer in an extravagant way, as well as his nasal vocal delivery. Only in 1979 did Pick receive some esteem from the critics, with the songs "Ne'esaf Tishrei" ([The month of] Tishrei ended, also known as "Met av u-met elul") and "Lo ani hu ha-'ish" (I'm not the man), both from the album *Musiqa*. Both were ballads based on poems by canonic poets Nathan Yonathan and Alexander Penn, delicately treated much like ballads sung by elite members of the rock community.

Parallel to his own recording career, Pick was also a prolific and successful composer of songs for other performers. Two of his most memorable successes as a composer were Ofra Haza's "Shir ha-freha" (1978), and Dana International's hit "Diva," which won the 1998 Eurovision song contest. As a performer, however, Pick's career declined during the 1980s. Various attempts at a comeback failed, as did attempts by some young critics in the 1990s to belatedly canonize his work. Thus Tzvika Pick's presence in the field has been characterized by the complaint, from both critics and Pick, that he was neglected and underestimated in the dominant discourse of popular music in Israel:

> Let me tell you the truth. Because of the special character of the music that I brought into the local Israeli market, because of the visual aspect that has always been salient, initially the media were shocked. They did not know how to accept it. . . . Of course, when it comes from abroad, David Bowie, Mick Jagger, it is accepted and understood. When it is

something Israeli, than it is strange and exceptional. And this has been true throughout the years. They never played my music on the radio as much as they played other musicians. I was never embraced by the media. It is a fact. (Tzvika Pick, interview on Reshet Gimmel, October 1986)

The cultural and social determinants at work in the consecration and legitimization of Israeli rock are reflected in the stories of the Churchills and Tzvika Pick. Members of the Churchills achieved legitimacy as "Israeli" musicians through their association with Arik Einstein and modification of their rock sensibilities; Tzvika Pick has never been truly canonized as "the originator" of Israeli rock. In the same way as Anglo-American rock was divided into various substyles and subcultures that reflected class divisions in the United Kingdom and United States (see Wicke 1990), so was Israeli rock. Its emergence was a general expression of revolt against SLI, but it still reflected some of the class and other social divisions that characterize Israel. Hence, neither their social background, nor their "imitation" of rock idioms—even when artistically appreciated—could provide the Churchills (or any other lehaqat qetzev) or Tzvika Pick with legitimacy and recognition as "proper" Israeli musicians, makers of authentic Israeli music. In order to gain such recognition, Israeli rock had to be made within different cultural and social determinants.

THE "ELITE" OF ISRAELI ROCK

For rock music to gain legitimacy as Israeli music, to become "Israeli" rock, it had to be made by musicians who possessed the cultural capital and habitus of "proper" Israeliness. In the case of popular music as a profession, "proper" meant knowledge of and close acquaintance with the spirit of Shirei Eretz Yisrael and apprenticeship in the lehaqot tzvayiot or other dominant institutions of Israeli popular music of the period. The latter also functioned as social capital and provided musicians with the necessary contacts with professionals in the media and the music business. The few musicians who did not possess such cultural or social capital and still entered the elite group of the founders of Israeli rock—mainly members of lehaqot ha-qetzev—did so through association with musicians who possessed that capital.

Israeli rock emerged around 1970 as the conscious, heretical response of musicians who had served in lehaqot tzvayiot to the ideological and nationalist nature of SLI and to the affirmative nature of the rest of Israeli popular music. It was invented by musicians and catered to audiences who wanted to open up Israeli music, and thereby, Israeli culture, to what they believed was a new, exciting, and artistic form of popular music. Fascinated by the sounds and images of the rock culture of the 1960s, musicians and audiences wanted their own rock in Israel and sung in Hebrew.

Thus the musicians who graduated from lehaqot tzvayiot and turned to rock were committed to Israeliness. Their quarry was not the notion of national music, but the dominant type of popular music, as embodied in SLI. They wanted a new form of national music that integrates the developments of rock. Consequently, when the incorporation of rock music in Hebrew gained legitimacy as Israeli music, key members of this elite group modified the rock elements in their music and recorded various tributes to SLI, in effect blurring the sharp difference that initially existed between their music and SLI. Their status as heretics quite rapidly changed to that of inheritors and innovators of the SLI tradition. This cultural process is demonstrated in the careers of several key members of the elite group of musicians—Arik Einstein, the band Kaveret (and its individual members), Shalom Hanoch, and the musicians who created a local variant of progressive rock.

Arik Einstein

Singer Arik Einstein recorded three albums between 1969 and 1971—*Poozy, Shablool* (with Shalom Hanoch), and *At Avigdor's Grass* (with Miki Gavrielov)—that marked the emergence of Israeli rock. Of these, *Shablool* is considered by leading reviewers, critics, and musicians to represent the "moment of the birth" of rock music in Hebrew and therefore as a cardinal turning point in Israeli popular music. Yaakov Gilad, for example—a major lyricist, record producer, and rock commentator during the 1980s—writes:

> [Compared to Israeli music of the time], *Shablool* was like a sudden thunderstorm on a clear day. A real boom. The music of Shalom Hanoch, his lyrics, and those he wrote with Arik Einstein. The Churchills. The most important and best album that came out to date of new Israeli music. Eternal hits. Rock and roll in Hebrew. Here, at this point exactly, Israeli rock was born. Here is where the acceleration begins. *Shablool* is the artistic peak of a cohesive group, at a specific time that will probably never return. (Gilad, *Ḥadashot*, May 12, 1986)

Shablool is a collection of twelve songs, all composed by Shalom Hanoch. He also wrote most of the lyrics. Members of the Churchills—whose collective name is not mentioned because of contractual obligations—are the backing musicians, augmented by a few session players. Band member Miki

Gavrielov is credited as "recording manager," probably meaning musical producer.

In addition to its authorship, two elements made this a "rock" album in Israeli ears. One is the undisciplined style of vocal delivery by both Einstein and Hanoch. Guttural enunciation of the lyrics and expressive shouts at the end of phrases dominate most of the songs. Another is the way the Churchills played the music. Abandoning their typical use of distortion and fuzz, they opted for an electric pop/rock sound with almost no solo guitar. The result is an atmosphere of fun that radiates from most of the songs, especially those based on a typical rock'n'roll beat. This album is clearly indebted to the work of the Beatles. Their influence is evident in the blues song "'Al tevatri alay" (Don't give up on me), similar to the Beatles' "Don't Let Me Down"; in the sequence of verses in "Lama li laqahat la-lev" (Why should I take it to heart?), which alternates between a ballad (sung by Einstein) and up-tempo rock'n' roll (Hanoch), very much like the Beatles "A Day in the Life"; and in the *musique concrete* piece "Shonot"—a collage of sounds inspired by the Beatles' "Revolution No. 9." But the songs also sound very local, very Israeli. The lyrics are not only in Hebrew, but most are written in the vernacular, unlike the prevalent tendency to florid language in lyrics. Also, the humor in some of the songs echoes the popular skits in Israeli culture. The album opens with Arik Einstein mimicing a well-known radio program of morning exercises and ends with a typical Eretz-Yisraeli song about early Zionist settlement in Palestine, "The Ballad of Yoel Moshe Salomon" (lyrics, Yoram Tehar-Lev).

Shablool thus came to be perceived as the work that shaped the Israelization of rock and the rockization of Israeli music. It established a formula of fusion that influenced and inspired many musicians in subsequent decades. It also demonstrated that the criticism embodied in Israeli rock toward SLI was more in the sphere of the form and aesthetics of popular music than in content and meaning. The point was to reformulate the sound of Israeli music.

Shablool was the culmination of Arik Einstein's quest for a new sound for his own work and for Israeli music, different from what he had grown up with and connected to the cutting edge of 1960s popular music. Until then, his career had followed the conventional path of Israeli popular music of those years.

Arik Einstein was born in 1939 in Tel Aviv. His father was a theater actor, and Einstein grew up surrounded by Hebrewism as a native culture. His home was frequented by actors, poets, and other cultural figures. In 1957, after a successful audition, he was recruited into lehaqat ha-nahal, the leading lehaqah tzvait. There, his lead vocal on the memorable song "Ruaḥ stav" (Autumn wind) established him as a prominent singer. After his military service he recorded an EP with four songs (1960), two of which became his first hits as a soloist: "Ha-sha'ot ha-qtanot shel ha-layla" (The small hours of the night; music, Yohanan Zarai; lyrics, Yossi Gamzu) and "'Ir levana" (White city; music and lyrics, Naomi Shemer). In the 1960s, he was a member of the highly successful Shlishiyat Gesher ha-Yarkon (Yarkon Bridge Trio), with which he made two albums (1964–65); his first album, *Shar bishvilekh* (Singing for you; songs by Dafna Eilat), came out in 1966; he won first prize in the Israeli Song Festival in 1965 with the song "Ayelet ha-ḥen" (Graceful gazelle) and in 1966 with "Leil stav" (Autumn night). In all these projects, Arik Einstein was a vocalist in the "popular song" tradition. His repertory was eclectic, inspired by the French chanson, American folk, Greek music, jazzy lounge music, and SLI. He worked with traditional, non-rock composers and arrangers. His crystal clear, silky voice, clearly articulated lyrics, restrained and disciplined style of vocal delivery, as well as his good looks made him the "most popular singer in Israel," according to the sleeve notes on the compilation album *Yashan ve-gam ḥadash* (Old and new [1968]).

Einstein, it seems, was unhappy with the musical material offered him by mainstream Israeli composers. Familiar with the new sounds of rock, he began to explore the possibility of "Israelizing" them. But because he lacked the necessary rock dispositions, he was not in a position to make the transition to rock on his own. Consequently, his quest for a new musical sound was also a search for partners, musicians who possessed the necessary rock habitus.

His first attempt was a collaboration with arranger David Krivoushey. They assembled a band—Arik and the Einsteins—and recorded an EP of four songs. The highlight was "Mazal," a quasi-humorous translation of the Beatles' "Do You Want to Know a Secret." Dominated by the sound of Krivoushey's Hammond electric organ, it was not clear if the song was meant as a joke or if it was an honest attempt to make Israeli rock. In later years, Einstein expressed antipathy for this project.

Shmulik Kraus was the person with whom Arik Einstein made the definitive transition to the sphere of rock. Kraus, an unknown musician who performed with his wife (Jozi Katz) in nightclubs, became acquainted with Einstein sometime in 1966 and introduced Einstein to some of his original songs. Consequently, Einstein, Kraus, and Katz formed the ha-Ḥalonot ha-gvohim (the High Windows Trio), which recorded an album in early 1967. All the songs on the album were composed by Kraus. Although the arrangements were mainly acoustic, the vocal harmonies and the sound of Kraus's guitar were clearly inspired by American bands of the period, such as the Turtles and the Mamas and the Papas. However, the rhythmic drive of most of the songs, dominated by Zohar Levi on drums, made the album stand out as the first rock-inspired record to come out of the mainstream of Israeli popular music. The partnership with Arik Einstein and the songs of the High Windows paved the way to canonization for Shmulik Kraus as a major figure in Israeli popular music. In subsequent years he wrote successful songs for various performers and occasionally recorded as well. His albums *Galgal mistovev* (Turning wheel [1982]) and *Aharei 'esrim shanah* (After twenty years [1988]) further established his stature. For Arik Einstein, the work with Kraus served as an apprenticeship on his way to Israeli rock.

In 1968 Arik Einstein met Shalom Hanoch, at the time a member of lehaqat ha-nahal. Impressed by Hanoch's songs, Einstein began a musical partnership with him that resulted in the album *Mazal gdi* (Capricorn [1969]). One of the first productions of Israeli music by CBS, the company was hesitant about the rock sound sought by Hanoch and Einstein. Instead, the company paired the two with arranger Alex Weiss, whose traditional approach to popular music emphasized strings and horns. *Mazal gdi* is the album that introduced Shalom Hanoch to the Israeli public. Although in later years his name became indistinguishable from Israeli rock, this album barely hinted in that direction. Many songs from the album eventually became classics of Israeli pop. But in 1969, within the context of Arik Einstein's quest for rock sounds, it was a step sideways.

Poozy was the album in which Arik Einstein finally found the rock sound he had been looking for. Well acquainted at this point with the rock aesthetic and frustrated by the inability of mainstream popular-music arrangers to provide him with the sounds he sought, he turned to where he knew such sounds existed: the clubs of lehaqot ha-qetzev, where he was introduced to the Churchills.

ARIK EINSTEIN: We were quite square for the period. . . . [T]here, in the clubs, the Churchills, the Blue Stars, and other bands were tearing the place apart . . . and me, what did I sing [he sings his schmaltzy ballad from 1965, "Ayelet ha-hen"]. . . . It was quite preposterous.

MIKI GAVRIELOV: We did not know him. He came to the club to hear us. This is a place where you play loud. And when there is no audience, it is really loud [laughs]. We showed him what we knew. We blew the place apart.

ARIK EINSTEIN: Suddenly there were [electric] guitars. I never had
such a thing in my life. I grabbed them.
(Excerpts from *Sof ʿonat ha-tapuzim*, pt. 2)

With the Churchills backing Arik Einstein, *Poozy* became the first Israeli
rock album. Letting his voice soar, groan, and grunt in a way he had never
done before, immersed in the production work of Stan Solomon (half the
songs) and Misha Segal, and surrounded by the twin electric guitars of Rob
Huxley and Haim Romano, Arik Einstein made an album with a strong
"psychedelic" rock feel, unprecedented in Israeli music.

A year later, Arik Einstein made *Shablool*. Perceived as more coherent
and consistent, mainly because of the collaboration with Shalom Hanoch,
this album achieved more acclaim than its predecessor. Einstein made a second album with Hanoch *(Plastelina* [1971]) and then *At Avigdor's Grass*,
with Miki Gavrielov. Including hits like "Ani ve-ata" (Me and you; a song
along the lines of John Lennon's "Imagine," about changing the world) and
"Qafe Turqi" (Turkish coffee), the album established Gavrielov as a legitimate Israeli musician. It was also the last album of Einstein's heretical phase,
when he invented Israeli rock.

Except for one album with Miki Gavrielov in which the rock spirit was
maintained *(Sa Leʾat,* Drive slowly [1974]), Arik Einstein's major effort during the rest of the 1970s was revitalizing SLI. Having established and consolidated his mastery of a certain rock habitus, he took upon himself to
apply this habitus, or at least elements of it, to old SLI. His intention—
which proved artistically and commercially successful—was to refresh
some of the old songs and record them in a modern way that would render
them accessible and "listener friendly" to pop audiences. A series of three
albums called *Good Old Eretz Yisrael* (vol. 1, 1973; vol. 2, 1976; vol. 3, 1977)
and the album *Songs* (1975) were mainly old SLI. His associates on the project—Avner Kener, Shem Tov Levy, and Yoni Rechter, all graduates of
lehaqot tzvayiot—had formal musical education. They were involved in
experimental projects influenced by progressive-rock and jazz-rock fusion
of the period. Combining their various musical inclinations, they arranged
the songs as fusions between chamber music, light jazz, and soft-rock ballads, in contrast to the pompous full orchestration or the forced folkism of
other recordings of such songs. Most important, Einstein's vocal delivery
emptied the songs of the pathos and drama typical of earlier performers.
These new recordings of the songs transformed them from ideological icons
to nostalgic ballads and gave them renewed popularity. Although this move

seemed to be a sharp departure from the rock'n'roll of *Shablool,* the Eretz-Yisraeli project manifested Arik Einstein's commitment to Israeliness.

Arik Einstein's Eretz-Yisraeli albums also included several original songs composed by Shem Tov Levy and Yoni Rechter. Levi was also his major associate on the album *Jasmine* (1972), and Rechter on a full album of original songs, *Ha-ahavah panim rabot la* (Love has many faces [1976]). The ability of these two musicians to combine a sophisticated song structure with a tranquil ballad, their tendency to compose music for existing poems, as well as for original lyrics (written by Einstein, Yaakov Rothblit, or Yonatan Geffen) about peace and other aspects of Israeli life, and the fact that these songs were interspersed with covers of old SLI all gave these songs an almost immediate status of continuity. That is, through their original songs for Einstein, Shem Tov Levy and Yoni Rechter emerged as latter-day, rock-influenced successors of Eretz-Yisraeli composers like Mordechai Zeira, David Zehavi, Sasha Argov, and the like. The Eretz-Yisraeli project affirmed Arik Einstein's stature as an all-Israeli singer, whose voice and repertory express innovation together with continuity and the perpetuation of Israeliness. Nowhere was this better expressed than in the glorification of the song "'Atur mitzhekh zahav shahor" (Your forehead is embellished with black gold; lyrics, Avraham Halfi; music, Yoni Rechter; original recording in the album *Good Old Eretz Yisrael* [vol. 3, 1976]). The song was twice selected as the "best Israeli song ever" by juries of experts. First in 1988, in a poll conducted by the magazine *Musica* (no. 12, March 1988) and again in a poll by *Yedioth Ahronoth* (April 12, 2002).

"'Atur mitzhekh" is a unique ballad in all its musical components. Despite its basic A-B-A form, it provides the listener a feeling of a through-composed "lied" quite unlike standard pop/rock songs. This feeling is created by variations in the length of the repetitions of each phrase (achieved by developing, shortening, or recombining melodic motifs), by constant rhythmic shifts (the melody is very syncopated although it does not swing), and by an unusual harmonic development (from D minor in the first section to E minor in the recapitulation through F minor in the middle section). The melody moves in jagged lines starting with a sharp plunge of a ninth echoing the opening measures of "Gute Nacht" in Schubert's *Winterreise.* Moreover, a long instrumental interlude precedes the recapitulation. The canonic recording of this song by Arik Einstein (there are numerous other recorded versions) is orchestrated for a unique acoustic ensemble (piano, string quartet, woodwinds, acoustic guitar, and bass) with the fagot (whose register and timbre delightfully recalls Einstein's voice) playing an important role, especially in the interlude. As a contrast to Einstein's baritone, this arrangement also employs (from its outset) a female duo singing almost a capella in a high register alternating with him on the low register. To sum up, this evocative love song, with its unique form, harmony, and instrumentation is a rock ballad in the vein of those by Randy Newman and the like. Considering its peculiar literary and musical qualities, the selection of this ballad as the "best Israeli song" speaks strongly in favor of its authenticity in the ears of many Israelis. Perhaps because it sounds different from any other easily recognizable foreign style of popular music and, at the same time, from the older Eretz-Yisraeli music styles, it is perceived as quintessentially modern Israeli.

With his sound formula of soft rock now firmly established as "Israeli," Einstein's work after 1980 was characterized by the addition of new albums in the same vein. Alternating between his regular associates, he made an album almost every year until 1989, but only three albums in the decade between 1989 and 1999. Most of his albums were acclaimed by critics and sold well. However, in 1980 Einstein stopped performing in concert and, except for obligatory marketing interviews and occasional music videos to support new albums, he stayed out of public eye. This retreat into privacy and his reportedly simple lifestyle only enhanced the valorization of his work as the corpus of songs and performances that best captured what Israeliness is basically about. He represented what Israeliness meant to the generations who unwillingly demythologized sabra culture and Hebrewism and who embraced the Western counterculture spirit of the 1960s. That is, Arik Einstein's work came to stand as the ultimate musical embodiment of the attempt to invent a fusion between the sabra culture and the 1960s spirit.

Kaveret

Kaveret (Beehive; known abroad as Poogy) was a band formed in late 1972 by Danny Sanderson (guitar, vocals), Gidi Gov (vocals), Alon Olearchik (bass), Ephraim Shamir (guitar, vocals), and Meir Fenigstein (drums), who served together in lehaqat ha-nahal. They were joined by Yoni Rechter (keyboard), who served in another lehaqah tzvait, and Yitzhak Klepter (nicknamed Churchill and founder of the Churchills, guitar), whose reputation as a local "guitar hero" was already established. The group made three albums, *Sippurei Poogy* (Tales of Poogy [1973]), *Poogy be-pita* (Poogy in a pita [1974]), and *Tzafuf ba-ozen* (Crowded in the ear [1975]) and then broke up. Their success was unprecedented and unexpected, especially for a rock group. Concert halls sold out, and the enthusiastic audience response during performances was unparalleled in the Israeli entertainment market of the period. The album sales were also remarkable, even by later local standards. The first album sold 80,000 copies, and all three together sold 200,000 copies. All three albums were still in Hed Artzi's active catalog in 1999. Kaveret returned three times after breaking up—in 1984, 1990, and 1998— for single concerts that drew audiences of hundreds of thousands, including young people who were born after the band broke up.

Repeated attempts over the years to explain and analyze the success of Kaveret and its enduring impact were characterized by a debate about whether Kaveret was a real rock band, or just an electric incarnation of typical Israeli pop groups like the Ha-Tarnegolim, or, indeed, the lehaqot tzvayiot. The reason for this ambivalence lies in the unique combination that Kaveret introduced into Israeli culture and popular music. It was an electric group, working within the sound and stylistic idiom of rock—that is, electric guitars, amplification, shouted vocal delivery, rock'n'roll rhythms in many songs, and so on. Yet the band was also perceived as strongly embedded within Israeliness. Its use of Hebrew in the lyrics as well as in skits (in themselves a very common feature of Israeli entertainment of the period), to produce what has often been described as nonsense humor, was practically untranslatable into other languages, or explainable to anyone not familiar with various elements of everyday culture in Israel. In addition, the songs had a merry, joyful feeling, highly resembling the spirit of songs by lehaqot tzvayiot. Thus Eldad Shrim, arranger and composer for various musicians, says, "Kaveret was more a lehaqah tzvait than a beat group. It was in fact a rock band, but the effect of rock [in the music] was secondary— the rhythms were very simple, and there was no kassah [brutality and anger]. It is impossible to call it a rock band, no way. They were a pop band, an excellent pop band" (interview on Galei Tzahal, September 1996).

Preoccupation with the rock character of Kaveret reflects the obvious fact that Kaveret was a successful merger of Israeli pop and rock. It was a rock band of particularly Israeli character, and it is exactly this trait that provides the key to understanding its success. Kaveret adopted cultural materials from earlier forms of local pop, which were already established as signifiers of "authentic Israeliness," and fused them with elements of rock, both in sound and in patterns of creativity. As a rock band, Kaveret was a self-contained creative unit. With band members composing the songs and writing the lyrics, playing the instruments and singing, arranging and producing the music in the studio, the band first introduced the notion of collective authorship common in rock to the mainstream Israeli popular-music community. The music was theirs not only as performers but also as authors, which gave the music the aura of personal authenticity, so central to the ideology of rock. The band thus catered to the emerging identity of new or global Israeliness, which sought to incorporate recent developments in Western/global culture, yet maintain its sense of national identity and local culture. Kaveret was there for the new Israelis, at the right point in time, as a rock band "of their own," with a well-crafted formula that combined a balanced dosage of rock and Israeliness. Kaveret's ability to achieve this formula was the result of its members' rock habitus on the one hand, and their apprenticeship in lehaqot tzvayiot on the other.

Kaveret was the brainchild of Danny Sanderson. In their first two albums, he wrote all the materials—music and lyrics—with some collaboration from other members (in fact, the "democratization" of authorship in the third album, *Tzafuf ba-ozen*, with almost all members contributing original songs, and the ensuing stylistic change, caused its relative failure and the consequent break up of the band). As a teenager, Sanderson spent most of the 1960s in New York. He therefore experienced, more closely and in a less mediated form than most Israelis, the pop/rock scene of the decade. His knowledge of rock music inspired his concept of Kaveret as a band with two or three electric guitar players: "My model for Kaveret was two bands: the Allman Brothers Band and Moby Grape. What impressed me was that these were two bands with a number of guitarists who all sang. This was my dream. To make a band where everyone plays and sings" (Danny Sanderson, in *Sof 'onat ha-tapuzim*, pt. 3).

Indeed, as various critics note, one of Kaveret's signature tunes, the instrumental "Lamrot ha-kol" (Despite everything), with its twin guitars, is reminiscent of the Allman Brothers Band hit "Jessica." Another concept that influenced Sanderson was the rock opera. *Tales of Poogy* was originally written and rehearsed for several months in early 1973 as such a work.

Other members of Kaveret were also rock musicians. Ephraim Shamir, for example, had his own rock band in Poland before emigrating to Israel in the late 1960s; Alon Olearchik, Gidi Gov, and Yoni Rechter noted in various interviews that as teenagers they had been rock fans; and Yitzhak Klepter joined Kaveret fresh from the band Aharit ha-yamim (Apocalypse), whose artistically adventurous 1972 album—a commercial failure, but much beloved by critics—was dominated by his virtuoso guitar playing inspired by Jimi Hendrix and Jimmy Page.

The band, however, was channeled away from these definitive rock dispositions for two major reasons. One was their desire for commercial success, and the perception of the Israeli cultural market held by their manager, Avraham Deshe (Pashanel). Pashanel was an extremely successful manager, associated mainly with the Gashash Hiver Trio, which for more than twenty years made tens of enormously popular humorous skits that made them a pillar of Israeli humor. Pashanel, who invested the capital that enabled Kaveret to perform and record, was convinced that the Israeli audience at large wanted humor and was not prepared for artistic experiments with popular music. The band went along with this perception and dropped the rock-opera framework, but left in some of the funny dialogs between songs. It thus replicated the typical Israeli entertainment pattern, especially in performance, of song-skit-song. Band members, newly graduated from lehaqot tzvayiot, needed no adjustment to this pattern; they were accustomed to it.

In addition, Sanderson's material clearly fit the pattern. By examining the minute details of everyday life in Israel and using word games to illuminate their absurdity, he created lyrics, dialogs, and one-liners that generated references to him as a "musical Woody Allen." This humorous attitude permeated the music as well, as evident in the decontextualized use of oriental elements in songs such as "Ha-tmanun ha-'iter" (The left-handed octopus) and "Shir ha-mehiron" (Song of the price list) and the salient presence of the rhythmic pattern known in Israel as *esta*. Esta is a pattern used by arrangers for lehaqot tzvayiot and by wedding musicians to standardize songs of various genres, giving them a cheerful Mediterranean/Balkan/ oriental spirit. First used in the music of Kaveret as parody, the electric "rock *esta*" that underlies some of the band's major hits—"Ha-magafaim shel Baruch" (Baruch's boots), "Yo-Yah," and "Shir ha-makolet" (The grocery store song)—eventually became one of their most distinctive features.

In its nuanced parody of lehaqot tzvayiot and in its unique humorous and reflexive look at the awkwardness of the Israeli experience, the work of Kaveret is sometimes interpreted as a kind of social critique. Moreover, this indirect humorous criticism is considered the reason for its breakthrough in October and November 1973, immediately after the traumatic experience of the Yom Kippur War. "Suddenly reality fitted the poetics of Kaveret. The songs' names gained additional meanings. 'Despite Everything,' 'We Didn't Know What to Do,' 'Old Child.' The texts of Kaveret expressed more than they were meant to. They told of confusion and pain, but offered an outlet as well: they were optimistic and full of life" (Gidi Avivi, *Koteret Rashit*, June 1984).

Thus—to the dismay of rock aficionados in Israel—Kaveret did not produce the pure rock that it seemed capable of, but rather a cute and joyful kind of rock, which proved to be very Israeli in spirit. "Their popularity was in many ways positive for Israeli pop: they proved that it is also possible to succeed when you play rock; discovered that it is possible to fuse foreign and local influences and to achieve a unique personal expression. They made Israeli pop more normal" (Gidi Avivi, *Koteret Rashit*, June 1984).

Kaveret's mark on Israeli rock did not end when it broke up. Building on their reputation, most members continued on to have successful careers that further refined Israeli rock as a distinctive hybrid of the SLI legacy, the merry spirit of lehaqot tzvayiot, and various elements of the rock aesthetic. Danny Sanderson continued, with diminishing success, his unique formula of humorous rock, first with two bands, Gazoz and Doda, both with Gidi Gov as lead singer, and then on his own. Yitzhak Klepter, the only member for whom Kaveret was not the first phase of his career, continued in collaboration with other musicians—most notably in the album *Tzlil Mekhuvan* (Tuned tone [1979]) with Shem Tov Levy and Shlomo Yidov, and two albums of his own compositions with Arik Einstein. He also made four acclaimed solo albums. Each of these projects included songs that fused his characteristic guitar playing, rock/blues influences, and pastoral Eretz-Yisraeli inspiration into distinctive Israeli rock ballads. Alon Olearchik left the country and resumed his career in the mid-1980s, making five albums into the 1990s and engaging in production work. His most successful songs typically mixed oriental flavors reminiscent of earlier attempts at East-West fusion by Eretz-Yisraeli and musiqa mizrahit composers.

Singer Gidi Gov also embarked on a solo career. He made four successful albums, all with original material written for him by leading composers and lyricists. His first two albums—*Gidi Gov* (1978) and *40:06* (1983)—were produced and arranged by Yoni Rechter, who also composed most of the songs. These albums, and Rechter's own solo albums, combined soft jazz–rock arrangements and precise studio production with complex melodies. Rechter's work with Arik Einstein and with Gov further established his position as a pop/rock inspired inheritor of Eretz-Yisraeli composers such as Sasha Argov or Mordechai Zeira.

Shalom Hanoch

Shalom Hanoch is the musician who successfully introduced the notion of rock auteur to Israeli music. Moving through various patterns of creativity, singing his own songs (music and lyrics) and covering a range of musical styles, he has firmly maintained his position as the leading artist of Israeli rock since the early 1970s. Most important, as a self-conscious local rock artist, he often functioned as speaker and ideologist for Israeli rock.

Shalom Hanoch grew up on a kibbutz. He was member of lehaqat ha-nahal during the Six-Day War in 1967. He started his civilian career as Arik

Einstein's protégé and collaborator. After their classic album *Shablool* and its follow-up *Plastelina*, Hanoch spent some years in London, attempting to build an international career. He recorded one album there in English, *Shalom* (1972), and its failure led Hanoch back to Israel. In 1975, together with Ariel Zilber, he fronted the band Tamuz, which made one album, *Sof 'onat ha-tapuzim* (The orange season is over). From 1977 to 1998, Shalom Hanoch released ten solo albums. Between them, they covered a range of rock styles from soft acoustic ballads to hard-guitar rock and pompous dramatic stadium rock. Three consecutive albums in the early 1980s best represent his work: *Ḥatunah levanah* (White wedding [1981]), *Al pney ha-adama* (On the face of the earth [1983]), and *Meḥakim le-mashiaḥ* (Waiting for messiah [1985]). Hanoch composes all of his songs and writes the lyrics for most of them. They include open exposure of personal feelings, romantic love songs as well as bitter songs of breaking up and divorce, philosophical reflections, political statements, and social commentaries. He sings in a cracked and rasping voice, plays the electric guitar, and is always supported—in performance and recording—by a rock band. Hanoch is also credited with the musical production in some of his albums. In sum, he is a prototypical male rock artist.

The major aspect of his career and presence in the field of Israeli popular music is the fact that he is generally considered to be the first musician to introduce artistically successful rock into Israeli music. He is therefore considered a pioneer, and his music is an important turning point in Israeli music. This, for example, is an assessment of his stature by a classical-music critic: "Shalom Hanoch was born into a definite Israeli style: the epic of the Russian sentimental song, the aching minor [scale], the emotional fervor of melody. . . . But he was the one who dared to do the unbelievable: he cut the umbilical cord of the zemer 'ivri from the minor key. An analysis of 22 of his songs demonstrates that they are in major keys, and some are even bitonal" (Ron 1988). In other words, Shalom Hanoch's work as a rock musician is glorified for its relevance to Israeli music. It is legitimate—Israeliness includes rock. This is related to Hanoch's own insistence on being considered Israeli in terms of what he does in music. In countless interviews he outlined his convictions about the Israeliness of his rock music:

> Here, a [national] culture is still being created. Anyone who says that he knows what Israeli culture should be like is simply a fool. This belongs to history. Time will tell. Anything that is being done in this country is Israeli until further notice. . . . The more that people will stop discussing it, and everyone will do what he feels like, the more we shall gain from the process of fusions between styles. As for myself, I do rock as an

artistic experience. This is my mode of creativity. I feel right with it. It fits me. I love rock. In fact, I have done everything. I wrote many quiet songs. In rock you go through the whole range of feelings. There is everything in rock. I don't like the attempt to be ethnic very much. It is good for folklore. I don't do folklore. I am engaged in contemporary creation. I deal with my life today. I don't search for roots in this regard. My roots are within me. I don't have to justify anything. I don't have to add oriental flavor for people to know that I am from the Middle East. If people would take rock more directly, the meaning of rock, not as a musical style, but as a conception—because this is what rock is for me, a conception, a form of expression—then everything can get into rock. In the world, oriental music has long been incorporated into rock. Israel cannot invent anything new here. (Interview on Reshet Gimmel, 1988)

Hanoch first realized his rock-as-art attitude in full with the band Tamuz and especially in its only recorded album, *Sof 'onat ha-tapuzim*. Although not as successful in terms of sales as *Shablool* or Kaveret's *Poogy* albums, this album had a strong impact on Israeli rock and the local field of popular music. It marked the arrival of the music producer as an artistic entity and the emergence of studio craftsmanship as a major aesthetic component of Israeli popular music.

Given his zeal for making rock in Hebrew and changing the aesthetics of Israeli popular music, forming a hard-rock band was almost imperative for Shalom Hanoch. The result was Tamuz. Ariel Zilber was second front-person. Zilber, son of singer Bracha Zefira, countered and balanced Shalom Hanoch's tendencies toward the rough and angry aspects of rock with his strong emphasis on fun. The other band members were Yehuda Eder (guitars), Eitan Gidron (bass), both graduates of lehaqot tzvayiot, and Meir Israel (drums), who had a long history with various lehaqot qetzev. Also present, although not as band member, was lyricist (and later singer/songwriter) Meir Ariel (1942–99), who is sometimes credited as doing for Hebrew popular music what Bob Dylan did for American music (Sheffi 1989). But the most important presence in the album was that of producer Louis Lahav. Lahav had just returned to Israel from years in the United States where he studied sound engineering and, most significantly, worked closely with Bruce Springsteen (he is sound engineer on the first two Springsteen albums: *Greetings from Asbury Park* and *The Wild, the Innocent and the E Street Shuffle*, both from 1973). He was recruited by Hanoch to work as musical producer with Tamuz on their concerts and then on the album. Utilizing the new 16-track facility at Triton Studios in Tel Aviv, Lahav produced a rock sound for Tamuz that excited rock aficionados in Israel: "He did an excellent job that makes this album the most superb of the few rock albums produced in Israel. Lahav's contribution is dominant in the high quality of the album in terms of sound and technical level—marvelous rock—it is hard to believe that it comes from an Israeli group" (Yossi Harsonsky, *Maariv*, January 15, 1976).

Tamuz established Shalom Hanoch's authorial position as the prime performer of his own songs. His exploration of rock styles from this point onward served the field of popular music in Israel as proof that it was possible to make rock in Hebrew that matched artistic standards of Anglo-American rock, yet maintain a strong element of local authenticity, of Israeliness.

Israeli "Progressive" Rock and the Eretz-Yisraeli Heritage

In 1983, a group of musicians that included Gidi Gov, Alon Olearchik, Ariel Zilber, Yehudit Ravitz, Shlomo Gronich, and Yitzhak Klepter recorded an energetic cover of the song "La-ʿavoda ve-la-melakha" (To work and labor). The song was originally a children's poem by national poet Haim Nahman Bialik, composed by Nahum Nardi. The song is a classic Eretz-Yisraeli song that praises hard work and labor as the cornerstones of the Zionist project. The fun and enthusiasm that radiate from this recording testify to the strong emotional connection of these Israeli rock musicians with SLI. Their gathering for this recording is a manifestation of the sense of heritage and continuity of SLI that underlies much early Israeli rock.

Indeed, as noted above, while the emergence of Israeli rock initially seemed like a heretical break with SLI, the musicians eventually turned to continuity. In addition to Arik Einstein's project of *Good Old Eretz Yisrael* albums, this tendency was most evident in the work of those musicians sometimes referred to as Israeli "progressive-rock" figures, including Yoni Rechter, Shem Tov Levy (who both closely collaborated with Einstein on his project), Shlomo Gronich, and Matti Caspi.

In various collaborations, this particular group of musicians—all of them with formal, mainly piano, musical education—produced a series of albums in the 1970s that contained sophisticated, complex, and sometimes even experimental music. These albums were consciously inspired by U.K. "progressive-rock" bands of the period, especially Gentle Giant, King Crimson, and Genesis (see Macan 1997). Thus Yoni Rechter, while still member of Kaveret, made the album *14 oqtavot* (14 octaves [1975]) with Avner Kener. In 1975, Shem Tov Levy, together with Shlomo Gronich and Shlomo Yidov, recorded the album *Qetzat aheret* (Slightly different), and in 1977 formed the jazz-rock band Sheshet. Shlomo Gronich made his own, highly experimental, album *Lama lo amart li* (Why didn't you tell me?) in 1971. In 1973 he and Matti Caspi released their joint project *Me-aḥorei ha-tzlilim* (Behind the sounds).

The complexity and avant-garde feeling of these albums was played down in later projects. In their albums of the late 1970s and 1980s, these musicians emerged as authors of sophisticated ballads, very much in the tradition of SLI composers such as Sasha Argov, Moshe Vilensky, Mordechai Zeira, and others. Unlike those composers, the "progressive" group also performed their own music. In addition, they were highly conscious users of recording studios and electronic keyboards and were often involved as arrangers and producers when other performers recorded their songs. In other words, in their overall musical output, the progressive group created a direct link between the Eretz-Yisraeli tradition and rock practices. They became the rock-inspired inheritors of the Eretz-Yisraeli tradition, thus forming a cultural link and a sense of continuity between SLI and the Israeli rock of the elite group.

Yoni Rechter is a musician whose versatility best exemplifies this link. With his own work, his projects with Arik Einstein, and his albums with Gidi Gov, he gained wide acclaim as a latter-day successor of Sasha Argov. Another highly versatile musician is Matti Caspi. For his first solo album—*Matti Caspi* (1974)—he played all the instruments, sang, arranged, produced, and composed all the music. This was followed by four more albums of original material, dominated by his partnership with lyricist Ehud Manor. In 1982 he made an album of covers of classic Sasha Argov songs; in 1984 he made another of new songs together with Argov. In 1977 he was the producer and major creative force behind *Eretz tropit yafah* (Pais tropical), songs from Brazil translated into Hebrew. With Yehudit Ravitz and Corinne Alal participating, this was a huge commercial success. Some of Caspi's other projects include work as producer, singer, and composer with the folk duo Ha-Parvarim; composer, arranger, and producer for female rock singer Ricki Gal, for the female trio Shokolad, menta, mastik, and for singer Gali Atari.

Taken together, in terms of stylistic diversity, Matti Caspi's versatile musical output made him one of the most influential musicians in Israel for several years, and his impact has been perceived as located between Sasha Argov and the elite group: "The question is not what draws Matti Caspi to perform Argov songs. 'Ve-'otakh' [And you], one of Caspi's early songs, is one of the most beautiful tributes by the younger generation to Argov" (Gidi Avivi, *Koteret Rashit*, May 1984). And Caspi himself asserts:

> Now, when I came to do it, I knew that it had to be all the way. The truth is that until I don't see how far I can go, I do not move. But now, there is Kaveret with excellent instrumentation, and Tamuz with techni-

cal improvements, great sound and professional brilliance—and I knew that whatever I do had to be as good. *(Yedioth Ahronoth,* March 17, 1978)

Musicians that I like are Ariel Zilber, Yoni Rechter, Shalom Hanoch, Yitzhak Klepter. *(Ha-'Ir,* January 10, 1986)

With ballads like Matti Caspi's "Brit 'olam" (Covenant of love; from his second album [1976]), Yoni Rechter's "Dma'ot shel malakhim" (Angels' tears; from *14 oqtavot),* Shem Tov Levy's "Ha-nasikh ha-qatan" (The little prince; from *Qetzat Aheret),* and many other songs, the progressive musicians of Israeli rock provided the music that linked Israeli rock to SLI, and sometimes even blurred the difference between the two.

• • •

In their various projects during the 1970s, the elite members created a body of work and established a position in the local field of popular music that can certainly be called Israeli rock. They created a typical sound, hybridizing SLI and lehaqot tzvayiot elements with rock, and received legitimacy as "Israeli" music by the media and others in the field.

In the late 1970s, however, Israeli rock was only one popular-music style, together with Festival ha-zemer, Eurovision-inspired mainstream pop, and contemporary SLI inheritors such as Yehoram Gaon, Chava Alberstein, Ilanit, and others. It was only during the 1980s that Israeli rock further developed to attain a dominant position in the field.

8　The Coming of Rock

By the early 1980s the field of popular music in Israel was ready to complete its transformation into a rock-dominated field. This was the result of two major factors. First, Israeli culture made another huge leap, following the one a decade earlier, by further opening up to the most recent trends of Western culture. This can be attributed to the combined effects of the collapse in 1977 of the Labor movement that had held political power in Israeli society since the early 1930s, the consequent rise to power of liberal-capitalist forces, and the first-ever peace treaty of Israel with a neighboring Arab country, Egypt, in 1979. Import and availability of material and cultural goods increased, and Israeli consumer culture rose sharply. Second, a generation was coming of age whose members could claim that "rock and roll was the soundtrack of our lives" (to use the famous phrase associated with U.S. rock critic Greil Marcus). These young people were making their presence felt in various key positions in the field of popular music.

As the market for popular music expanded, and as the major record companies grew in size and sales, the cultural and aesthetic perceptions of the young professionals who came to occupy key positions in the field were directly derived from the rock aesthetic. This was evident in the industry as well as in the media. Thus new young directors of artists and repertory divisions at Hed Artzi, CBS, Phonokol, and, later, Helicon were anxious to apply the most recent aesthetic and marketing standards of Anglo-American pop/rock to Israeli music. The emerging young and authoritative popular-music columnists in the daily and weekly newspapers were also "professionalized fans" of the rock aesthetic—believers in the artistic value and progressive message of rock. The influential music editors and DJs in the recently established Reshet Gimmel, as well as in the expanded Galei

Tzahal, were committed to encouraging local Israeli music that followed any of the current trends in Anglo-American pop/rock.

In addition, the 1979 decision to abolish the lehaqot tzvayiot resulted in new directions in the search for talent, by providing opportunities for musicians who fit the aesthetic perceptions of the new professionals in the field. Of major importance was the work of the elite group in the 1970s. This provided evidence that rock in Hebrew is artistically possible, that it has a record-buying and concert-attending audience, and that it is ideologically justifiable as "authentic Israeli" music. The elite group brought with them a professional community of session musicians, sound engineers, musical producers, composers, lyricists, singers, and musicians whose aesthetic habitus lay within rock.

During the first half of the 1980s, the field of popular music in Israel witnessed the appearance and success of a series of albums, by new as well as known musicians, all with a "rockier" sound than most of the albums made earlier. Major examples include Shalom Hanoch's *Ḥatunah levanah* (White wedding [1981]), Tislam's *Radio ḥazak* (Strong radio [1981]), Benzeen's *Esrim ve-arbaʿ shaʿot* (Twenty-four hours [1982]), Shlomo Artzi's *Tirqod* (Dance [1984]), Yehudit Ravitz's *Derekh ha-meshi* (Silk road [1984]), and Rami Fortis's *Plonter* (as early as 1978). These and other albums reflect the stylistic and cultural diversification that was taking shape within Israeli rock as it emerged to dominance in the field. The "rockization" of Israeli music was taking various paths, following different artistic images, career patterns, and genres or styles. By the 1990s the "coming of rock" to Israeli popular music was complete, as the field came to be predominantly comprised of a series of scenes, styles, sound textures, and career patterns associated with the rock aesthetic. The overwhelming presence of rock in Israeli popular music by the 1990s manifested itself most strongly in the annual Arad Festival. Starting in 1982 as an annual meeting of ḥavurot zemer (singing ensembles) who performed SLI, the festival was gradually transformed and became a three-day rock festival, with all variants of the local rock scene participating.

HEIRS

We use the term "heirs" to refer to a group of musicians who, during the 1980s and 1990s, retained the basic sound formula of Israeli rock, invented by members of the elite group. This was a sort of melodic rock fused with the lyricism of Shirei Eretz Yisrael. They are therefore the heirs to the elite group. The path of inheritance is best exemplified in the career of Yehudit

Ravitz, the rise of female rock auteurs to prominence, and the "star text" of Aviv Geffen.

Yehudit Ravitz and the Rise of Female Rock Auteurs

Yehudit Ravitz's relationship with the elite group began through support and collaboration as a participant in joint projects with members of the elite such as Arik Einstein. In fact, although her career began around 1980, in retrospect she could be included in the elite group itself. Her career exemplifies a significant consequence of the emergence of a rock artistic consciousness among Israeli musicians, namely, a change in the position of female musicians. The rock aesthetic, with its emphasis on authorship of performers, facilitated a transformation of female musicians. From being mainly performers of musical products and carriers of images designed for them by males, they became auteurs who composed their own music, wrote lyrics, played instruments, and in general had much more control over their images and careers (O'Brien 1996). During the 1980s and 1990s, inspired by the commercial and artistic success of Ravitz (as well as Corinne Alal), a growing number of female rock auteurs and performers gained prominent positions in the field. Asthar Shamir, Mazi Cohen, Sharon Lipsitz, Nurit Galron, Ricki Gal, Leah Shabat, Etti Ankeri, Ronit Shahar, and Dana Berger are some examples.

Three different moments mark the start of Yehudit Ravitz's career in 1977 (after graduation from a lehaqah tzvait): membership in the band Sheshet; vocals with Arik Einstein in the song "Atur mitzhekh zahav shahor"; and an appearance in the Israeli Song Festival. Between these three poles, her position in the field was clearly defined as both "Eretz-Yisraeli" and "rock." Sheshet was a band led by Shem Tov Levy that was greatly inspired by British "progressive"-rock and American "jazz-rock" styles of the period. With the band, Ravitz participated in musical exploration and even experimentalism embedded in the rock aesthetic; her vocals (together with Corinne Alal) with Arik Einstein on the song "Atur mitzhekh" are a salient component of the sonic texture of that recording. Her participation in the recording placed her at the core of the fusion between Israeliness and rock aesthetic elements, as pioneered by the elite group. In 1977 Ravitz also appeared at the Israeli Song Festival with the song "Selihot" (Forgiveness), a poem by Lea Goldberg, composed by Oded Lehrer. Accompanied by a full symphonic orchestra, she chanted softly and played her acoustic guitar; her performance of the song was pure Israeliness, as defined by SLI.

Ravitz's first albums in the 1980s included a balanced dose of "Israeli" and "rock" songs. Some were her own compositions; others were especially written for her by other prominent composers. By her fifth album—*Derekh ha-meshi* (Silk road [1984])—she opted for clear rock. Except for her interpretation of one classic Eretz-Yisraeli song, all the songs were her own compositions (she rarely writes lyrics). Her authorial position was also evident in her responsibility for the arrangements that emphasized a funky electric-guitar sound throughout the album. "Ravitz today can sing rock or Shirei Eretz Yisrael and the audience will go with her. 'Industrial post-punk' fans and lovers of land and country believe her. She radiates sympathy. . . . [S]he has a pleasant combination of power and vulnerability, openness and shyness, and above all directness" (Gal Uchovsky, *Ha-'Ir*, April 25, 1986).

Her next album, *Ba'ah me-'ahavah* (Coming from love [1987]), was even rockier. Inspired by the trendy Bruce Springsteen sound of the period, it had a pompous rock sound, full of "synthesizer walls" and echo-laden drums and vocals. An accompanying tour found her on stage, dressed in black leather, playing her electric guitar and fronting a large rock band.

Successful as this album was in terms of sales, Ravitz was criticized for her exaggerated "rockization"—especially after a second album in the same vein proved a commercial failure. After a long hiatus, in 1993 Ravitz came out with the album *Ve-meod lo pashut le-ḥakot* (And it is not easy to wait). Taking credit for musical production and arrangements and composing all of the songs in this album, she merged rock and Eretz-Yisraeli idioms completely. This was most clearly audible in the hit song "Tmunah" (Picture). Originally a poem by Dalia Rabikovitch, it reminisces on early girlhood anguish, countered with pastoral descriptions of sheep, fields, and the sea. Ravitz's yearning vocals perfectly match the lyrics. The composition—an up-tempo ballad—completes the almost traditional SLI character of the song. The sweet sadness of the song is accentuated throughout by her doubled voice at the end of each verse (typical rock practice for signifying softness, pioneered by Buddy Holly in his song, "Words of Love" [1958]), the consistent heavy drumming and bass pulse, and the sound of a slightly distorted, "dirty" electric guitar in the song's "intro," between phrases, in a solo interval, and at the end of the song. The formula of "Tmuna" was successfully repeated in other tracks on the album, and in her subsequent album, *Eizoh min yaldah* (What kind of girl [1996]), particularly in the title song. Thus the soft Eretz-Yisraeli female singer, who takes lyrics from a quasi-pastoral poem and composes a matching ballad, and the rock auteur, who—through studio production practices of multitracking and carefully arranged electric instrumentation—creates a contemporary sound texture, become inseparable in the work of Yehudit Ravitz.

Projecting a slightly more avant-garde image in her dealings with the rock aesthetic, Corinne Alal also emerged from collaborative projects with elite members to become a leading female rock auteur in the 1980s and 1990s. In albums such as *Antarctica* (1989) and *Zan nadir* (Rare species [1992]), she merged her unique expressive vocal style and rock arrangement with melodicism in the Eretz-Yisraeli spirit and with lyrics (written for her by Yaakov Rothblit) that commented critically on the Israeli social and political reality.

Other female rock auteurs, such as Asthar Shamir, Sharon Lipsitz, and Mazi Cohen, made notable albums throughout the 1980s. Also important were female performers such as Nurit Galron, Ricki Gal, and Dafna Armoni, who strengthened the female presence in Israeli rock by making successful albums, mainly through collaboration with elite members, who acted as composers, arrangers, producers, and so on. Although many of these female musicians failed to sustain long-lasting careers, their artistic and commercial success had an impact on the field. This was also the case when a veteran singer such as Chava Alberstein "converted" to rock authorship, or when in the 1990s, musicians such as Leah Shabat and Etti Ankeri each made several successful albums. With the addition of younger musicians Ronit Shahar, Mika Karni, Dana Berger, and others, the presence of female rock auteurs became an enduring feature of the field.

Aviv Geffen

In 1999, at the age of twenty-six, Aviv Geffen had a seven-year career behind him that included eight albums (one of them a compilation), all certified "gold" (sales of more than 20,000 copies), and some even "platinum" (40,000 copies)—an exceptional achievement by Israeli standards. With his music, lyrics, and image, Geffen was not only one of the most successful rock musicians in Israel but also the emblem of a generation and an often controversial public figure.

The "glam" rock pyrotechnics in his shows and videos, as well as occasional morbid and nihilistic visual and verbal elements, were the major elements that made Aviv Geffen controversial. With his dyed orange hair, heavy makeup, and extravagant, sexually ambiguous clothing (long black skirts, for example), he sang about betrayal and existential meaninglessness and strongly criticized Israeli militarism in both his lyrics and interviews to the press. Although this type of image was familiar to Israelis from foreign rock acts (and, in fact, passé by the 1990s), in the Israeli cultural context, Geffen's cultural package projected a strong image of rebellion. With the exception of Tzvika Pick's quasi-successful attempt at "glam" rock in the 1970s, there had never been a "star text" of this sort in the Israeli field, and it was an image alien to Israeli rock. Geffen's success and the accompanying phenomenon of "Geffen-mania" among his teenage fans therefore stirred up not only the field of popular music but also Israeli public culture in general. However, despite his rebellious image, Geffen's arrangements and sonic textures were consciously inspired by the work of early Israeli rockers, especially Shalom Hanoch. Smooth, harmonious, and pleasing, his typical sound was far removed from that of his contemporaries in the alternative Israeli rock scene. "I'm still stuck with the music of past times. I see myself as a late-blooming flower. I love old stuff, direct and without hints, very kitsch, very banal, very penetrating. I adore nature, the Kineret [Sea of Galilee]. Don't like *techno, thrash [metal]*. . . . [T]he Kineret is my creative power, my inspiration, a place that reminds me of past times" (interview in *Rosh 1* [youth magazine], February 1993).

With a strong tendency toward melodicism and softness, Geffen's biggest hits were ballads that allowed his audience to join him in concerts in a rock variant of shirah be-tzibbur. In other words, Geffen made Israeli rock at its best. His phenomenal success should be understood as directly stemming from the tension between his subversive image, as expressed in his visual texts (music videos and concerts) and some of his lyrics, and the traditional and conservative rock sound of most of his songs. For his fans, this duality produced a genuine sense of subversiveness and radicalism, completely immersed in a familiar and beloved sonic idiom. Moreover, his music was eventually embraced by veteran musicians, who glorified his talent for composition, and by a wider cultural and political establishment, who viewed Geffen's concerns about Israeli social reality as an ideological commitment in the Zionist tradition; hence, his position as "heir."

Aviv Geffen's rebellious image manifested itself in his lyrics, public statements, and some of his videos. Beginning with his first album, Geffen took on the role of spokesman for a generation of Israeli youth wondering about and questioning the ideological imperatives of Zionism, including the widely consensual, obligatory military service. The practice reached a certain peak with the chorus of the song "'Akhshav me'unan" (It is cloudy now; the title song of his second album [1993]), that included the line "Anaḥnu dor mezuiyan" (We're a fucked-up generation). It became a slogan and was much quoted to describe Geffen's cultural stance. In interviews, Geffen strengthened this position by making statements against the military that were supported by the well-publicized fact that Aviv Geffen had not served in the army. "I'm against the supremacy of the establishment called 'army.' Against taking an eighteen-year-old boy and shutting his innocence in green [the color of the uniform]. My aim is to divert the stinking machoist

Israeli line into a more delicate direction. Open, external, deeper" *(Maariv,* February 1993).

Although it was made public that he had been discharged on medical grounds, Geffen used the discharge in his antimilitary statements, saying that he was glad that he had not served. Another confrontational expression was his occasional use of morbid images. His video for the song "Bokhe ʿal ha-qever shel imma sheli" (Crying on my mother's grave) contained "gothic" images à la Roger Corman and other horror movies, including a coffin with a woman in it. The publicity apparatus around Geffen made it well known that the "actress" in the video was his real (and living) mother, thus supposedly blurring the difference between the fictive video and lyrics and Geffen's true feelings.

But in spite of his oppositional stance, Geffen was playing on familiar ground and according to the rules of Israeliness. His constant use of the collective "we" in his lyrics and statements was one more in a long procession of commentaries in Israeli culture about "our" lot as Israelis, where "we" have been culturally, and where "we" are now. In addition, Geffen always emphasized his love for some of the long-established emblems of Israeli culture, most notably the Kineret (the Sea of Galilee—as noted in the quote above).

His role as "heir" in terms of Israeli rock and his commitment to Israeliness culminated in the circumstances surrounding the song "Livkot lekha" (Crying for you). Geffen originally wrote the song in memory of a friend who was killed in a car accident. However, the structure of the lyrics made it a lament on the death of any man, in any situation. Initially, Geffen did not record the song himself, but gave it to Arik Einstein, who included it in his album *Yesh bi ahavah* (I have love), released in early 1995. Arik Einstein's recording quickly gained popularity, and the song was given much airplay on that year's Memorial Day (mourning soldiers who died in all of Israel's wars). It perfectly fitted the typical playlists of the day, which contain mainly old SLI, lehaqot tzvayiot songs, and "classic" Israeli rock ballads, with emphasis on songs eulogizing the soldiers who died. Aviv Geffen the songwriter thus entered this ideologically charged national ritual day via his connection to the elite group of Israeli rock.

On November 4, 1995, Aviv Geffen performed "Livkot lekha" at a rally in support of the peace process between Israel and the Palestinians in which Prime Minister Yitzhak Rabin participated only moments before his assassination. During Geffen's performance, Rabin was still backstage, waiting to close the rally by singing "Shir la-shalom" (Song for peace) with all the participants. A photo of Rabin and Geffen emotionally embracing was widely

circulated following the assassination. A week later, at the massive com-
memoration rally held in the same square, Geffen again performed "Livkot
lekha" (see Vinitzky-Seroussi 1998). The song, both in the Arik Einstein
recording and as performed by Aviv Geffen, consequently came to connote
the national trauma of the assassination, and Aviv Geffen became fixed in
Israel's collective memory as a serious, politically committed musician.

Following or parallel to Geffen, a series of other "sensitive" male rock
auteurs emerged to become prominent in the field. They sang mainly ballads, wrote confessional lyrics about their innermost feelings and experiences, relied on smooth and soft-rock accompaniment, and in their vocal
delivery projected fragility and desperation. While not necessarily committed in their lyrics to collective issues (as was Geffen), the sound produced by
these musicians was squarely within the typical Israeli rock tradition.
Notable among these are Ivry Lider and the brothers Meir Banai and Eviatar
Banai. The most prominent name here, however, is that of Russian-born
Arcadi Duchin. First as a major creative force and singer with the band Ha-
ḥaverim shel Natasha (Natasha's Friends) and later as a singer-songwriter,
Duchin made a string of albums of melancholic songs beginning in 1989.
The band's sophisticated melodic structure, careful arrangements, and witty
lyrics endeared Duchin to critics and commentators in the field, and his
music was soon canonized as an artistic achievement of Israeli rock and popular music in general.

CONVERSION/TRANSFORMATION

The emerging dominance of the rock aesthetic was most clearly demonstrated in the conversion or transformation of musicians and others holding
major positions in the field from "nonrock" to "rock." That is, the emerging
equation of "authenticity," "creativity," and "art" in popular music with
patterns and sounds associated with the rock aesthetic propelled a change in
the sound and production work of various musicians. Performers or musicians who functioned within the Eretz-Yisraeli or Festival ha-zemer traditions became rock musicians. One notable example is Chava Alberstein.
During the 1980s, with a more than ten-year career as a folk performer
behind her, she gradually became a politically and socially conscious female
rock auteur. Her "rockization" culminated with the album and song London
(1989), that included a critique of Israeli policies and bitter commentary on
the general atmosphere in the country during the first Intifadah (the
Palestinian uprising against Israeli occupation).

There were a number of other middle-of-the-road (MOR) performers whose general sound changed during the 1980s from orchestrations in the popular song and Festival ha-zemer tradition to rock-inspired arrangements. However, foremost among the musicians who converted to rock was Shlomo Artzi.

Shlomo Artzi

Shlomo Artzi's career can be divided into two distinct phases. The first began around 1970 with several leading vocal roles as a member of lehaqat ḥeil ha-yam (the Navy Ensemble). During this phase, his work was strongly associated with the Festival ha-zemer pattern and with new songs in the Eretz-Yisraeli tradition. The second phase began in 1978, when he made the album *Gever holekh le-'ibud* (A man getting lost) and became the most successful rock auteur in Israel. By the late 1980s, each of his albums typically sold more than 100,000 copies. Even a triple-CD set, a compilation of songs only from his "rock" phase, sold some 150,000 copies in 1993. His performances before tens of thousands of enthusiastic fans often last for several hours.

An interesting fact about the early phase is that it has almost completely been deleted from the history of Israeli popular music. Most of the albums he made between graduating from the lehaqah tzvait and 1978 have never been reissued on CDs. With the exception of his very first album and a small number of songs that somehow made their way into compilations, most of Shlomo Artzi's recorded catalog before 1978 is unavailable to the public (though the old vinyl albums circulate as collectors' items). Artzi's early career was deliberately deleted; he is said to have purchased the rights to all his early recordings and refused to allow their reissue. This reflects the view held by Artzi and various rock critics that the 1978 album was not merely a turning point, but the actual starting point of his career. More important, it exemplifies the strength of the belief in the rock aesthetic as the major creative framework for making artistic and authentic popular music that eventually came to dominate the field of popular music in Israel. Music made before the conversion to rock became an object of contempt or ridicule. Music inspired by and created within the cultural framework of rock became the "real thing."

Indeed, from 1978 onward, the overall sound of Shlomo Artzi's songs and albums changed drastically. This was evident not only in the instrumentation and the general sound of his albums, but most clearly in the grain of his voice. His voice in the 1970s albums was soft, smooth, pleasant. His pronunciation of lyrics was always clear and punctilious. With his transition to rock, Artzi's vocal delivery changed completely. His singing voice became husky, rough, laden with emotion. His pronunciation gained conversational qualities. Again, this was a very conscious act of learning and adjustment that stemmed from Artzi's conviction that his early music was ridiculous and that Shalom Hanoch's way of making music was the "right" mode in terms of authenticity and artistry. Starting with the album *Tirqod* (Dance [1984]), his growing mastery of rock patterns was guided by producer Louis Lahav: "I still did not understand how to do rock'n'roll in Hebrew. I think that what Shalom understood, in Tamuz for example, . . . I mean, I did not know how to match a guitar riff with Hebrew [lyrics]. . . . It was Louis who pushed me to other places, to match the words differently to the melody" (Shlomo Artzi interviewed in *Sof 'onat ha-tapuzim*, pt. 9, 1998).

The new authentic quality of his voice joined a switch to writing confessional, intimate, semibiographical lyrics. Expressing the typical Israeli male themes of soldiers' comradeship or jealousy and possessiveness toward women in a sensitive and introspective style, for thousands of fans he came to personify the romantic and gentle qualities hidden in Israeli masculinity. "Layla lo shaqet" (Unquiet night), from the album of the same name (1986), nicely captures some of these themes.

LAYLA LO SHAQET (ARTZI)

Again at night I dream of you
In the army uniform that was your uniform
The helicopter circles in the hot desert air
And you are frightened
And she already has a child here
She calls me to come over
And I dodge it, and I try
But she's not just anyone

[chorus]

I tell her it is coming back
Yes, it does not leave
She gives me hot coffee
And caresses me all over
And then she asks: "Does it help?
Have a smoke and woo me"
She undresses though it's not warm
And seduces me

But at night I dream about you
Of the face that was your face
And those tiny whiskers which you
Never had a chance to shave

And I get out of bed
And I commune, but not with her
Yes, I dodge it, I try
But she is watching

Again at night I dream of you
Wake up because I dreamt how they
Shot at you and hit you
And you cry
Maybe you found rest
Among soldiers, you are allowed
Yes, I take comfort and sleep with her, yes
As though instead of you.

Unquiet night
And you are dead.

Initially, Artzi's new form of expression met with criticism because it was perceived as pretentious. But by the end of the 1980s, Artzi gradually gained the approval of the critics as well, who came to appreciate his unique melodic strength, lyrical ability, and acquired rock dispositions.

> Artzi is in fact a sort of fascinating mixture of Bruce Springsteen and Julio Iglesias. He comes on stage in a white t-shirt and faded jeans. He sways his ass, even raises a fist, but unlike Springsteen or Shalom Hanoch, the arrow he shoots at the audience does not come from his crotch. Like Iglesias, he actually hands them a rose, an invitation to dinner by candlelight, a sense of intimacy that could lead to a night-long kiss, but not to wild sex in the dressing room. (Gal Uchovsky, *Hadashot*, August 19, 1988)

His albums *Layla lo shaqet* (Unquiet night [1986]), *Yareaḥ* (Moon [1992]), and *Shnaim* (Two [1996]), and especially *Ḥom yuly ogust* (July–August heat [1988]) firmly consolidated Artzi's position as a voice of Israeliness, as an "embodiment of Israeli tribalism. The army, the women in our lives, the friends we lost. An album that became a pillar of his work" (Amos Oren, *Haaretz*, April 28, 1998).

Middle of the Road

Another prominent niche that underwent conversion to the rock aesthetic during the 1980s was MOR popular music. This refers to the sort of pop music aimed at a wide audience of all ages, with strong emphasis on entertainment. As Gammond defines it, with some mockery of rock, MOR is "a loose term that has come into use to cover all the popular music that is not in the current rock idiom and thus appeals to an older and middlebrow audience who still hanker after melody and harmony" (1991: 382). Indeed, until the mid-1970s, Israeli MOR producers and arrangers tended to use sound patterns associated with the general popular-song tradition—full symphonic orchestration and only occasional use of drums and electric bass. The prototypical formula of the Israeli MOR found expression in the songs of the Israel Song Festival, which itself was influenced by European song contests such as the Italian San Remo Festival and the Eurovision.

By the 1980s, various MOR singers, mainly females, moved toward rock arrangements and instrumentation: electric guitars and keyboards, solo intervals with such instruments, rhythm sections of bass and drums, and so on. The change occurred because with the emergent perception that the rock aesthetic was more appealing to contemporary audiences, a growing number of arrangers and musical producers could do the actual work of "rockization." Elite members and associates (producers, session musicians, and so on) were increasingly recruited to compose, arrange, play, and produce music for MOR singers.

Singer Gali Atari is a salient example of this transition. Her early career, during most of the 1970s, consisted of a series of successful songs, mainly in the context of various festivals. She achieved a certain peak when, as the prominent member of the Milk and Honey vocal group, she won first prize in the Eurovision contest of 1979 (held in Israel), with the song "Halleluyah." After leaving this group, she began to work with rock-oriented arrangers and producers. In 1988, with the acclaimed album *Emtza September* (Mid-September), her conversion to rock-inspired songs was complete. In the album produced by Ilan Virtzberg and Yaakov Gilad and played by top session musicians, Atari's voice was placed within well-crafted soft-rock arrangements. "After the big success of 'Halleluyah,' there was a decline. . . . I tried to move away from the Eurovision image. I was considered a singer for the whole family, who sings nondisturbing songs—and suddenly rock'n'roll. I wanted to be released from the synthetic image. . . . I would not record such songs today" (interview in *Hadashot*, October 1987).

Gali Atari was one of a number of performers who converted to the belief that within a rock context their pop image would gain more artistic credibility, an image of seriousness, and a touch of personal authenticity. Yardena Arazi and Ofra Haza are two other examples of this. By the 1990s, Israeli MOR pop became synonymous with moderate, soft, and light adaptations of the rock aesthetic. There were no more midcareer conversions—MOR acts were constructed within a rock-inspired framework from the very start of the artists' careers.

PRODUCTS

The emergence of rock as the major context for making popular music in Israel in the 1980s took shape through practices of music production and artistic creativity, as well as in practices of marketing, image construction, and, in general, the whole notion of career management. The perception of "rock" among record company managers did not relate only to sound but also to carefully planned images and marketing strategies. After analyzing how directors of major international record companies planned, constructed, and launched rock stars, Israeli managers began to copy and implement these practices. Throughout the 1980s and 1990s, the field witnessed a series of carefully constructed "products" of popular music, in the form of individual musicians or groups, some of whom became highly successful and gained wide critical credibility as authentic artists.

An early case in point was Tislam. The launching of the band's first album, *Radio ḥazaq* (Strong radio [1981]), was an early exercise in the import of rock marketing practices. One element of the campaign involved a deal between CBS-Israel and Bank Leumi (Israel's largest bank). The bank purchased 15,000 copies of the album before its actual release, for free distribution among teenagers when they opened a new account. As a result, only a few more sales were sufficient to certify the album as 'gold' immediately on its release. In addition, the album cover depicted the band members staring at a naked female, as well as other publicity photos, creating a male-sexual, macho image for the band, which purportedly suited the hard-rock sound of the album's title song. With the massive sales and an image of desirability, the publicity apparatus evoked the phenomena of hysteria and fandom (when in fact the band was still scarcely known).

Tislam became highly successful in the two years that followed. Their images tarnished by the marketing devices that initially surrounded their career, band members have been trying ever since to gain credibility as serious artists by denouncing those devices. One who succeeded in this effort was Yizhar Ashdot, who made several albums and became a leading producer (his most famous projects were the electro-dance remixes of Ofra Haza's Yemenite songs—"Galbi" and "Im nin'alu"—that made her world famous).

By the mid-1990s, the marketing skills and career-management techniques of the local music industry had reached much higher levels of sophistication and proficiency. Professionals and experts in various aspects of a pop/rock career implemented patterns and practices directly borrowed from the global pop/rock scenes. Launching and managing a career came to be a carefully planned professional project. This aspect of rock practices attained a peak with the launching of the High Five band in 1997. Modeled after "boy groups" such as Take That, Boyzone, and the Backstreet Boys, the band was assembled by Hed Artzi with much attention to detail. Members were recruited according to a formula combining the different "looks" required. They were trained in singing and in dance by a choreographer before recording began. Musicians from the local rock scene were engaged as musical managers, to compose, write, arrange, and produce the typical sound formula of boy groups for the band. As soon as the band began to record, the publicity department at Hed Artzi issued news items and photos of the upcoming phenomenon. High Five members became stars before they sang a note. When their first album was released, commercial success was practically guaranteed.

Rita

When considering the set of music industry practices that include career launches, image construction and management, and long-term planning, marketing, and maintenance of a "star text," the case of Rita is probably the best example in Israel. Rita was spotted by Helicon director Roni Braun when she and her partner (later her husband) Rami Kleinstein, were performing as a duo during their military service in the early 1980s. They were given a long-term recording and career-management contract. Her first album—*Rita*—was released in 1985. Almost fifteen years later, in 1999, Helicon released her fifth album, the double-set *Tiftaḥ ḥalon* (Open a window). By this time, Rita was the diva of Israeli popular music, with thousands of fans eagerly awaiting her new release and flocking to her concerts. Rita's albums typically include well-produced songs, in which her dramatic vocals are surrounded by soft-sounding electric guitars and synthesizers. Many of her songs are composed and produced by Rami Kleinstein, who, at the same time, has a successful singing and recording career of his own. Rita's career was carefully constructed and maintained around the contrasting images of her stage persona and her private life, counting on long intervals between albums and tours to help create anticipation.

Rita's stage persona is that of feminine, sensual, and emotional abandon. In performances and videos, her dramatic and soulful vocal delivery is enhanced by expressive choreographed body movements and gestures, transmitting the feeling that she is completely overwhelmed by the power and meaning of the music. This is heightened by her lavish costumes, which cover a range of feminine images associated with constrained, yet soon-to-be-loosed sensual, erotic energy.

This stage persona contrasts with what is known about her private life, information that is constantly disseminated by her career managers and herself—in interviews, press releases, gossip columns, and so on. Here, the major element is Rita's happy marriage to Rami, following their high-school romance. Their fruitful artistic partnership and the fact that they are not envious of one another are also emphasized.

This contrast between domestic tranquility and stage vigor was intensified by the long intervals between her albums and tours. That is, by keeping her career dormant for a few years after each album or tour, interest in Rita's absence and curiosity about her next creative eruption were easily stimulated and enhanced. Thus, for example, after the success of her second album, *Yemei ha-tom* (Days of innocence [1988]), she was barely heard from for six years. When *Tzipor zarah* (A strange bird [1994]) finally appeared, it was surrounded by a publicity campaign that made Rita's new album, tour, and videos into news. In fact, a thirty-minute documentary, produced by her own record company, about the making of the video for the album's title song, was broadcast during prime time on Channel 2.

It should be stressed that staging images and careers, timing album releases, as well as many other marketing and management practices, had invaded almost all sectors of popular music in Israel by the late 1980s and into the 1990s. As a result, this aspect of rock culture has rendered all Israeli musicians susceptible to the tension between personal authenticity and the artificiality that these practices evoke.

ALTERNATIVE SCENES

Perhaps the most vivid expression of the rise of the rock aesthetic to dominance in Israel was the emergence of alternative rock as a salient phenomenon in the field and as a major supplier of new talent to Israeli music in general. Alternative refers to musicians and groups who express and manifest an ideological and artistic commitment to what they perceive to be the cutting edge of aesthetic and stylistic innovation in rock. Alternative rock scenes are therefore the cultural contexts where Anglo-American rock trends are most strongly emphasized and where distance from anything Israeli is most prevalent.

An alternative rock scene has existed in Israel since the mid-1960s. Lehaqot ha-qetzev, in their commitment and uncompromising approach to playing rock were certainly an alternative scene. But lehaqot ha-qetzev lacked the media and industry support needed to gain recognition and legitimacy beyond their narrow scene. Thus the change in the 1980s was reflected in the public presence and media coverage, in the recognition and legitimacy, of young rock musicians as a sort of avant-garde. By the early 1980s, new popular-music columnists in the *meqomonim* (local newspapers) of Tel Aviv and Jerusalem, *Ha-'Ir* and *Kol Ha-'Ir*, as well as some music editors in Galei Tzahal and Reshet Gimmel, were anxious to discover and encourage rock musicians (see Maroz 1990). They were especially eager to present to the public what they believed to be music that was artistically better. This reflected the wish to perceive the Israeli field of popular music as a worthy participant in the international field, as containing music of the same artistic quality and as innovative as any Anglo-American rock. This collective professional and artistic-ideological enthusiasm among music editors and critics was best reflected in the attempt to publish a high-quality local rock magazine, *Volume*, which appeared between March and November 1983.

Initially, this newfound enthusiasm for alternative rock was a marginal phenomenon. Record companies were cautious about signing recording contracts with fringe musicians fostered by the critics. But when the few musicians who did get a chance to record proved successful, and as some of the directors at the record companies themselves became aficionados, alternative rock in Israel became a prominent feature of the field. In a sense, by the late 1980s the alternative-rock scenes had replaced the lehaqot tzvayiot as the locus where managers of record companies searched for and recruited young, new, promising musicians.

There were three major moments in the rise to prominence of alternative rock: the initial "breakthrough" moment in the mid-1980s, often referred to as *tqufat ha-mo'adonim shel Tel Aviv* (the Tel Aviv club era); the early to mid-1990s, sometimes called "the sound of Sheinkin" (after the street in the heart of Tel Aviv where musicians used to hang out in cafés); and the electro-dance scene of the mid- to late 1990s, with successful dance clubs in Tel Aviv and Jerusalem and its associated phenomenon of trance music. The most prominent names to emerge from the alternative contexts were the band Mashina and musicians Rami Fortis and Berry Sakharof.

The Club Scene of the 1980s

Between 1982 and 1985 three clubs in Tel Aviv—Penguin, Liquid, and Qolno'a Dan (Cinema Dan)—laid the stage for what came to be known as *tequfat ha-mo'adonim* (the club era). The period remains in the collective memory of rock cognoscenti in Israel as a moment of a thriving alternative rock, mainly associated with "postpunk" and "new-wave" rock styles. The clubs hosted a string of contemporary and older rock bands and musicians such as Siouxie and the Banshees, Tuxedomoon, Peter Hammill (of Van Der Graaf Generator), Jack Bruce, Bauhaus, Shriekback, and others. The appearance of well-known (to rock aficionados) alternative rock musicians in a club context was unfamiliar to Israelis—most foreign rock acts that visited Israel up to that period gave concerts in halls. The appearance of these musicians in clubs enhanced the belief in the cosmopolitan nature of the scene and projected an avant-garde and alternative aura on the local bands that played in the clubs.

Most of the local bands that played in the clubs were short-lived. Some existed for only a few months. Others were able to leave their mark through a few singles or even an album or two that later gained a kind of legendary status among critics. But by 1985, journalist Eyal Halfon wrote that the clubs were in decline as performance venues and that the young teenagers were turning to discotheques:

> New wave has died. It has weakened. The avant-garde which we loved to read about, write about, and believe is here with us, in Liquid, Penguin and Qolno'a Dan, like in Camden Palace and the Marquee [famous London clubs], was strangled by the hora and hit-parade disco. The years 81–85 created a temporary illusion in Israel culture. It seemed as if a growing circle of people played, listened to, and absorbed contemporary music. . . . A relatively adult audience that could be defined as intelligent, open-minded, and sophisticated was gathering each Tuesday and Thursday to listen to local and foreign bands. (*Ha-'Ir*, July 19, 1985)

In retrospect, the scene proved to be an embryonic context for musicians who later became highly regarded and busy producers and session players. Lehaqa Retorit (Rhetoric Band), for example, made one minialbum. Its front-person, Yossi Elephant, later became lead guitarist and producer with Ehud Banai and Ha-ḥaverim shel Natasha (Natasha's Friends). In 1991 he collapsed and died on stage at the Logus Club in Tel Aviv. Another example is Oved Ephrat, who played bass with the Clique—a band that made two albums—and who in the 1990s became a sought-after musical producer.

Alternative Rock in the 1990s

The 1980s club scene caused some rock aficionados to believe in Tel Aviv as a global city, like New York or London. It also provided a reference point for musicians and journalists who nurtured hopes for the revival of the aura of those times. This Tel Aviv aura suited processes of gentrification that were taking shape in certain Tel Aviv neighborhoods, not unlike processes taking place in neighborhoods in New York City such as SoHo and the East Village

(Zukin 1995). By the late 1980s, Tel Aviv city planners and entrepreneurs began to encourage the development of a young artistic and bohemian street culture in what was called the heart of Tel Aviv, particularly in the neighborhood of Sheinkin Street. Consequently, the area drew aspiring young musicians from other towns and parts of the country who believed that this was the place for them to be if they wished to participate in the alternative scene of Israeli music and culture.

Directors of local record companies shared a belief in the creative and artistic potential of the alternative scene. Among them Haim Shemesh, who throughout most of the 1990s was director of the Israeli department at Hed Artzi, is notable. He initiated the release of a large number of albums by alternative bands and musicians, with other companies soon following his lead. Most of these bands were guitar-based, male, hard-rock units that emphasized melodic and harmonic aspects. The sound, image, and success of the "grunge" phenomenon in Seattle were clearly inspirational, not only in terms of style but also as a model for discovering fresh talent and constructing a career.

Nos'ei ha-migba'at (Top-Hat Carriers, originally from Jerusalem), Eifoh ha-yeled (Where Is the Child), Niqmat ha-traqtor (Tractor's Revenge), Mofa' ha-arnavot shel Doctor Kaspar (Dr. Kaspar's Rabbit Show), Rockfour, Ziqnei Tzfat (Elders of Safed), Asaf Amdurski, Yirmi Kaplan, Dana Berger, and Ha-mekhashefot (The Witches, an all-female band) were some of the more prominent names that emerged during this decade. For some years, it seemed as if a rock tide had swept over Israeli music.

Like similar phenomena elsewhere, and like the elite group twenty years earlier, the Israeli alternative rock scene of the 1990s was a collaborative effort, carried out by a network of musicians. The musicians constantly formed and re-formed bands, assisted and participated in each other's albums, and often performed together on stage. The musical producers of many of the albums were veterans of the 1980s scene, most notably Rami Fortis and Berry Sakharof, who in turn recruited many of these younger musicians to play on their own albums and in concerts.

During the 1990s this network of musicians, consisting of twenty-five to thirty solo artists and bands, released more than fifty albums. By the end of the decade when many of them were finding it increasingly difficult to sustain long-lasting careers, the scene declined.

Mashina

In the eyes of many commentators, the huge success of Mashina undermined its image as an alternative-rock band. Yet, throughout its ten-year existence, the band embodied the almost unbreakable ties that connected the alternative-rock scene with issues of Israeliness. That is, with all its artistic ideology of avant-gardism and the construction of a global sense of identity, alternative rock in Israel was entrapped within Israeliness. The fact that an alternative scene did exist and flourish, for example, was sometimes portrayed by scene members in terms of national pride (that is, "We have an alternative scene of our own"). Moreover, when an alternative band or musician succeeded beyond the relatively narrow audience of the scene, they needed to come to terms with themes of Israeliness, the underlying demand made on them by the field. It was a tension not unlike that of rock musicians vis-à-vis the music industry and its demands for stylistic standardization (Frith 1981).

Emerging from the 1980s club scene, where it underwent several personal and stylistic changes, in 1985 Mashina released its eponymous debut album. Tinged with ska and reggae influences, and including the hit "Rakevet layla le-Qahir" (Night train to Cairo; reminiscent of the song "Night Boat to Cairo" by the British ska band Madness), it was an instant success. An attempt to refute the critical image of imitators and light pop by including somewhat more complex songs in their next two albums resulted in commercial failure. Their fourth album, *Gvirotai ve-rabbotai* (Ladies and gentlemen [1989]) was a compilation of hits and four new songs. From that point until its breakup in 1995, Mashina retained its position as the top Israeli rock band, commercially and artistically.

In its next four albums—*Ha-'amuta le-Ḥeker ha-tmuta* (Death-rate research association [1990]), *Miflatzot ha-tehillah* (Monsters of glory [1992]), *Si ha-regesh* (Climax of emotion [1993]) and *Le-hitra'ot ne'urim, shalom ahavah* (Farewell youth, hello love [1995])—the band managed to maintain a balance between jerky, ska-inspired tunes (that often resembled the hora, with its SLI connotations) and somber, dark guitar rock ballads. Each album contained successful hits and anthemlike songs, much beloved by their fans. The lyrics growingly commented on and implicitly criticized issues of Israeliness. "Az Lama li politiqa akhshav" (So why do I need politics now [1990]) stood out in its bitterness.

AZ LAMA LI POLITIQAH AKHSHAV (BRACHA)

Thousands of mercenaries concentrate in a mosque
They talk about me but not with me
And an uncle of my neighbor was promoted to battalion vice-commander
So said the wife of my sister's son
Shamir [dill, and the name of the Prime Minister] and parsley meet in
   the dark

To solve the current situation
And in New York they invented a new kind of disease
And someone claims he is my brother

I lied when I said everything was so wonderful
Because nothing was actually true
Even our ball that became square
Forgot it is round
The rock'n'roll business
(I'm in rock'n'roll)

In San Francisco the bridges need recovery
In Russia another train disaster
The masses in Berlin destroyed the wall
And you and I can only hope

Why does a stone in Ramallah divert from its course
You and I in a case
I'm singing and you dance in the middle

I lied when I said everything is so wonderful
Thousands of mercenaries concentrate in the dark
And in New York they invented a new kind of disease
I feel so wonderful
We are a chosen people

So why do I need politics now?
> (From the album *Ha-'amota le-Ḥeqer ha-tmuta*
> [Death-rate research association] [1990])

Announcing their breakup in May 1995, the band was to give its farewell concert at the Arad Festival in July. But as the band began to play, the dense crowd pushing its way into the concert site crushed three teenagers to death. The tragedy was followed by public discussion about rock, aggression, and "what is happening to our youth." The failure of the organizers to install proper gates and fences was overlooked (at least initially; later they were taken to court), and the music was viewed as the source of the trouble. The incident came to show that—for all its widespread presence and dominant position in the field of popular music—rock music was still seen by some educators and politicians as a foreign element in Israeli culture. The band finally gave its farewell concert in October to 40,000 people in HaYarkon Park in Tel Aviv.

Rami Fortis and Berry Sakharof

Together and separately, Fortis and Sakharof were the ultimate heroes of the alternative scene. Generally regarded as the most successful and sustained embodiment of Israeli rock music in Hebrew, they did not compromise on their aesthetic and artistic values in favor of Israeliness of any sort. Throughout their careers, the output of these musicians has been considered the most authentic and original rock music made in Israel.

With the release of his first album, *Plonter*, in 1978, Fortis established his image as the enfant terrible of rock in Israel. At times deliberately dissonant, rough, lyrically blatant (at least by Israeli standards), dominated by a loud and hard guitar sound, the album was clearly inspired by punk rock. In concert, Fortis consolidated his "mad" image with additional elements. When the club scene emerged a few years later, Fortis became its best-loved native son. Performing on his own, or with different bands (Jean Conflict, the Emergency Room Unit), he consistently incorporated recent sonic and stylistic elements (electronic, ethnic, morbid imagery, "Goth" melancholy) and never lost his "mad" image. His role as hero of the scene reached its peak when he joined the band Minimal Compact. The band consisted of Sammy Birnbach, Malka Spigel, and Berry Sakharof, friends and associates of Fortis who had participated in *Plonter*, but then the band left Israel in search of other opportunities. They formed Minimal Compact in Amsterdam in the early 1980s. Singing in English, they had recorded two albums by 1983 and gained some reputation in clubs in Europe and even in Japan. The band frequented the Tel Aviv club scene, playing to small, enthusiastic audiences. Fortis often joined his friends on stage, participated in their second album, and became a band member in 1984, in time to record their acclaimed third album, *Raging Souls* (1986). Their music was described as "tasteful, elegant art-pop and dance-rock" (Steve Huey, in the *All Music Guide* Web site, http://allmusic.com; see also the entry in the *Touser Press Record Guide*). Minimal Compact gave the Tel Aviv club scene a genuine aura of cosmopolitanism. The band became the pride of town, as it linked the local scene to its foreign equivalents.

After the band broke up, Fortis and Sakharof returned to Israel, not before recording together, as Foreign Affair, an album of ethnic rock—*The East Is on Fire* (sung in English). In Israel they recorded *Sippurim me-ha-qufsa* (Stories from the box [1988]) and *1900?* (1990). With these two albums, they endeared themselves to critics and audiences and finally achieved cult status with larger audiences. These two albums are considered by critics to be among the best rock albums ever made in Israel.

During the 1990s, Fortis and Sakharof parted ways. Fortis made albums that continued—with diminishing success—his typical energetic and soulful hard-guitar rock. Sakharof became one of the most appreciated and valorized musicians in Israel. His four albums—*Ha-kol o klum* (All or nothing [1991]), *Simanim shel ḥulshah* (Signs of weakness [1993]), *Ḥam al ha-yareah* (Hot on the moon [1995]), and *Negi'ot* (Touches [1998])—proved to fulfill local rock aficionados' dreams about Israeli alternative rock.

> *Negi'ot*, Berry Sakharof's marvelous last album, placed him on the front line of local rock. It is followed by a concert that ranks him as the prime Israeli rocker at the moment. Drawing on his developing work, and assisted by an excellent group of players, the humble prince accumulates power and magnitude beyond his modest appearance. Sakharof of winter 1999 is a fascinating demonstration of power, assurance, sweeping energy and excellent songs. Urban and pungent Tel Avivian rock, yet cosmopolitan in its colors and qualities as well. Combines an aroma of distortion with a psychedelic tendency and a connection to the East, and climaxes with an astonishing performance of "Kama Yossi" [How many Yossi, from his second album]. (Amos Oren, *Yedioth Ahronoth*, January, 25, 1999)

Trance and the Electro-Dance Scene

A salient component of the alternative scene in Israel throughout the 1990s was the so-called electro-dance scene. While in many ways it paralleled club cultures in cities around the world (Thornton 1996; Straw 1991), the local electro-dance culture gained its unique character through its offshoot, the trance-music scene.

Discotheques playing the most recent electronic dance music began to open in Tel Aviv by the late 1980s. By the mid-1990s, major local record companies, as well as some new small labels, were regularly releasing compilations of the latest club hits in house, techno, drum'n'base, jungle, and so on. In cities all over the country, young entrepreneurs were opening new, ever-larger, and more lavishly designed clubs. Allenby 58 in Tel Aviv and Ha-oman 17 in Jerusalem became major attractions, drawing hundreds of clubbers on weekends. In the clubs, local DJs built their own reputations while foreign DJs frequented the scene as well. Clubbers in Tel Aviv took special pride in the claim that Allenby 58 created "a musical environment which is comparable with Europe. So that Allenby is now known all over the world, mentioned in all [dance] magazines. . . . Everyone who understands, knows that today the hard-house or club-trance the one can hear in Tel Aviv is as good as anywhere else" (*Haaretz*, November 26, 1999). But for all the salience of club culture as an ultrahedonistic phenomenon, the scene that gained much more public attention was that of trance.

Trance music, also known as Goa trance or psychedelic trance, is characterized by its mythologized origins in the area of Goa, India, an ideology that mixes elements of utopian futurism, Indian mysticism, and psychedelic vocabulary. It also features typical electronic sound, musical structure, and high-speed rhythms. Its visual aspect consists of animated colorful computer graphics that resonate the futuristic mysticism (Cole and Hannan 1997). By 1997, speakers for the local scene, using the phrase "Israel is a trance power," were claiming that the trance scene in Israel was one of the most prominent in the world.

This claim was substantiated by the large number of privately organized secret or underground weekend raves in forests, on beaches, and in desert valleys, attended by thousands. Also, two events—the rave in the Ganei Huga Park in the north of Israel in June 1997, and the rave in the beach area of Nitzanim a month later, each drawing tens of thousands of participants— were proudly described as the "biggest trance raves" in the world. The Israeli scene was frequented by some of the world's most prominent trance DJs, and the number of Israeli trance musicians and album releases grew steadily. Some of the Israeli trance musicians—most notably the duo Astral Projection—gained an international reputation and was often invited to perform around the world. The companies that produced trance in Israel— Phonokol, Krembo, and BNE—reported export sales of hundreds of thousands of items.

Media reports on trance rapidly evolved from glorious reviews of CDs by Israeli artists and late-night programs of trance music on a few radio stations, to a full-scale moral panic concerning the trance scene. Police raids of trance raves and regular use of the phrase "drug parties" to describe the raves in the media placed the trance scene at the focus of a public debate about Israeli youth and drug use. The trance scene responded with various defense tactics that culminated in a demonstration, which turned into a large rave, in Rabin Square in the heart of Tel Aviv. There, on a Thursday evening in July 1998, approximately 20,000 people danced to live performances by the most famous Israeli trance musicians.

Perhaps paradoxically, the moral panic had the effects of bringing trance to the attention of a wider audience and of increasing its popularity. By late 1998, although the police still caused difficulties, trance raves became an almost regular commercial enterprise, like any other musical event. Trance tracks also became part of all kinds of dance parties, including weddings.

ETHNIC ROCK

A pinnacle of the Israelization of the rock aesthetic during the 1980s and 1990s was the emergence and crystallization of ethnic rock. In the Israeli context, "ethnic" for the most part means "oriental." In other words, the emergence of ethnic rock related to the appearance of a hybrid style that merged rock components with various Mediterranean and Middle Eastern musical elements. From the outset, ethnic-rock musicians and their supporting media apparatus distinguished their music from musiqa mizraḥit, which in many ways can also be perceived as ethnic rock. Considered by the musicians themselves, as well as by the critics, as artistically superior to musiqa mizraḥit, ethnic rock has been perceived as the Israeli authentic contribution to "world beat" or "world music" (Mitchell 1996; Regev 1997b; Taylor 1997). It was only in the mid- to late 1990s, with the massive success of the collaboration between the band Ethnix and musiqa mizraḥit singer Eyal Golan, and with the success of the band Tea-Packs, that the difference between the two genres was slightly blurred.

Indeed, leading Israeli ethnic-rock musicians took their cultural (though not necessarily stylistic) inspiration from styles such as reggae, Algerian rai, various African pop/rock idioms, and so on in order to create their own Israeli variant of world beat. Their work can thus be interpreted as keeping pace with major artistic trends in the world of international rock while fulfilling the national task of creating local authentic music. This explains the enthusiasm that surrounded some of the albums made by ethnic-rock musicians in Israel. In fact, it was the artistic and commercial success of some major ethnic-rock musicians that inspired a large sector of the field. By the mid-1990s, ethnic touches and nuances of sound came to be present in much of the rock music made in Israel. It can be argued that by the late 1990s, Israeli rock as a whole underwent a certain degree of "ethnicization."

The "rock" in ethnic rock typically relates to the mode of vocal delivery, use of electric guitars, often with fuzz and distortion, the basic instrumentation of a rock band, and emphasis on studio production values of "clean" and accurate mixes. The "ethnic" represents the reliance on rhythmic patterns borrowed from various oriental and Mediterranean music traditions, occasional use of instruments from such traditions, and generating electric or electronic sounds that imitate these instruments. The differences between particular musicians lies in the type of traditions they turn to for influence and the extent to which actual traditional elements are present in their sound. The most prominent musician in this context throughout the 1980s and 1990s is Yehuda Poliker.

Yehuda Poliker

In early 1997, Yehuda Poliker released his live double album, *Live at Caesarea*. "Yehuda Poliker's first live album is everything that one could hope for. The 45-year-old local icon serves up a satisfying 31-song overview of his impressive career covering his days in Benzeen, his forays into Greek music, and his deeply personal reflective rock, which has earned him the title of 'the conscience of Israel'" (David Brinn, *Jerusalem Post*, March 7, 1997). This live album was released almost ten years after *Efer ve-avaq* (Ashes and dust [1988]), the album that determined Poliker's artistic stature. That album was an exploration by Poliker and Yaakov Gilad—Poliker's creative partner, writer of the lyrics of most of Poliker's songs, and musical producer of his albums—of their experiences as young men growing up in Israel in the 1960s as sons of Holocaust survivors. Pain, rage, despair, and hope were the adjectives used to describe the music and, in particular, Poliker's vocal delivery. On the album Poliker played electric guitars and also bouzouki, accordion, keyboards, and baglama. Intensive production work mixed a range of influences and sources—hard rock, progressive rock, electronic musique concrete, Greek ballads, and Arabic rhythms—into one coherent stream of songs. The critics raved, and the album immediately gained the status of a masterpiece.

> In this album Poliker and Gilad distill from their joint work a personal and universal album. Touching, penetrating, delicate. An album that has everything. (Noga Tal, director of Hed Artzi, *Haaretz*, April 28, 1998)
>
> The Holocaust and its impact on the second generation. The basic rock of Benzeen is assimilated into Poliker's Greek roots. Combined with Gilad's lyrics, one of the most important works of the 1980s was born. (*Yedioth Ahronoth* critics, April 14, 1995)

In a sense, *Efer ve-avaq* salvaged Poliker's original image as a serious rock artist. His career began in 1981—somewhat belatedly, as he was already thirty-one years old. Poliker was at that point leader of Benzeen, a hard-rock band that mainly played at weddings in the Haifa area. Forming a partnership with Gilad, who was already a well-known figure in Israeli rock circles (mainly through his joint work with Yehudit Ravitz), Benzeen made two albums of mainly Poliker/Gilad compositions. The albums revealed Poliker as a soulful singer, a talented pop/rock composer, and, most importantly, an extraordinary electric-guitar player. Their first album was a great success. The band's roots in a working-class industrial area and its rough sound caused critics to hail Benzeen as a "genuine" rock band.

However, to the dismay of many aficionados, the band broke up in 1984, and Poliker turned to his Greek roots, to the country where his parents were born. For his father, this was a second family after he lost his first wife and son in the Holocaust. Poliker grew up in a home where the traumatic experiences of the Holocaust somehow merged into nostalgic memories of prewar Greece. In 1985, under the influence of emerging "world music" and looking to Greek superstar Yorgo (George) Dallaras for inspiration, Poliker made *Eynaim sheli* (Eyes of mine), an album of Greek songs, mainly in the laika and *rembetiko* styles, translated into Hebrew by Gilad. The songs were played and arranged as rock, but in many of them, Poliker preferred the bouzouki to the electric guitar. The album enjoyed massive success and brought Poliker to a wide range of audiences, including those of musiqa mizrahit. But his rock fans were disappointed. "This week Israeli rock'n'roll received a 'knock-out.' It was overpowered by two of its best artists: Yehuda Poliker and Yaakov Gilad. . . . I saw Israeli rock crumbling. . . . If devoted rockers are doing 'Greek' music in such an excellent way, who will carry on the rock wagon?" (Amos Oren, *Yedioth Ahronoth,* November 21, 1985).

Poliker made a second album of Greek songs and in 1988 came up with *Efer ve-avaq.* Back to original rock compositions and the electric guitar, the Greek influence had by now become a major and permanent component of his music. Greek and other Mediterranean influences were completely integrated into his Hebrew rock music: "It's just that growing up, I simply came to love the Beatles, rock'n'roll, and all this hard sound. But Greek music was there all the time, inside. . . . [My music] is rock all the time. It is Greek music that has rock'n'roll in it. It is not Greek music done in an authentic way" (Yehuda Poliker, excerpts from an interview with Shimon Parnas, Reshet Gimmel, February 13, 1988).

Poliker's subsequent albums—*Pahot aval ko'ev* (Less, but still hurts [1990]), *Le-eyneikha ha-kehulot* (To your blue eyes, an instrumental album [1992]), *Ha-yeled she-bekha* (The child in you [1995]), *Meuhar ulai muqdam* (Late maybe early, yet another instrumental album [1998]), as well as his live retrospective album *(Live at Caesarea)*—further explored the possible mixes of rock sounds and energy with Mediterranean and occasionally Arab influences and electronic sound textures. They also consolidated his stature as one of Israel's most successful and beloved musicians.

The "Ethnicization" of Rock

Poliker may have been the most successful of the creators of Israeli ethnic rock, but he was certainly not the only musician to make such music. The practice of mixing oriental elements with rock was increasingly adopted by musicians during the 1990s. Beyond suiting the aim of participating in the recent "world beat" trend, the practice, in a way, closed a circle in the history of Israeli music. It embodied a return to the Zionist "melting-pot" idea of East-West fusion that informed much of the work of early SLI composers. Only this time around, given the "nativeness" of the musicians and their rock aesthetics habitus, the fusion was perceived not as stemming from a conscious ideological-national commitment, but rather as a spontaneous expression of Israeliness.

A prominent musician in this context was Ehud Banai. Beginning in 1986 with *Ehud Banai ve-ha-plitim* (Ehud Banai and the refugees), by 1999 he had made five albums that earned him the high esteem of critics and a devoted audience, based on his Dylanesque lyrics and his folk-inspired approach to rock.

From another angle, the band Ethnix emerged in 1990 with a mixture of oriental-sounding electronic keyboards and pop tunes that made them a huge commercial success during the 1990s. Although often looked down on by critics for the "formulaic" nature of their music, the band reached a peak when it collaborated with musiqa mizrahit singer Eyal Golan, thereby producing the most impressive crossover success of a mizrahi musician.

The band that drew the most enthusiasm—not only among music professionals but also in the wider cultural field—for its ethnic rock and East-West fusion, was Tea-Packs. Originally from the southern development town of Sderot, Tea-Packs was the most successful of the bands to emerge from that small desert town in the 1990s (others being Sfataiym [Lips] and Knesiat ha-sekhel [Church of the Mind]). Tea-Packs was essentially a vehicle for the creative force of its leader, Kobi Oz. Between 1992 and 1999, Tea-Packs made six full albums and one minialbum, in which diverse influences such as rock, electro-dance, musiqa mizrahit, Moroccan-Jewish-Arab songs, and early Israeli rock (mainly Kaveret) were integrated into one typical sound. A major ingredient in the band's success was the lyrics, in which Oz often depicted life in the periphery, characterized by neglect and marginalization by hegemonic Israeliness. He achieved this by cleverly combining various styles and registers of Hebrew, thereby assuming the voice of peripheral Israeliness, while at the same time commenting on it, mainly in a quasi-humorous way. By mixing rock, which is associated with hegemonic, Western-oriented Israeliness, with expressions of mizrahiyut and peripheriality in a musically innovative mode (which was quite different from typical musiqa mizrahit), the music of Tea-Packs, "although talking in the language of the cultural center and created according to the 'melting pot' model, decentralizes Israeli culture and cancels its one-dimensional categories and labels. . . . [It] defines an additional type of local native cultural practice" (Saada 1999: 74).

Indeed, with ethnic rock becoming one of its major modes of expression, by the late 1990s Israeli rock—willingly or unwillingly—came to embody a realization of the major element of Zionist-national ideology, namely, the invention of an authentic native Israeli culture.

Yet, at the same time, in various forms, rock music also functioned as a cultural tool for creating and maintaining different microidentities in Israel. Thus, for example, a group of youth scattered around the country maintained a tiny scene of "extreme metal" rock, which gave rise to bands such as Salem and Orphaned Land, which released albums on European labels (see Harris 1999); youth of the large Russian immigrant community that emerged in Israel in the 1990s created its own vibrant scene of Russian rock, with very close ties to its parent scene in Russia; and youth of the Ethiopian community, with some participation by West African foreign workers residing in Israel, created a local rap and reggae scene of clubs and events (Shabtay 2001).

Between its SLI-inspired soft sounds, its alternative variants, its ethnic-oriental textures, and other manifestations, Israeli rock at the turn of the century has become the major musical tool through which Israelis perceive the variants of their identity as being at once "national-local" and "global-cosmopolitan."

PART IV

Musiqa Mizraḥit

9   Musiqa Mizraḥit

Origins, Style, Production, and Public

Israeli rock and SLI, the music cultures that express the variants of Israeli-ness we have labeled global Israeliness and Hebrewism, are conventionally associated with the dominant sectors of Israeli society, that is, the establish-ment, or the secular Ashkenazi middle and upper classes. Musiqa mizraḥit (lit., Eastern or oriental music) is the popular music associated with mizraḥiyut, the cultural variant of Israeliness created by Jews who came to Israel from Arab and Muslim countries in North Africa and the Near East. Referred to in earlier periods as *'edot ha-mizraḥ* (the Eastern communities), these Jews were relegated by the dominant Western perspective to an "eth-nic" component of Israeli Jewish culture and typically occupy the less-privileged socioeconomic positions (Arab-Israeli Palestinians are another such component).

Musiqa mizraḥit is a major expression of a profound process of social change that has affected mizraḥi Israelis since the 1970s. However, despite its long-standing presence in the field of popular music in Israel, its precise definition still remains elusive. Basically musiqa mizraḥit incorporates var-ious ethnic "colors" (for example, Yemenite, Arabic, Kurdish, Persian, Moroccan, Greek, and Turkish; on the concept of "color," see Racy 1982) within the standardized forms of Western popular music. Musiqa mizraḥit's association with low-status Middle Eastern and North African Jews and its ethnic colors originally gave it the immediate image of "otherness." Until the mid-1980s leading forces in Israeli popular music therefore perceived it as "non-Israeli." In this position of otherness and cultural inferiority, musiqa mizraḥit was initially consigned in the netherworld of "cassette cul-ture" (see Manuel 1993). It was transmitted through live, often informal, performances (at wedding parties, or *haflot*, celebrations consisting of food and entertainment on various occasions, such as farewells) or through cheap cassettes and videotapes, rather than via formal media such as television, radio, or LPs.

Until the mid-1980s, this marginal status was reflected in the terms used by the media to describe musiqa mizrahit: *musiqat qasetot* (cassette music), or the equally derogatory term, *musiqa shel ha-tahana ha-merkazit* (music of the Central Bus Station), which is a reference to the old Central Bus Station in south Tel Aviv, where most of this music was sold at open-air cassette stands that played the music over loudspeakers.

Since its inroads into the national arena in the second half of the 1980s, musiqa mizrahit has developed into a major form of popular culture in Israel. The modes of dissemination (CDs instead of cassettes), the technical quality of the recordings, and its presence in the media have changed dramatically. This shift in the position of musiqa mizrahit vis-à-vis other types of Israeli popular music was symbolically reflected in the new labels that its producers, practitioners, and the public used to refer to it: *musiqa mizrahit yisraelit* (Israeli Eastern music) or the more emblematic *musiqa yisraelit yam tikhonit* (Israeli Mediterranean music; see Horowitz 1994). However, musiqa mizrahit still remains a common term of reference to this music in the media and in the vernacular. In the 1990s musiqa mizrahit became a major actor in the struggle for the definition of Israeliness in the field of popular music. (On the social frameworks, its performers and public, its contexts of performance, and its special language, we draw substantially on our early study of musiqa mizrahit; see Halper, Kidron, and Seroussi 1989.)

SOME PRELIMINARY REMARKS

Musiqa Mizrahit and Other Ethnic Music in Israel

Although the role of music as a reflection of social change has been discussed frequently, its ability to predict and perhaps even influence social change has been subjected to less discussion. It can safely be said that, after thirty years of development, musiqa mizrahit has had an affective power in Israeli social life by being instrumental in defining mizrahi Israeliness. Music in itself does not determine social relations, but in specific situations within relatively limited periods—such as the period of mizrahi Jewish identity-formation in Israel—it does have a certain role as an agent of social change. For instance, attempts by many mizrahi performers and composers to both draw on Arabic music and yet distance themselves from it by developing a unique "Israeli mizrahi style" for the *amkha* (common people, a euphemistic reference to the working class of which the mizrahim comprise a relatively large majority), indicates how this popular music helped to define identities and group boundaries.

From the outset one should distinguish musiqa mizraḥit from the traditional music heritage of the mizraḥi Jews who immigrated to Israel from Arab and Muslim countries. However, in spite of the clear differences between the modes of creation and transmission and the contexts of performance of traditional and popular music, there are persistent links between both fields. For example, tunes drawn from traditional repertories, such as songs from the *diwan* (Yemenite Jewish religious poetry), became popular mizraḥi songs.

One should also draw a line that separates musiqa mizraḥit from various forms of ethnic popular music in Israel that are beyond the scope of this study. Musiqa mizraḥit should not be conflated, for example, with "ethnic" rock (for example, the case of Yehuda Poliker). It should also be distinguished from works by Israeli artists operating within the "world music" context, of which Shlomo Bar is a pioneer and major representative. Starting with their first album (1977), Shlomo Bar and his band Ha-brera ha-tiv'it (Natural Gathering) aspired to fuse a wide variety of ethnic styles (including jazz, perceived as ethnic Afro-American music) into a multifaceted avant-garde sound set to socially committed texts (Kutner 1986). Bar and his band also reinterpreted in a provocative manner several mainstream Israeli and traditional Jewish songs (both Sephardi and Ashkenazi). Despite the mizraḥi origin of some of the artists (Bar is originally from the Atlas Mountains in Morocco), musical materials and texts, Ha-brera ha-tiv'it always distanced itself from musiqa mizraḥit and its audiences (Horowitz 1997: 90). Instead, it targeted the elites who are sensitive to ethnic discrimination in Israel while aiming "to achieve recognition for the distinct Oriental style of this music as equivalent to Western fine art music" (Cohen and Shiloah 1985: 209).

However, the sounds of Yehuda Poliker and Shlomo Bar helped open paths for the acceptance of musiqa mizraḥit as an authentic type of Israeli music and therefore as an alternative expression of Israeliness. Moreover, as musiqa mizraḥit gained legitimacy, various patterns of "crossing over" took shape between different music styles, and some mizraḥi musicians were involved in hybrids of musiqa mizraḥit and rock, most notably the bands Ethnix and Tea-Packs.

The Narrative of Musiqa Mizraḥit and its Research

Musiqa mizraḥit is the form of Israeli popular music that has attracted the most attention from the scholarly community within and outside Israel. It presents all the elements that turn a topic into a heaven for analysts from diverse fields: anthropologists (Jeff Halper); sociologists (Tova Benski, Eric Cohen, and Motti Regev); folklorists (Amy Horowitz); linguists (Malcah Yaeger-Dror); and ethnomusicologists (Amnon Shiloah, Edwin Seroussi, Pamela Squires-Kidron, and Eliezer Finegold) have all approached musiqa mizraḥit. Israeli rock, a form of music that appeals to a wide audience and has strong inbonds yet less clear semiotic and social connotations, was a less "appealing" and more complex subject of inquiry to handle, theoretically and methodologically. Musiqa mizraḥit, on the contrary, appeared as a prolongation of the music of the ethnic communities of Israel, the classic subject of local ethnomusicological inquiry.

Musiqa mizraḥit renders itself to theoretical issues such as perceptions of cultural identity and social borders of producers and publics, confrontation between center and periphery, conflicts of classes and/or of taste publics in a multicultural society, a dissenting subculture within a new nation trying to forge its cultural identity, reflections of political stances in a popular art, eclectic or exotic popular-music styles with strong ethnic elements, and so on. Moreover, from the point of view of methodology, this field offered the scholar several advantages: great variety, but a numerically tolerable group of outspoken key informants, abundant "native" literature, and a manageable musical repertory. Finally, the creators of musiqa mizraḥit, performers, composers, and producers alike formed, even institutionalized, a lobby eager to attract the attention of scholars interested in their art. Consciously or not, they recruited scholars to forward the interests of their music industry. For these reasons, research of musiqa mizraḥit turned sometimes into a naive mobilization of writers who were dragged in by the rhetoric of promoters of this music. Much of the rhetoric of musiqa mizraḥit, which attracted scholars with social and political agendas, is of recent vintage, the result of social processes that are extremely subtle.

Musiqa mizraḥit is also a type of Israeli popular music whose social and cultural connotations have been intensively debated in the Israeli media, outside academic circles. This debate can be attributed to the public activism of musiqa mizraḥit producers as well as to media critics who used this music as a metaphor to express their own views about Israeliness. A result of this peculiar situation has been the oversimplification of extremely complex issues. Thus genuine musical creativity was mixed with shrewd economic interests, and sincere social passions were intermingled with manipulative politics geared to attain financial success that could not be obtained through conventional means, such as large sales of records.

Despite the impressive amount of research on this subject, several issues in the study of musiqa mizrahit remain to be studied. First of all, a question demands investigation: whether musiqa mizrahit is a defined musical genre or a "mishmash" of songs of diverse styles, a social movement expressed in the commitment of its followers to certain songs and contexts of performance or a space of contradictions, "ours and theirs," "authentic and imposed," where the nature of mizrahiyut is negotiated. Second, the narrative of musiqa mizrahit, which emerged in its most articulate form in the 1990s, with its mythological figures and events, needs a critique. Understanding of the evolution of this narrative and its uses as part of the musiqa mizrahit cultural system must be refined. Moreover, the influence of scholarly research should also be incorporated into a critical reading of musiqa mizrahit.

Some commentators have stressed that the musical pluralism of musiqa mizrahit is characteristic of the oppressed "Levantine" culture in Israel. The essay *After Jews and Arabs: Remaking Levantine Culture* (Alcalay 1993) offers an example of this type of interpretation:

> Despite the efforts to extricate Israel from the Middle East . . . there is probably nowhere in the Levant where such a vast variety of music from the region can be found. Against great odds, each group of immigrants either preserved or, if it is possible, continued to follow the trajectory of their musical culture from afar. In the alleys of the open marketplaces, at the central bus stations, out of suitcases, kiosks, flimsy stalls, or tiny shops, virtual walking encyclopedias of popular culture sell cassettes and videos, in every dialect of Arabic, in Turkish, Greek, Persian and Kurdish. . . . But it is here, as well, where the very real political and cultural schism creates a true split. In this sense, the majority of Levantine and Arab Jews are still hostage to policies and hierarchies of power they did not institute: social, political and economic structures and realities directly confront cultural limits, memories, affinities and events. . . . One can hum the tunes of Farid al-Atrache, Umm Khulthum, or Muhammad Abdel Wahab one minute, and serve as an interrogator in which the Palestinian subject becomes an object of misplaced rage the next. Such is the nature of Israeli working-class dislocation and each turn of the screw in both hegemonic cultural structure and the continuing occupation . . . only serves to further mutilate memory itself as an entirely new history and set of relations is constantly being produced. (Alcalay 1993: 253–54)

Heavily politicized and yet scholarly interpretations of musiqa mizrahit as an underprivileged style of popular music need to be refined. Political subversion or cultural rebellion were not, and are not, at the forefront of the agenda of most producers, performers, and consumers of musiqa mizrahit.

THE ROOTS OF MUSIQA MIZRAḤIT

The Yemenite Jewish Model

The incorporation of "oriental" elements into the new Israeli music culture was an integral part of the agenda forged during the Yishuv period by the European Jewish musicians who arrived in Palestine (this process is discussed by Hirshberg 1995: ch. 11). This ideal has its roots in the orientalist fascination of these musicians with the exotic "other," which they inherited from the late romantic schools of Western European art and music, and in their vision of the new Hebrew identity as having certain "colors" of Middle Easternness. These trends are reflected in their use of modal frameworks and oriental rhythms in their compositions, as well as in the adoption of local Arabic, Bedouin, and Druze melodies for some of their folk songs.

The incorporation of authentic oriental music by the Jewish composers of the Yishuv into their new works was also the result of direct contacts with Eastern Jews, particularly with the Yemenite Jews. In their studies of the Yemenite-born singer Bracha Zefira, Hirschberg (1984) and Flam (1986) stress her particular role as a "mediator" between the Eastern Jewish music traditions and Western European music in the formative stages of Israeli music. Zefira, who was an orphan raised by families of diverse ethnic origins in Jerusalem, included in her repertory traditional Sephardi and Eastern songs, many taken from religious contexts (see Zefira 1978). She sang arrangements of these songs on the stage in the early 1930s accompanied on the piano by Polish-born composer Nahum Nardi. Zefira also issued a moderately successful series of recordings of these Eastern songs. Later on, after parting from Nardi, she added to her repertory more sophisticated arrangements of the same traditional Eastern songs that were prepared for her by distinguished Israeli composers who immigrated just before World War II, such as Paul Ben Haim from Germany and Oeden Partos from Hungary. Zefira aspired to be an opera singer; therefore, her commitment to Eastern music was only one aspect of her creativity. Late in her life, after having been forgotten by the public for three decades and outshined by the success of other Yemenite Jewish female singers (particularly Shoshana Damari), Zefira attempted to construct a narrative in which she positioned herself as a pioneer in introducing European Jews in Israel to "oriental" music (see Zefira 1978: 24).

Although the precedent of Zefira is far removed from contemporary musiqa mizraḥit, her public presence during the Yishuv period has to be considered as the first case of the "orientalizing" tendencies in emerging Israeli popular music. It is not by chance that a singer of Yemenite origins such as Zefira was the first to make inroads into the European audiences of the Yishuv. The Yemenite Jew became, for Ashkenazi Zionist intellectuals, emblematic of the imagined "noble native" Jew (see Berlovitz 1981) who never abandoned the cradle of ancient Jewish civilization, the Near East. In their minds, the Yemenites preserved traits of an authentic Jewish lore that could inspire the invention of new patterns of Hebrew culture (for a critique of these views, see Druyan 1981). The Yemenite singing voice was one of these sources of inspiration; indeed, Zefira was only the first in a gallery of successful Yemenite female artists who were active in Israeli popular music as both performers and composers beginning in the 1940s. This list includes Esther Gamlielit, Sara Levy-Tanay, Hana Aharoni, and Shoshana Damari. Eventually, Yemenite singers (including women such as Ahuva Ozeri and the young Ofra Haza before her breakthrough) became the leading figures of musiqa mizraḥit in the early 1970s.

The image of Yemenite Jewish music as "authentic" was fostered not only by the presence of "native" performers. Musicological research on traditional Yemenite music between the 1910s and the 1940s, carried out by Eastern European Jewish scholars such as Abraham Zvi Idelsohn, Menashe Ravina (Rabinovitch), and Shlomo Rosowsky, indirectly supplied Yemenite Jewish music materials for use by composers and arrangers.

The attraction to performers of Yemenite music and the availability of musical notation of Yemenite music influenced the incipient field of popular music in the Yishuv. Of particular significance were the Yemenite motifs in several early songs by Moshe Vilensky, who reminisced that shortly after his immigration from Poland to Palestine in 1932, he was attracted to the music of the Yemenite Jews. He used to attend services at Yemenite synagogues in the Kerem Ha-teymanim neighborhood of Tel Aviv in order to capture the spirit of their traditional music that later inspired him in some of his works. One of his earliest songs composed in Palestine, "Elimelekh," dating from 1935, is a tango that includes a pseudo-Yemenite motif in the refrain. In the same year, Vilensky also began his collaboration with young Yemenite singer Esther Gamlielit, in a pattern similar to the Nardi-Zefira partnership. This was the first of several collaborations between Vilensky and Yemenite singers. Several years later, he began his lifelong artistic relationship with singer Shoshana Damari, for whom he composed a number of his better-known songs of the 1940s. Vilensky included "Yemenite" numbers in scenes related to Yemenite Jews in the musical theaters and cabarets where he worked. Examples are the songs "Be-karmei Teyman" (In the vineyards of Yemen [1945]) and "Miriam bat Nissim" (Miriam, daughter of Nissim [1947]) written for the Li-la-lo theater company. Vilensky's

"Yemenite" output continued into the statehood period, with songs such as "Marvad ha-qsamim" (The magic carpet [1950]), celebrating the mass immigration of Yemenite Jewry brought to Israel in an operation of the same name, and "Zekharya ben Ezra" (1954, text by Yaakov Orland), which describes life in the immigrants' temporary camps and the warm, paternalistic relations between Prime Minister David Ben Gurion and the Yemenite Jews. Vilensky composed this song for Yemenite singer Ḥana Aharoni.

The Yemenite model as an inspiration for the orientalist stream within emerging Israeli culture did not relate exclusively to the field of music (Aharoni 1986: 167–68; see also Lewis 1989). During the Yishuv period, Yemenite arts and crafts became a source of inspiration for emergent Israeli art (Ofrat 1998) and in the invention of Israeli folk and art dances. The Yemenite model would remain a persistent component not only of Israeli mizraḥiyut but also of musiqa mizraḥit.

However, the Yemenite component in Israeli musical orientalism should not be overemphasized. There were other key elements in the complex expression of mizraḥiyut in popular music. Various streams of Eastern Jewish musical creativity, besides the Yemenite one, had coexisted in the Yishuv since at least the 1930s. These genres and styles were beyond the horizons of European musicians striving for an East-West synthesis in emergent Israeli culture and, as a result, are usually absent from the narrative of Israeli music. One example is Ezra Aharon, one of the most distinguished Iraqi Jewish musicians, who immigrated to Israel in 1934 and opened the doors to the performance of Arabic art music by Jews in Israel. In 1936 Aharon was commissioned by the recently inaugurated Palestine Broadcasting Authority to establish an ensemble of Arabic music. Arabic music thus became a component, though a minor one, of the early Eretz-Yisraeli soundscape.

Another example is the music of composer Rahamim Amar. A Jerusalemite of Moroccan origin, he performed Arabic music at coffeehouses together with Arab musicians. He also composed many popular songs of religious content, some of which remain in the repertory of Sephardi synagogues in Jerusalem to this day. Although isolated from the established cultural activities of the Yishuv, these musicians maintained an Eastern Jewish musical scene based on Arabic music, which inspired later generations of mizraḥi musicians.

Why was the music of the Yemenite Jews favored over Arab music by European composers as an oriental component of their new music? It appears that in the eyes of Ashkenazi Zionists, Yemenite Jewish culture was viewed as a preservation of ancient and authentic, perhaps even biblical, elements of Jewish culture, untainted by Arab or other influences. Given the growing antipathy of the Hebrewist cultural establishment for using purely Arab materials for its orientalist purposes, the Jewish Yemenite model was seen as the perfect source of such components. Indeed, the problematic status of Arab music will remain a permanent dilemma for musiqa mizrahit. Only in the 1990s, with the expansion of the peace process between Israel and some of its Arab neighbors did the presence of Arabic music in the Israeli soundscape acquire some degree of legitimacy (Regev 1995).

Eastern Music in the First Years of Statehood

After the establishment of the state, Eastern Jewish musical activities proliferated in different venues. Commercial records of unedited traditional Yemenite music became available from minor record companies in Tel Aviv in the early 1950s. Certain venues in the Tel Aviv area, in particular, Café Noga in Ramat Gan (a satellite city of Tel Aviv), offered popular Arabic music performed by the best of the immigrant Jewish musicians from Iraq. Iraqi Jewish singers, such as Albert Chetrit, better known as Filfel al-Masri, recorded popular songs that attained certain success and were popular with the growing population of Jewish immigrants from North African and Middle Eastern countries. His successful song "Ha-kol be-tashlumim" (Everything [paid for] in installments [1959]), for example, in which a husband complains about his wife's overspending due to her constant purchases on credit (a financial novelty for Jews from Arab countries), has an Arabic ensemble accompaniment, and the Hebrew text, pronounced in a heavy Eastern accent, is spiced with many Arabic words. No sound could be farther removed from the ideal of Israeli music in the 1950s than this song by al-Masri (see also Perlson 2001).

Even more popular than al-Masri was Moroccan-born singer Jo Amar. Some of the songs that Amar recorded attained wide popularity, particularly those with grassroots appeal such as "Barcelona," "Shir hashikor" (The drunk's song), "Yismah Moshe" (Moses shall rejoice), and "Shalom le-ben dodi." The latter, a religious song that turned into a popular one, became one of the first musiqa mizrahit hits of the early 1970s in cover versions by Lehakat tzlilei ha-'ud and Zohar Argov. The overall style of these songs by Amar is Andalusian, that is, drawing on both Spanish popular music of the 1950s (for example, the *paso doble*) and urban Moroccan Jewish music traditions. His arrangements incorporate Arabic instruments (such as the qanun and the 'ud), improvised passages in free rhythm (usually in a pseudoflamenco style), and the mizrahi pronunciation of the singer that differs greatly from the sanctioned Israeli pronunciation of modern Hebrew.

These popular-music activities "by Orientals for Orientals" found very little expression on Israeli radio, the only mass-communication medium in the 1950s. For the most part, this music remained within the boundaries of the traditional venues of performance of Eastern Jews, such as weddings or haflot and in coffeehouses.

The Greek Wave

The status of popular Eastern music changed dramatically in the 1960s, with the eruption of the "Greek" wave of popular music in Israel. "Greek popular music" in this context should be understood as the sound of hybrid nightclub music styles from Athens and Thessaloniki, generally referred to as *laika* (DeBoer 1996). A dominant feature of this sound is the presence of the bouzouki. This type of Greek music became a favorite style for Israeli-born Eastern Jews as well as for many non-Easterners. This wave is particularly connected to the rise to stardom of Greek singer Aris San. A seventeen-year-old non-Jew from Thessaloniki, San began to frequent Israel after 1956 and to appear in clubs in the port city of Haifa, which was populated by many Jews of Greek origin. Following a love affair with an Israeli girl, San settled in Israel and began to appear at the main venue of Greek music in Israel, the Arianna nightclub in Jaffa, owned by Shmuel Barzilay, a Thessalonician Jew. General Moshe Dayan, at the peak of his political power and popularity in the 1960s, is said to have been a fan of Aris San and even to have intervened to formalize the singer's legal status.

Aris San's success and that of other contemporary Greek singers who landed in Israel was not a total breakthrough because the presence of Greek popular music in Israel predated his arrival. Nightclubs in Jaffa, such as Arianna, regularly hosted live Greek music and musicians in the 1950s. One may hypothesize that the success of Greek music of the laika style among mizrahi Jews was their way of eluding the quasi boycott of Israeli public culture on Arab music. Sometimes similar in sound and affective appeal, Greek laika music provided a legitimate way to publicly enjoy the type of sounds beloved by Jews from Arab countries.

Individuals who became the major producers of musiqa mizrahit in the 1970s, such as Asher Reuveni (personal communication), were exposed to the music of these clubs in their youth and became avid consumers of it. Consequently, the "Greek sound" became one of the main stylistic inspirations of musiqa mizrahit.

San's influence on later musiqa mizrahit cannot be overestimated. One pivotal element was his use of the electric guitar in a high-pitched staccato mode, as an amplified imitation of the sound of the bouzuki. The sound was later copied and became a signature sound of leading musiqa mizrahit guitar players such as Moshe Ben Mush and Yehuda Keisar. The song "Boum-pam" (in Greek), a huge hit for San in Israel, is exemplary here. In addition to a long guitar solo, the song also includes a short quote from Um Kulthum's song "Enta Omry" (composed by Mohammed Abd el Wahab), hinting at the proximity to Arab music that his work contained.

San's hit songs in Hebrew, such as "Sigal," conquered the charts in the 1960s, paving the way in the Israeli public to a new "Mediterranean" sound. San's songs were simple and light, in sharp contrast with the patriotic content of many popular songs produced during the same period, in the aftermath of the Six-Day War (1967). In terms of melody, "Sigal" is based on a few two-bar motifs repeated in sequence. The minor scale in the verses is not melancholic, as is the case in many mainstream Israeli songs, and the contrasting beginning of the refrain in major sets the spirit of the entire song. Its "Greekness" rests mainly on the sweeping instrumental introduction by San on the bouzouki.

SIGAL (LYRICS, KATZ; MUSIC, SAN)

Water I did not sip
Eyes I did not close
Food I did not taste
I dreamt and dreamt
By the moonbeams
I deceived my heart
I am not myself
Since you are mine, Sigal.

Refrain

My innocent Sigal, Sigal,
My love Sigal, Sigal,
I am your lord Sigal,
I am your slave Sigal,
How suddenly, so much, so much,
[It is] only you, you, you.
[It is] only you, you, you.

By the early 1970s, San's songs became part of mainstream Israeli popular music. Five of his songs are included in the printed collection *Lehitim bo'arim* (Hot hits; see Kedar 1971) together with popular songs by leading Israeli composers such as Moshe Vilensky, Dov Seltzer, and Nurit Hirsh.

The Mediterranean Tinge

Another antecedent of musiqa mizrahit can be found in the activities of several mizrahi singers whose main performance venues were the nightclubs of the city of Ramla, a mixed Jewish-Arab city 20 kilometers east of Tel Aviv. These singers were in fact part of the early rock phenomenon of lehaqot ha-qetzev. The musical ideal of these singers, or, more precisely, "crooners," was similar to the style heard at the San Remo song contest in Italy. They added the southern European romantic ballad to the typical English rock repertory heard in the clubs. The mixture of rock and sentimental ballad lay the groundwork for the adoption of rock instrumentation in musiqa mizraḥit. The style of ballad singing by mizraḥi singers was slightly more dramatic than its European counterpart, and, of course, the pronunciation of the Hebrew texts was mizraḥit. This taste for European popular ballads among mizraḥim was rooted in the musical culture of the North African Jewish bourgeoisie, which had been exposed to French popular songs in Morocco and Algeria and Italian ones in Tunisia and Libya. Moreover, Jewish singers in North Africa were ballad-singing stars in their countries of origin; hence, performers such as Shimi Tabori, Avner Gedassi, and Nessim Saroussi are conventionally considered pioneers of musiqa mizraḥit, despite their obvious sentimental pop style.

Critics, such as Oren (1998), suggested that the origin of musiqa mizraḥit as a challenge to mainstream Israeli popular music occurred in a mythical interview given by one of the most notable of the mizraḥi "crooners" of the early 1970s, Nessim Saroussi, to journalist Yaron London in 1975. The interview was held on *Tandu,* one of the earliest talk shows on Israeli television. London, a writer and TV host, was the archetypal representative of Ashkenazi, Western-minded Israeli intelligentsia in the media. He openly described Saroussi's music as "tasteless" before a national audience. Following the interview, critic Emanuel Bar Kadma wrote, "Saroussi . . . is one of the phenomena that perpetuates all the gaps in education and provides a fictional and destructive pride . . . to the sectors of the under-educated in the Israeli society" (Emanuel Bar Kadma, *Musag* 2, 1975). Upset by the media messages, Saroussi chose to leave Israel and settle in France. The echoes of this interview reverberated until the late 1990s, when London publicly apologized for his "lack of political correctness" in his early television career.

CRYSTALLIZATION AND MAJOR FEATURES

Musiqa mizraḥit emerged from the traditional and popular musical styles of Eastern Jews, especially the Yemenites, and partly from the southern European popular-ballad tradition that was widespread in North Africa and the Levant. Beginning in the 1930s, a vigorous and fluid scene of different types of non-Western music, popular and traditional, whose goal was to entertain ethnic Jewish audiences, coexisted in Israel. This music market was stylistically eclectic and included, most prominently, Arabic (Egyptian and Iraqi), Yemenite, Moroccan, Kurdish, Turkish, Greek, French, Italian, Spanish, and Persian elements.

These music traditions were joined to the influence of Shirei Eretz Yisrael that had been conspicuously included on the agenda of mizraḥi musicians since the 1940s. Mizraḥim were exposed to Israeli songs through socializing agents, such as the school system, the youth movements, the army, and the state radio. Also significant was the presence in the mizraḥi singers' repertory of Anglo-American pop-rock, from which many musicians drew their inspiration for amplified sound and their perception of musiqa mizraḥit as popular rather than traditional music.

This wide variety of musical sources set the ground for the eclecticism of musiqa mizraḥit in its formative years (the 1970s and 1980s). This eclecticism supports our assertion that musiqa mizraḥit, though based on elements of a popular-music genre, was from the outset a cultural context, a social framework for musical activities where songs from diverse sources were given a particular interpretation.

The social feature that unified all the proto-mizraḥi musical styles under one roof in the 1950s and 1960s was their almost total absence from Israeli radio programming. If Eastern Jewish music was broadcast at all, it was usually in the framework of "folklore" programs. Arab music could be heard on the Israeli Arabic network (essentially a propaganda channel aimed at audiences in neighboring Arab countries), which had its own home orchestra of Arab music, that included many Jewish musicians who came to Israel from Iraq and Egypt. Arab radio stations, especially Egyptian ones, which could be heard in Israel, were popular among mizraḥim because of the music they broadcast. In spite of the wide availability of all forms of Arab music, popular and classic, its presence in the institutionalized field of Israeli music was banned, as anti-Arab sentiment reached its peak after 1948.

Due to the unavailability of conventional mass media as a means for diffusing their sound, mizraḥi musicians relied on live performances and on close physical contact between performers and listeners. Because the practitioners of this music were not professionals, for the most part, they made their living through other occupations, including some musical ones like, in the case of male singers, synagogue cantors.

By the late 1960s, a well-developed venue for different kinds of Eastern popular musical performances existed in social clubs, cafés, nightclubs, and wedding halls, especially in neighborhoods in south Tel Aviv. The predominance of Yemenite Jews in these areas of the city led to the pervasive presence of Yemenite singers in the emergent musiqa mizraḥit, a trend that continues to the present. By the early 1970s, different mizraḥi singers, such as Shalom Shubeli, Moshe Meshumar, and others, began to form new bands. The most successful were Lehaqat tzlilei ha-qerem (The Sounds of the Vineyard Band, named after Qerem ha-teymanim, the "Yemenite Vineyard" neighborhood in south Tel Aviv), fronted by guitarist Moshe Ben Mush and singer Yossef Levi (better known as Daklon); and Lehaqat tzlilei ha-ʿud (The Sounds of the ʿUd Band), fronted by guitarist Yehuda Keisar and singer Rami Danoch. These early musiqa mizraḥit ensembles were very active and became well-known in south Tel Aviv and beyond. They experimented on secular and religious repertories from diverse sources, including Yemenite and Moroccan Jewish, Greek, and Middle Eastern musical styles and European ballads coupled with mainstream. They consolidated the eclectic "sound" of musiqa mizraḥit through a combination of Eastern and Western musical instruments, adding *muwwalim* (improvised passages in free rhythm) and singing with silsulim (lit., waves or spirals; vocal inflections of long pitches).

In spite of its popularity with its constituencies, mizraḥi music remained peripheral to the field of Israeli popular music until the mid-1970s. From the perspective of its consumers, these non-Western styles of popular music fulfilled the traditional social functions of live entertainment in urban venues, especially in wedding halls.

The Mythological "Birth" of Musiqa Mizraḥit

Musiqa mizraḥit existed long before it was conceptualized as a distinct field within Israeli popular music. However, until the 1970s the idea of popular music as a commodity for mass distribution to an amorphous and anonymous audience was not yet, for the most part, considered by mizraḥi musicians. The conceptualization of musiqa mizraḥit as a commodity emerges with the arrival of cassette technology in Israel. The cassette brought musiqa mizraḥit into the center of the public debate around the definition of Israeliness in popular music.

The mythological "birth moment" of musiqa mizraḥit as a style of popular music occurred at the wedding party of music producer Asher Reuveni in 1974 (see Horowitz 1997: 45–46, quoting *Haaretz* journalist, Michael Ohad) and is connected with cassette technology. Reuveni and his brothers owned a record and electric hardware shop in Shekhunat ha-tiqvah (lit., the neighborhood of hope), one of the best-known working-class neighborhoods in south Tel Aviv. The area was then mainly inhabited by mizraḥi Jews, with a relatively high percentage of Yemenite Jews. The image of this neighborhood was that of an impoverished slum, with a high rate of delinquency.

Reuveni was forced to postpone the celebration of his wedding (though not the religious ceremony) because of the Yom Kippur War in 1973. When the party took place a few months later, it included, as did most Yemenite weddings at that time, live musical performances by Yemenite musicians. Since many of his friends were still at the front and could not attend the party, he decided to record it for them. The recording was reproduced manually on cassettes and became an instant hit, with an unprecedented demand for more copies than anyone had expected.

This story includes three main elements of the musiqa mizraḥit narrative: (1) its origins in a working-class, mizraḥi neighborhood; (2) its close link to events of traditional Jewish life, the wedding party; and (3) its dependence on a new technology, the cassette. Not coincidentally, this story also emphasizes the "Cinderella" syndrome: "from humble beginnings to stardom." In 1981 Reuveni told the story for the first time to a journalist from *Haaretz*, the elite daily newspaper of the upper and educated classes, at a time of rising interest among mainstream media in musiqa mizraḥit as a "curious phenomenon." The interview followed a feature about musiqa mizraḥit on the prestigious Friday night newsmagazine of the only television channel on the air in Israel at the time. What Reuveni concealed in this interview was that musiqa mizraḥit had actually existed long before his wedding, in the entertainment venues of south Tel Aviv, Ramla, and elsewhere.

The crucial element that explains the absence of musiqa mizraḥit from the public ear in Israel until the late 1970s was the artistic downgrading and stigmatization of almost anything overtly Arabic in Israeli culture. Especially in the public sphere, the presence of significant Arab components was beyond the scope of cultural producers in Israel. To the Western ear of dominant cultural producers in Israel, the sounds of musiqa mizraḥit resembled those of Arab popular music; hence, this music was not a candidate for public presence. In other words, cultural power was the major determinant in the absence of musiqa mizraḥit from radio broadcasting in Israel in its early years.

Still another important element that explained the absence of musiqa mizraḥit from radio and record stores was the self-perception of its practitioners. Until the late 1970s, many musicians did not entertain the idea of commodifying this music, which in their eyes still functioned along more traditional functional patterns. As Moshe Meshumar, one of the founders of musiqa mizraḥit, noted in an interview: "The truth is that we did not record because we did not have a predisposition for it. We played [at parties] until the early morning hours. We went to sleep and got up to play [again]. We sang naturally, from the heart, not artificially. Who thought about recordings and money?" (Levi 1998: 49).

The idea of commodifying mizraḥi songs to attain economic profit is then what differentiates between the pre- and post-Reuveni periods of musiqa mizraḥit. Realizing the potential of mass distribution of cassettes of a music that until then was heard only at live performances at weddings and parties led Reuveni to found one of the first—and, to this day, major—recording companies of musiqa mizraḥit.

Why is the formidable success of the Reuveni brothers and other producers of musiqa mizraḥit, such as the Azoulay brothers and Ben Mush Productions, different from the mainstream Western popular-music production system? One answer, of course, relates to the new cassette technology. These producers were attracted both by the low price of the software (the cassette) and by the mobility of the hardware, the portable cassette player, which revolutionized the consumption of popular music in many small countries (see Wallis and Malm 1984). In addition, considerations of quantity overcame quality. But these are only partial answers. One needs to look into deeper motivations. Quick profits were certainly a factor in the launching of musiqa mizraḥit as a popular-music industry. But to this financial motivation, a new social dimension was added: the idea of orchestrated discrimination against mizraḥi musicians and their music by the establishment-dominated media and the consequent shrinking profits of producers and artists. The growing awareness of the social dimension surrounding musiqa mizraḥit led to a series of events that soon became the core of the public debate over Israeliness.

One of these developments was the institution of the Festival ha-zemer veha-pizmon Lamnatzeaḥ shir mizmor by the Israeli Broadcasting Authority. This festival was established at the initiative of Yosef Ben Israel, then head of the Folklore Department of the Israeli Radio (Kol Israel). By arguing that Eastern music had been discriminated against at the Israel Song Festival produced by the IBA since 1960, Ben Israel succeeded in promoting the first oriental song festival in 1971. It is noteworthy though that Ben Israel, a graduate of the Rubin Academy of Music in Jerusalem and one of the few mizraḥim high up in the hierarchy of the IBA, devised the festival with a double purpose: first, to serve as a kind of affirmative action; and second, as a reaction to the emerging low-quality musiqa mizraḥit, which in the 1970s was mainly denoted with the pejorative label of musiqat qasetot.

In 1979, the festival of oriental songs was nationally televised for the first time, raising interest in it on the part of musiqa mizraḥit performers and composers who sought entrance into the core of the IBA. In 1982, the future icon of musiqa mizraḥit, Zohar Argov, won first prize at the festival with the hit song "Ha-peraḥ be-ganni" (The flower in my garden), composed by the most distinguished composer of this music, Avihu Medina. One of many young Yemenite singers on the nightclub and wedding hall circuits of south Tel Aviv, Argov experienced a rise to stardom on state television, which proved to be another high point in the evolution of musiqa mizraḥit as a genre of Israeli popular music on a national level.

Musiqa Mizraḥit, Technology, and the Music Industry

The rise of musiqa mizraḥit coincided with technological developments that made the recording of music on cassette tapes easy, inexpensive, and more accessible to an expanding taste public (Gans 1975). Thus singers who had made musiqa mizraḥit popular at ḥaflot and weddings, but who had no access to record companies or radio stations, were able—with the help of small mizraḥi entrepreneurs—to produce cassette tapes.

Musiqa mizraḥit was recorded almost exclusively on cassettes rather than on records, the latter being the main medium of the mainstream pop industry in the 1970s and 1980s. This was a technological handicap that kept the musiqa mizraḥit industry marginal. Moreover, until the late 1970s, many musiqa mizraḥit performers produced cassettes mainly to bolster their live appearances. One reason for this, besides the question of access itself, was that musiqa mizraḥit artists did not make much profit from recordings, but rather used them to generate more performances.

The profit structure of the musiqa mizraḥit cassette industry promoted artistic mediocrity. Producers made most of their profits not on their well-known stars, but on the tens of smaller singers (who paid for their own master tapes) whose cassettes could be produced with a minimum of investment. Producers needed to sell only 250–500 copies to make a profit. Since almost anyone could make a tape, the turnover in singers was rapid, with many performers making only one tape. Moreover, there was no formal marketing or packaging of the cassettes. They were not directly marketed to stores, little if any promotion accompanied their release, and widespread pirating was tolerated. This approach to marketing kept musiqa mizraḥit marginal to the wider popular-music scene in Israel even though by the mid-1970s it clearly possessed a large audience.

Since the 1980s, the technical quality of mizraḥi songs has gradually improved. The development of digital recordings and the CD and the constant decrease in the price of CD production began to close the gap between the mizraḥi and the mainstream popular-music industry. However, the recording quality of many CDs still reflects the quality of the cassettes (for an examination of recording technology in musiqa mizraḥit, see Finegold 1996: ch. 2).

Some Cultural Codes of Musiqa Mizraḥit

The production and consumption of musiqa mizraḥit is based on several codes, on an image and self-perception of the industry, performers, and audiences as part of the "common people." According to this image, the music belongs to the amkha, to the mizraḥi lower strata whose life is characterized by simplicity. Until the 1990s the performers were viewed not as distant figures, but as "one of us." They were expected to demonstrate an intimate and personal connection to the mizraḥi taste public.

The amkha quality of musiqa mizraḥit was clearly evidenced in the places where performances took place in the 1970s: gas stations and restaurants at prominent intersections, public halls and clubs often located in industrial zones, or family celebrations *(smaḥot)* held in neighborhoods or wedding halls. By the same token, cassettes of mizraḥi singers were sold in places clearly frequented by the amkha: the old Central Bus Station in Tel Aviv, the Maḥane Yehudah market in Jerusalem, and similar locations—not, for the most part, in record stores. Native terms used to describe the music in conversation also revealed its quality: *kef* (fun); *toseset* (effervescent); *malḥiva* (exciting); *meshagaʻat* (drives one crazy); *mefotzetzet* (explosive). The rapport of musicians with their audiences was expressed by such terms as performing *le-drishat ha-qahal* (at the audience's request), evenings filled with *sharim, okhlim, smeḥim ve-rokdim* (singing, eating, making merry, and dancing), and *le-sameaḥ et ha-qahal* (making the crowd happy).

While traditional cultural boundaries began to break down in the 1980s and musiqa mizraḥit penetrated Israeli mainstream popular music, until the 1990s there was still a clearly bounded public whose musical taste and concerns had little impact on the wider musical scene. On the monopolistic radio, musiqa mizraḥit was heard on special "corners" (ghettos," as the narrative of musiqa mizraḥit referred to this phenomenon), on programs with suggestive names such as *Libi ba-mizraḥ* (My heart is in the east), *'Agan ha-yam ha-tikhon* (Mediterranean basin), and *Meʻorav yam-tikhoni* (Mediterranean mix), more in recognition of the large listening audience and the pressure of interest groups rather than its acceptance by music editors as a genuine genre of Israeli popular music.

Musiqa mizraḥit became Western popular music overlaid with Eastern codes and ethnic colors that accurately reflected the general position of mizraḥi Jews in Israel. Marginalized by dominant sectors to become the lower and working classes of Israel, they had always aspired to full integration into Israeliness. Just as their ethnicity was instrumental in nature, in the sense that it was essentially a means of coping with a Western society that demanded conformity but was not open to them, so did early musiqa mizraḥit express their ambivalent feelings. On the one hand, musiqa mizraḥit expressed the need for identity and cohesion that lies behind ethnicity—a feeling of "us" and "them" when contrasted to mainstream popular music, often associated with Ashkenazim. On the other hand, they were socialized to Western popular music and were concerned that their music be seen as "Israeli."

The Musical Style of Musiqa Mizraḥit

Reflecting the dualism of contemporary Israeli mizraḥiyut itself, musiqa mizraḥit composers and performers developed a unique sound that was close enough to the Western tradition to be tolerated by taste-makers and yet possess a distinctly mizraḥi identity—even though this "Easternness" was neutral and could not always be associated with a specific *'edah* (Jewish ethnic group) or a particular Eastern musical style.

By the early 1980s, musiqa mizraḥit already spoke to its taste public through a series of musical codes that conformed to a style that can be called "mainstream musiqa mizraḥit." These codes cannot generally be ascribed to one of the specific musical styles from which musiqa mizraḥit emerged, such as Greek, Turkish, Arabic, or Jewish Yemenite music. These musical codes are:

- Standard Western forms of popular music, for example, phrases constructed of eight or sixteen bars of four beats, combined with short vocal and instrumental introductions or interludes recalling improvised, free-rhythm genres of Arabic or Turkish music (for example, the mawwal);

- The vocal "shaking" or "trilling" of the longer sounds in the melody (especially at the end of phrases), a phenomenon generally referred to by the musiqa mizraḥit musicians as silsulim (lit., waves or spirals);

- Static harmony;

- A cyclic rhythmic pattern in the rhythm section (usually the Arabic *masmudi*);

- Distinctive orchestration (combining Middle Eastern instruments within a rock ensemble);

- Avoidance of or blurring major/minor scales, especially by using the extremely widespread *Kurdi* and *Bayat* maqams.
- Nasal voice quality of the singers.

A similar process of conscious construction was involved in marketing a performer. Musiqa mizraḥit performers relied on live performances for their livelihood. Since they belonged to the amkha, their direct relation to their live audiences was an integral part of their music making, both in song-writing and in performance. Dialogue with the audience was essential, especially as musiqa mizraḥit was also conspicuously used for dancing. This closeness to the public could be found even in later years, in the popular television programs *Ba-taverna* (In the taverna; broadcast after 1995, and later renamed *Shishi ba-taverna*, or Friday at the taverna, on the Israel Channel 1) and *Etzel Parnas ba-taverna* (At Parnas's taverna), which opened in fall 2000 on Channel 2 (anchored by Shimon Parnas, one of the most learned media experts of musiqa mizraḥit). On these shows, which are dedicated to musiqa mizraḥit, the audience sits around food-laden tables, as would be the case at musiqa mizraḥit nightclubs, parties, and weddings, and interacts closely with the artists. Musiqa mizraḥit places more emphasis on participation than on originality, more on the use of music than its intrinsic musical qualities or lyrical content. It is essentially and consciously an art of pleasing and therefore tends to avoid explorations of aesthetic frontiers, of being avant-garde.

Mizraḥi audiences, while more or less united by class and ethnic characteristics, nevertheless come from different Middle Eastern backgrounds. Just as lyricists and adapters construct the music itself around the needs of the audience, so too do the performers build their repertories. They do this by varying the styles of the mizraḥi music they sing. While the mainstream style is based on Greek/Turkish/Yemenite music, many ethnic substyles, such as Persian, Kurdish, Indian, Moroccan, Arabic, or Spanish, are grafted onto it. These comprise the "ethnic colors" of a singer's repertory, stereo-typical musical elements that are immediately recognizable to an audience from a particular ethnic background and that create the excitement of the performance and the bond between the performer and the audience.

· · ·

Musiqa mizraḥit crystallized into a clearly defined cultural context for making popular music during the 1970s and 1980s. Chronologically, it followed the rise of the "Black Panthers," a militant group of young mizraḥim (inspired by African-American politics), who, in the early 1970s, led a series of demonstrations and riots to protest the wide socioeconomic gap between mizraḥim and Ashkenazim. The rise of musiqa mizraḥit thus coincided with the emergence of mizraḥiyut as a local sense of identity, a variant of Israeliness. This overlap made musiqa mizraḥit the quintessential cultural form associated with mizraḥiyut.

The very fact that mizraḥiyut has been articulated as a hybrid, as a mélange of various cultural sources, perfectly served the claim and insistence of its speakers that this is an Israeli creation, a Jewish native cultural construct that could have taken shape only in Israel. By insisting on mizraḥiyut as an experience of sameness, of collective identity, its speakers implicitly accepted the homogenized image of Eastern Jews portrayed by the cultural mechanism of Hebrewism, that is, an image that coalesces the differences between, for example, Moroccan, Yemenite, and Iraqi Jews and looks at them as one entity.

The difference between the self-image of mizraḥiyut and that portrayed by dominant Israeliness clearly lay in issues of meaning and legitimacy. While Hebrewist and later global Israeliness portrayals of mizraḥiyut tended to stigmatize and label the emergent cultural context as inferior, the cultural producers associated with mizraḥiyut took pride in their culture, insisted on its "authenticity" and Israeliness, and demanded legitimacy and recognition.

The single most crucial ingredient in the cultural hybrid of mizraḥiyut and musiqa mizraḥit, one that seems to lie at the core of the issue of legitimacy, is what can be called "Arabness." The cultural project of Zionism and Israeliness included a process of de-Arabization of Jews arriving in Israel from Arab countries (Shenhav 2002). Eastern Jews cooperated in this process and aspired to abandon their Arabness. But their strong link to their Arab past could not be completely erased. The continuing presence of Arab elements within the general construct of mizraḥiyut made it susceptible to "games of inclusion and exclusion that fixed the mizraḥi as a person who 'belongs-and-not-belongs' [to Israeliness], as 'one of us yet alien.' In this conflicting situation, mizraḥim in Israel attempted to construct practices of integration" (Shenhav 2002: 109). These practices included various forms of appropriation, juxtaposition, and bricolage of cultural elements. Thus, for example, derogatory terms such as *chaḥ-chaḥ* (low class, "greaser"), *dfuqim* (screwed up), and *freḥa* (an oriental chick) occasionally found their way into mizraḥiyut vernacular, transforming them into in-group symbols. The word freḥa underwent a memorable twist of meaning as a source of pride with Ofra Haza's hit "Shir ha-freḥa" (Song of the freḥa; lyrics, Assi Dayan; music, Tzvika Pick) in 1978.

As for musiqa mizraḥit itself, two parallel strategies of struggle emerged during the 1980s within this general cultural context. One was to increasingly "Israelize" the music by adding elements associated with SLI to the mix; the other consisted of retaining the typical sound of musiqa mizraḥit, yet insisting on the Israeliness of this type of music. The first strategy is associated with the work of singer Haim Moshe, the second with that of singer Zohar Argov and the musical and ideological work of Avihu Medina.

Through these struggles, the status of musiqa mizraḥit evolved continuously within the field of Israeli popular music, and with it, its musical contents, manner of production, and contexts of performance. By the mid-1980s, musiqa mizraḥit was a well-established component of Israeli popular culture, and a new era had begun in which the major issue at stake was, from the perspective of the mizraḥi artists, the positioning of this music within Israeli culture at large.

10 From "Neighborhood" to the Charts

Musiqa Mizraḥit and Legitimacy

Ever after its formative period (ca. 1970–85), musiqa mizraḥit continued to move into the national scene of popular music, battling the stigmas attached to it and expanding its public. This process reached its peak in the late 1990s, when musiqa mizraḥit contested other forms of popular music for the very definition of Israeliness.

MUSICAL PARADOXES: THE STORY OF THE SONG "ḤANALE HITBALBELA"

Haim Moshe and Zohar Argov were the singers whose careers served as the platform for musiqa mizraḥit's claim for legitimacy. However, insofar as the particular circumstances of individual figures during the crucial period of the late 1970s and early 1980s are exemplary, the eclectic nature of musiqa mizraḥit is best demonstrated through the study of the birth of one particular song. "Ḥanale hitbalbela" is an emblematic example of the complex processes that shaped the repertory of mizraḥi artists.

The "disputed territory" of Israeli popular music was often presented as a set of opposites, such as that between Shirei Eretz Yisrael and musiqa mizraḥit (see Horowitz 1994, 1997; Regev 1986). This opposition, however, is the result of the "narrative of confrontation" between the mizraḥi artists and the establishment that was constructed in later periods. The "founding fathers" of musiqa mizraḥit did include Shirei Eretz Yisrael in their repertory, simply because their perception of Israeliness was more integrative.

From this more integrative perspective of musiqa mizraḥit, one can understand how and why the song "Ḥanale hitbalbela" (Ḥanale was rattled; see Seroussi 1999), first recorded by Lehaqat tzlilei ha-'ud, became one of the first smash hits of musiqa mizrahit. The song was originally written as a pizmon by canonic poet Natan Alterman, for the Purim (Jewish carnival) celebrations held in Tel Aviv in the early 1930s. Alterman set his parodic poem, about a couple of out-of-towners arriving in cosmopolitan Tel Aviv for this festival, to the melody of a klezmer tune that he remembered from his home town in Eastern Europe. The song later circulated as an urban folk song (referred to as *shirei rehov*, street songs) with a surrealist text about a quarreling couple that finds itself facing an unwanted baby whose origins nobody appears to know. This new text, a remake by Alterman himself (personal communication with Nahumi Hartzion), departs from Alterman's original and retains only its opening stanza. Sung, for example, at youth movement gatherings, "Hanale hitbalbela" belonged to the invented Israeli urban folk culture.

The transformation of this song into a mizrahi hit is located in its new context and manner of performance, rather than in its musical or poetic content. As an urban folk song, it became a standard in the repertory of the early 1970s haflot held in Qerem ha-teymanim—the parties in the Yemenite neighborhood of Tel Aviv that served as the cradle of musiqa mizrahit. The recorded version of "Hanale hitbalbela" by Lehaqat tzilelei ha-'ud, a version that certainly reflected the actual performance of the song at parties and weddings, included the characteristic, driving mizrahi cyclic rhythmic pattern in the bass, the bouzouki-like electric guitar, the nasal vocal style, and typical Yemenite pronunciation of Hebrew. Moreover, in the recording, the song is linked to another, "Heviani el beit ha-yayin" ("He hath brought me to the banqueting-house," a verse from the *Song of Songs* 2:4), reflecting the live performances of the bands.

Thus, as one of the earliest (and rare for its time) instances in which a musiqa mizrahit song became a national hit, "Hanale hitbalbela" came to epitomize the hybrid nature of the genre: a traditional Eastern European Jewish tune, with its lyrics by the canonic Israeli poet, performed using a mixture of electric and traditional instruments, and arranged in an "orientalist" manner.

The seeming paradox of "Hanale hitbalbela" is symptomatic of the ambivalent musical codes of musiqa mizrahit. The Eastern European tune, whose form bore traces of its Romanian or Balkan origins, was easily transformed into a mizrahi one by means of its special delivery and orchestration. However, the barriers imposed by its ethnic contexts of performance were broken only after this "street song," which had previously circulated only in the oral tradition, was successfully recorded.

MIZRAḤIYUT IN SEARCH OF HEBREWISM: HAIM MOSHE

Studying the careers of individual mizraḥi artists illuminates the path of musiqa mizraḥit from the fringes of Israeli ethnicity into the mainstream. Haim Moshe and Zohar Argov are two of the most representative performers of musiqa mizraḥit. We selected them not only because of their widespread popularity, sales figures, and the shared opinions of mass-media critics, but also because the developments of their musical careers reflect a key social aspect of musiqa mizraḥit: the limitations imposed by the establishment and by the mizraḥi public on the attitudes, repertory, performance contexts, and lifestyle of mizraḥi artists.

Haim Moshe was born in 1956 in the humble working-class neighborhood of Morasha on the outskirts of Ramat Hasharon near Tel Aviv, to a Yemenite family that arrived in Israel in 1948. He studied at the local secular state-run elementary school but also attended the Yemenite *ḥeder*, the traditional religious school. His home was religious, and there he had the opportunity to absorb the traditional musical repertories of the Yemenite Jews.

From an early age his musical talents were apparent. By age six, he sang in the synagogue and at family parties. As a teenager, he sang Yemenite, Greek, Turkish, and Arab songs at local parties and weddings, but at this early stage he did not yet entertain the possibility of a singing career. He worked as a foreman in a print shop and enrolled in the army as a regular soldier; that is, like most other future musiqa mizraḥit performers, he was not a member of a lehaqah tzvait.

In 1976, after completing his military service, and while still working in the print shop, for a short time he joined the Lehaqat tzlilei ha-qerem ensemble, appearing with Moshe Ben Mush and Daklon. Like most mizraḥi singers, he performed at ḥaflot, occasional parties in rented halls or private homes, and weddings. His repertory was influenced by the Yemenite substyle of musiqa mizraḥit, reflecting his musical background as well as his audience's tastes. In 1976 and 1978 he released two cassettes that included Yemenite and Arab songs with Hebrew texts, some with religious content and others that included stigmatized terms of reference (such as freḥa) and themes conspicuously used by mizraḥi singers as in-group symbols—the mother, the neighborhood, the Jewish people *(ha-'am)*. It was the latter that put musiqa mizraḥit in a position that sometimes overlapped that of SLI. But musiqa mizraḥit uses quasi-biblical Hebrew terms to denote collective identity and, therefore, relates to traditional Jewish identity rather than modern nationhood.

Moshe's breakthrough onto the national scene came in 1983 with the release of his third cassette *Ahavat hayyai* (The love of my life), which sold an estimated 200,000 copies, a very large number in Israeli terms. This cassette, which followed Moshe's success at the Oriental Song Festival, included two smash hits: "Linda, Linda," a popular Lebanese tune (sung by Moshe in Arabic), and the Yemenite-tinged title song "Ahavat hayyai" (lyrics, Sasson Tzan'ani; music, Moshe Ben Mush), amidst other Hebrew songs and covers of Arabic and Greek songs. The arrangements on this recording were more sophisticated than in his earlier releases in the 1970s and appealed to a much wider mizrahi audience.

Between 1984 and 1989, Moshe released an average of two cassettes per year, selling between 30,000 and 60,000 copies of each. Following his success in 1983, he began a steady path in the direction of mainstream Israeli pop music (Halper et al. 1992). This process included:

- performing in mainstream venues, such as the summer concert series at the amphitheater in HaYarkon Park in north Tel Aviv, the children's song festival, kibbutzim, Independence Day festivities, and, on Independence Day in 1990, at the nationally televised ceremony of the prestigious Israel Prize ceremony;

- appearing regularly on the media, particularly on the IBA Channel 1 Friday night TV show that, before the liberalization of the media in the 1990s, had the highest viewer ratings;

- breaking off with the impresario who had "created" him and was identified with his more ethnic period and establishing his own marketing operation;

- introducing non-mizrahi musical styles into his repertory, particularly Shirei Eretz Yisrael and more neutral Mediterranean songs, such as the 1986 hit "Todah" (Thank you; originally a Greek song called "Ola Kala," written by S. Kouyioumtis and popularized by singer Yiorgo Dalaras; Hebrew lyrics by Uzi Hitmann);

- asking mainstream Ashkenazi composers such as Nurit Hirsh, Naomi Shemer, and Yitzhak Klepter to compose original songs for him, and, even more relevant to this process of change, being offered original songs by them (singing original songs replaces the common practice of most mizrahi singers of "constructing" songs by covering Arabic, Turkish, and Greek tunes or motifs with Hebrew texts); and

- using lavish arrangements in recordings and live performances including strings and woodwinds instead of the regular mizrahi backup group (drums, synthesizer, bass, electric guitar, and bouzouki).

Newspaper articles of the mid-1980s reflected the process of change in Moshe's career in published profiles with suggestive headlines such as "From Farid el-Atrash to Naomi Shemer," "Haim Moshe Changes Direction," and "Haim Moshe: Between Black and White." Moshe's mizrahi public and accused him of *ishtaknezut* ("Ashkenizing" himself) and of "betraying" his original followers.

This attitude requires interpretation. Haim Moshe's explosion into the mainstream of the Israeli pop scene contrasted with the growing perception by mizrahi artists such as Avihu Medina of discrimination by the Ashkenazi-dominated media. This dissatisfaction appears to be related to a web of boundaries that limited musiqa mizrahit and its artists. These boundaries seemed to be self-generated and self-limiting, particularly the idea that "you can't or shouldn't aspire to too much," and that "you will remain downtrodden no matter what you do." Texts on subjects such as mother, soccer, the beloved homeland, and the father reciting the sabbath prayers were stigmatized by middle-class Ashkenazim as signaling a low type of "common folk": close-knit families, sports fans, right-wing populism, and religious observance. The music very successfully consolidated this pan-Sephardi identity, and that was precisely the reason that it was self-limiting.

Musiqa mizrahit took the stigmas and stereotypes imposed by outsiders, and by using them prominently in songs, transformed them into positive in-group symbols. While these symbols were directed at mizrahim, at the same time they carried a loaded hostile message to the dominant group. For this reason, Moshe eliminated all references to most of these symbols in his recordings in the late 1980s, while adding to his repertory *shirei meshorerim* (lit., songs of the poets), a term used to refer to musical settings of poems by elite poets (as opposed to pop lyricists). He did not apologize for this attitude, but rather justified it as a natural outcome of his aspiration to be accepted: "My style did not really change because I was considered a mizrahi singer. It can be said that it developed. I added to what I had in the past. Just as an employee advances upward in the factory, so I progressed" (quoted in Levi 1998: 143).

Moshe's pragmatic attitude to the concept of success shows that the subversive element often attached to musiqa mizrahit is somewhat exaggerated. For more than twenty years and through sixteen albums, he slowly climbed the ladder leading to the hegemonic consensus of Israeliness. Yet, despite his efforts to conceal his Yemenite Hebrew accent, his voice remained easily identifiable to audiences as mizraḥi.

ZOHAR ARGOV

Despite the similarities in the general profile of their careers, Zohar Argov's story was entirely different from that of Haim Moshe. Argov's public career was short, meteoric, and eventful, lasting for only about seven years (ca. 1980–87). Born Zohar Urkavi in 1955, he grew up in a poor, delinquency-plagued neighborhood in the city of Rishon Le-Tzion (south of Tel Aviv), the first of ten children in a family with a dysfunctional father. Like Moshe, as a child Zohar sang in the local Yemenite synagogue. Because of his family's precarious economic situation, he had to leave home at the age of thirteen to become a construction worker.

Argov's rise to stardom began after he was discovered by studio owner and guitarist Yehuda Keisar (who was also one of the original members of Lehaqat tzlilei ha-'ud). Keisar released Argov's first cassette, *Elinor*, in 1980. Its title song was one of the greatest musiqa mizraḥit hits ever, parallel only to Moshe's "Linda Linda." In the same year, Argov appeared on a television feature on the prime-time Friday night magazine that dealt with the "phenomenon" of musiqa mizraḥit. This was the first time that the IBA had ever given any consideration to this musical genre.

Two years later, in 1982, Argov won first prize in the IBA-sponsored Oriental Song Festival. Since the festival was televised, Argov was exposed for the first time to a national audience. The winning song was one of Avihu Medina's greatest hits, "Ha-peraḥ be-ganni" (The flower in my garden). No less important than the song itself was the lavish pop/rock arrangement by Romanian-born Nansi Brandes, who coached Argov and produced two of his most important records: *Nakhon le-ha-yom* (True for today [1982]) and *Kakh 'ovrim ḥayyai* (This is how my life goes by [1983]). After his success at the festival, his ascent to stardom was meteoric. Argov was nicknamed "Ha-melekh" (the King), which reflected his status in the eyes of audiences and critics alike.

HA-PERAḤ BE-GANI (MEDINA)

I remember you from a clear and bright spring day,
And since then I knew very well that I would not give up.
Because you were the apple of my eye, every day and every night,
For me you were an angel of God appearing from the mist,

I wanted to ask for your hand, I wanted to tell you
The secret of the love which I jealously keep in my heart

I just wanted to say: I loved, I loved and it is over
But I did not dare, even when it was too late.

Refrain

You are my whole world at dawn, you are mine all day
You are my whole world at night, you are the dream
You are in my blood, in my spirit and in my heart
You are the sweet fragrance, the flower in my garden.

Unlike Moshe, however, Argov never consciously aspired to win the acceptance and approval of dominant Israeliness. He became consensual by remaining faithful to his voice and stage presence. His repertory was never committed to the mainstream of musiqa mizrahit. It was an eclectic repertory reminiscent of that of the grassroots founders of musiqa mizrahit and included canonic songs from the mainstream Israeli repertory, such as "Yerushalayim shel zahav" (Jerusalem of gold) by Naomi Shemer, as well as Hebrew translations of European ballads. Audiences were won over not by the contents of the songs that Argov performed, but rather by his unique and piercing mizrahi delivery and by his commanding stage presence. Anything he sang was cherished by his fans, particularly the women. Argov was thus a true heir to earlier generations of mizrahi (especially Yemenite) entertainers, who were concerned with the mizrahi style of delivery of the songs rather than their content.

Argov's untimely death in 1987 further intensified his heroic status. He committed suicide in jail, while awaiting trial on drug-related offenses. Following this event, his image came to be portrayed along the lines of a tragic hero who authentically expressed, in his songs and in his life, the feelings of a large, culturally discriminated against sector of Israeli society. This image was largely based on interviews of Argov in the media, in which he described the tensions he faced as a successful singer:

> What do I lack? Warmth! I live alone in Tel Aviv. I have no friends. . . . I have a Mercedes and a penthouse with a jacuzzi. Thus, am I another person? . . . I came from a poor neighborhood. . . . I can see the distance people take from me. . . . Sometimes I stop [the car] at a traffic light and people shout: "You are big now, ah, you made it!" . . . I want to tell them that my soul has not changed. (quoted in Levi 1998: 120)

Argov's death catapulted him to a level of national consciousness that no other mizrahi or popular artist had reached in the past. His stature actually grew after his death. His gravestone (in the shape of a guitar) became a site of pilgrimage and communion, not unlike the graves of international rock musicians who died prematurely or violently.

A further dimension was added to the cult of Argov that reflects patterns similar to the worship of saintly sages among mizraḥi Jews. On the anniversary of his death, a remembrance reunion of fans and colleagues is held, like the *hillulah* (remembrance ceremony on the date of death) for great rabbis (see Ben-Ari and Bilu 1987). Moreover, the attempt of his son Gili Argov to launch a singing career can also be interpreted as an endeavor (which failed) to create a dynasty, not unlike the rabbinical dynasties, by keeping the spirit (or rather the voice) of the revered artist alive through his direct offspring.

Several television documentaries; a play, *The King* (by leading playwright Shmuel Hasfari); and a feature film, *Zohar* (directed by Eran Riklis [1993]) further gave shape to the story of Argov's life as a humble Yemenite boy from a poor neighborhood who rose to stardom despite the marginality of his art. The film even added a layer to the martyrological narrative of Argov as the mizraḥi artist "making it" despite all adversity. It reasserted the legend of the "King" as an innocent victim of vicious impresarios who exploited his natural gift and relentlessly pressured him, eventually forcing him into the abyss.

Argov thus became a national icon of musiqa mizraḥit, a figure that defied all established boundaries in Israeli popular music and changed its map forever. Listening to Argov became en vogue even for the Ashkenazi elite, which only a decade earlier had scorned musiqa mizraḥit as a low form of popular music. The revival of some of his songs by mainstream rock groups and singers in the 1990s represent the de facto recognition of musiqa mizraḥit as mainstream Israeli culture.

ARTICULATING AN IDEOLOGY OF DISCRIMINATION: AVIHU MEDINA TALKS

The path paved by Moshe and Argov was followed in the 1980s and 1990s by performers such as Margalit Tsanani, Eli Louzon, Yshai Levi, Zehava Ben, and many others. The contest for the essence of Israeliness in popular music embodied in the music of these artists led to the articulation of what might be defined as a "narrative of musical discrimination." This narrative emerged from the sense on the part of musiqa mizraḥit artists and producers that they were rejected by the establishment, particularly by the state-funded media. This rejection was perceived as a de-legitimization of musiqa mizraḥit as an authentic form of Israeli popular music. The public airing of this narrative became the hallmark of a relentless campaign by Avihu Medina, one of the most influential composers of this style (more than four hundred songs) and, since 1991, one of its major performers as well.

Medina's dossier includes many of the canonic songs of the musiqa mizraḥit repertory, such as "Shabeḥi Yerushalaiym" (Praise Jerusalem), popularized by Daklon; "Ha-peraḥ be-ganni" (The flower in my garden), performed by Zohar Argov; and "Al tashlikheni le-'et ziqnah" (Do not abandon me when I get old), sung by Shimi Tabori. "Shabeḥi Yerushalayim" is an example of an archetypal musiqa mizraḥit song. The text is religious (Psalms 147:12–13) and has nationalistic connotations (the consensual topic of Jerusalem) and its ubiquitous melody is in maqam Kurd. The song was traditionalized and today can be heard in synagogue services.

Medina's dedication to the public cause of musiqa mizraḥit is apparent in his statement that his output as a composer was meager because "80 per cent of my time I was busy in the wars against discrimination" (Boaz Cohen, "Medina ze Ani," *Yedioth Ahronoth*, April 3, 1998). During the last two decades, Medina has expressed his grievances in many interviews given to major newspapers. Especially revealing interviews with Medina appeared on the occasion of Israel's fiftieth anniversary in 1998. Cleverly playing on the literal meaning of his surname *(medinah* in Hebrew means "state"), the articles were titled "50 to Medina" or "Medina is me"; the latter is a play on the famous saying by Louis XIV, "L'etat est moi." In these interviews, Medina stresses, in different ways, four basic, related ideas: (1) there is conspiratory discrimination against musiqa mizraḥit by music editors of radio (in particular, Galei Tzahal) and television stations; (2) this conspiracy dates back to a period when "Israeliness" equaled "Westernness," and this period is over; (3) until the start of his own public campaign there was no protest by musiqa mizraḥit artists against discrimination because Eastern Jews are submissive to structures of power due to their education in totalitarian regimes and their lack of experience in open democracies; (4) there is no power now that can halt the cultural integration of Israel into the Middle East, and this integration means adopting an orientalized culture: "Everybody here will be a Middle-Easterner. We are going in that direction and those who do not see it are blind" (Boaz Cohen, "Medina ze Ani," *Yedioth Ahronoth*, April 3, 1998).

As a result of this analysis, he concludes that musiqa mizraḥit is the only authentic Israeli music because it reflects "a synthesis of East and West" (Boaz Cohen, "Medina ze Ani," *Yedioth Ahronoth*, April 3, 1998). It should therefore be allowed slots of airtime in the media that suit this status.

> The [music] editors fight the zemer mizraḥi; they are afraid of it. They know that the moment they give air time to this music, there will not be room for their thing. . . . Because our music is the Eretz-Yisraeli [music]. . . . The media still does not broadcast consensus. It is the media

of the establishment. People work on behalf [of the establishment]. They do not reflect the existing reality. . . . They created ghettoes to play our music. . . . In my opinion the [music] editors and disk jockeys of these stations should be thrown out. . . . They betrayed the public's trust. (Shimon Ifargan, "50 shanah le-Medina," *Kol ha-darom*, August 28, 1998)

The campaign against alleged media discrimination led to the establishment of AZIT (an acronym for Amutat ha-zemer ha-yam tikhoni, the Mediterranean Song Association), an independent organization dedicated to promoting the interests of musiqa mizrahit. Some critics have pointed out that the heads of this organization, such as Avigdor Ben Mush and Asher Reuveni, own the largest recording companies of musiqa mizrahit. Thus their interest in creating a lobby to promote musiqa mizrahit in the media was interpreted as a concealed campaign to increase their profits. However, not only producers but also artists such as Avihu Medina are active in AZIT.

In support of its claims, AZIT recruited statistical research prepared by academics. Academic research "proved" the conspiracy against musiqa mizrahit with facts. Moreover, one scholar warned that "when [musiqa mizrahit] is removed from the consensus [for example, by not broadcasting musiqa mizrahit songs in prime-time programs], Israelis are stripped of their mizrahiyut ["Easternness"] and the mizrahim from their Israeliness. (Ayelet Ben-Zvi, quoted by Rami Hazut and Tamar Trabelsi-Hadad, "Nevadeh sheha-musiqa ha-mizrahit tushma' yoter ba-radio" [We shall ensure that musiqa mizrahit is heard more on the radio], *Yedioth Ahronoth*, November 11, 1997)

AZIT succeeded in creating a public debate on the issue of discrimination of musiqa mizrahit and even parliamentary intervention in this issue. The Knesset Education Committee debated AZIT's grievances in 1997 at a meeting in which the director-general of the Israel Broadcasting Authority and the head of the state radio stations participated. Politicians expressed, as expected of Israeli politicians when dealing with the hot issue of ethnic tension, their sympathy for the arguments of AZIT. However, they politely dodged the issue by not taking any specific action except for vague recommendations to the IBA and a promise to follow up on the issue.

The mistrust that Avihu Medina and AZIT members demonstrated toward the establishment should not, however, be interpreted as a subversive political agenda. Quite the contrary, Medina's goal was to become, or, more precisely, to replace, the establishment. In one interview, he praised former Prime Minister Shimon Peres for intervening on his behalf when he was banned from presenting a popular midnight radio show, Tziporei layla

(Night birds) on Galei Tzahal. When asked about his appeal to the office of a prime minister from the Labor Party (that is, the Israeli Ashkenazi establishment), Medina replied without any regrets, "This is what life in Israel has taught me. You do not receive rights, you take them, and by force." On another occasion he situated himself in the midst of the gallery of canonic Israeli poets. Complaining about the shallow texts of many musiqa mizrahit lyricists, he said, "There is a certain public who does not know who Bialik [Israel's national poet], Tchernichowsky, Avihu Medina, Naomi Shemer are" (Alon Caspi, "Mafsiq lehilahem," *Davar*, May 12, 1994).

This yearning to become "the" Israeli cultural establishment is backed by another argument, namely, that the label musiqa mizrahit was after all invented by the media, as part of its campaign of discrimination. Anonymous "systems" conspire against musiqa mizrahit because it has "Jewish roots or is ornamented by Eastern sounds." These "systems" are defined by Medina as "the Israeli culture as it is presented in the media." Thus "the very definition of [the label] zemer mizrahi is an invention of the media that derives from its lack of orientation in the field. The materials we are talking about are simply Israeli" (Caspi, "Mafsiq lehilahem," *Davar*, May 12, 1994).

Avihu Medina's rhetoric is not shared by all musiqa mizrahit artists. An attempt to boycott Galei Tzahal by recalling all the CDs of musiqa mizrahit from the station's record library was not supported by distinguished mizrahi performers, such as female singer Zehava Ben, one of the prominent musiqa mizrahit stars in the second half of the 1990s (see Eran Hadas, "Hazamarim ha-mizrahim le-Galatz: al tashmi'u otanu yoter" [The mizrahi singers to Galatz: Do not play our songs any more], *Yedioth Ahronoth*, October 10, 1998). Moreover, in the eyes of some journalists (for example, Caspi, "Mafsiq lehilahem," *Davar*, May 12, 1994), Medina is already a part of the Israeli consensus. After he published his book of songs (Medina 1994), an event perceived as the recognition or canonization of the work of a popular song composer, media critics wondered whether Medina's continuing and relentless attacks on the media were not part of a publicity strategy. Even radio presenter Shimon Parnas, who is considered a media pioneer for his programs dedicated to musiqa mizrahit (which in 1998–99 included an extensive prime-time radio series on its history), wondered about the goals of AZIT and Medina after he himself had been accused as being part of the establishment: "They [AZIT, Medina] want [to promote their] singers, not the music. They were not interested in the 'war of culture' [a term used for the battle over Israeliness in Israeli public discourse]. And in the present situation, when the musiqa mizrahit yisraelit—I rather prefer this definition—is the consensus, they are still not satisfied. Now they have no reason to fight" (quoted in Oren 1998). The continued dissatisfaction of Medina and his peers appears to be related to the self-generated and self-limiting web of boundaries described above, particularly the idea that you will remain downtrodden no matter what you do.

MUSIQA MIZRAḤIT AND RELIGION

Musiqa mizraḥit includes many musical expressions that challenge the link between contemporary popular music and secular society. Moving among synagogues, traditional weddings, and nightclubs is a characteristic of the careers of several stars of musiqa mizraḥit. The ambivalence between the realm of the sacred and the mundane in musiqa mizraḥit is reflected in the contents of the first successful commercial recordings by early mizraḥi singers such as Jo Amar, and by the first bands, such as Lehaqat tzlilei ha-ʿud and Lehaqat tzlilei ha-qerem. All include religious songs *(piyyutim)* mixed (sometimes in the same take) with secular ones.

Moreover, several notable singers of musiqa mizraḥit became *baʿalei teshuvah* (returnees in repentance, that is, orthodox Jews). This transformation is part of a movement of returning to roots by mizraḥim of the second and third generation, which has gained momentum since the early 1970s. The religious reaction of the 1980s followed the left-wing political activism of small militant groups within the mizraḥi community, such as the Black Panthers (see Cohen 1972). The Westernized culture of the absorbing Israeli establishment was blamed for the economic failure, social marginalization, and the loss of traditional cultural identity by the immigrant mizraḥi Jews. Groups such as the Black Panthers, however, were not successful in mobilizing the mizraḥi masses, who leaned more toward the conservative right wing of the political spectrum. They also underestimated the strong attachment of the mizraḥi Jews to tradition, even while they did not meticulously observe all the religious precepts.

The political expression of these deep and repressed religious sentiments can be found in the meteoric rise of the political party called Shas (an acronym that stands for Shomrei torah sfaradim, meaning Sephardi Torah Guardians), established in 1981, and which fifteen years later became the third largest political party in the Knesset. The leaders of Shas, many of them young ordained rabbis, shrewdly manipulated musiqa mizraḥit to attract nonobservant mizraḥi youth. For example, meetings dedicated to their missionary activities included appearances of musiqa mizraḥit singers and bands who had returned to religious observance. These rallies typically combined musical performances with homilies by leading rabbis, particularly by Rabbi Ovadiah Yossef, the spiritual leader of the Shas Party. Rabbi Ovadiah is well known for his predilection for Arabic music and even ruled in favor of setting religious songs in Hebrew to popular Arabic melodies (Yossef 1954–55).

Most of the songs performed at Shas meetings are, musically speaking, indistinguishable from mizraḥi secular songs. Only the texts of the songs shift entirely (usually to biblical verses) or partially (by changing few words of the original song). This represents the well-documented phenomenon of *contrafactum*, the transformation of a secular song into a religious one by changing the text while retaining the melody, which is typical of both Ashkenazi and mizraḥi Jewish music. The phenomenon can be found in Hebrew sacred poetry of the Sephardi Jews from the sixteenth century until the present (see Seroussi and Weich-Shahak 1990–91). In the case of musiqa mizraḥit, the practice was applied to modern-day popular music as well. A notable example of this process of composition in the mid-1980s was the hit "Ani ḥozer bi-tshuvah" (I return in repentance) by Rabbi Zion Waqnin. Originally a cover version of the Italian song "L'italiano" (The Italian) by Cristian Minelono and Toto Cotugno, who won second prize at the San Remo festival in 1981–82, it was first set to Hebrew lyrics in 1984 and performed by singer Doron Mazar as "Ani ḥozer ha-bayta" (I return home). By changing the word *ha-bayta* (home) to *bi-tshuvah* (in repentance) in the refrain, Waqnin created a song that represented the sentiments of the growing movement of "return in repentance" that had begun to spread among mizraḥi Jews. In this way, a mainstream European popular song was transformed into a mizraḥi song by a shift in the content of the text and the context of its performance.

This phenomenon created copyright problems. The following newspaper report, referring to Beni Elbaz, one of the most distinguished musiqa mizraḥit singers to "return in repentance" and the "house singer" of the Shas Party, vividly raises the issue:

> Beni Elbaz, who was previously a *yam tikhoni* [Mediterranean] singer, and is presently a *maḥzir bi-tshuvah* [preacher of repentance], found in the Bible the answer to the showy question "Where are those like that man / who was like a weeping willow" [Refrain of the popular song "Ha-ish ha-hu" (That man), by Nathan Yonathan, set to music by Shlomo Artzi]. One year ago he recorded [the song] "That Man" and provided it with a new name: "Ben Yokheved ha-tzaddik Moshe" [The son of Yokheved, the righteous Moses]. He strictly followed the melody by Shlomo Artzi, but instead of the lyrics by Nathan Yonathan, he sang,

"Where are those like Moses the righteous." This song and nine others
(including "Latet" by Boaz Shar'abi, and songs by Maria Carey and Jean
Jack Goldman) to which he also added "holy words" are included by
Elbaz in his album titled *Ḥozrim le-aba, mi l'Adonay elay* [We return
to the father, those who favor Adonay (come) to me]. (Anonymous,
"Aqum neged ha-ḥazarah bi-tshuvah shel Elbaz" [The Society of
Authors and Composers against the return in repentance of Elbaz],
Yedioth Ahronoth, 7 Leylot, April 4, 1998, p. 9)

The entry of musiqa mizraḥit into the religious experience of the Eastern
Jews is a logical consequence of its status as a representation of the pan-
mizraḥi identity. As this identity moved toward religious forms of expression, the musiqa mizraḥit system shifted to religious contents and contexts.
Thus spiritual assemblies replaced nightclubs, and biblical verses replaced
expressions of the mundane experiences of terrestrial love. Yet the music
shared by both contexts allowed performers to fluctuate between the two.

INROADS TO MAINSTREAM:
OFRA HAZA, ETHNIX, AND TEA-PACKS

Our examination of musiqa mizraḥit began in the previous chapter with a
discussion of the status and the perception by critics of ethnically oriented
artists such as Shlomo Bar and Yehuda Polikar, who have contributed to the
dissemination of "other" sounds within the non-mizraḥi sectors of Israeli
popular music since the late 1970s. In the late 1980s and 1990s various other
pop and rock artists continued this trend. Inspired by the growing success of
musiqa mizraḥit, these musicians blurred the dichotomy between pop/rock
and musiqa mizraḥit and thus paved the road that eventually led to the
breakthrough of musiqa mizraḥit into mainstream pop.

First and foremost among these artists is Ofra Haza. On the basis of her
humble beginnings as a young singer of Yemenite origin in the Shekhunat
ha-tiqvah neighborhood of south Tel Aviv, she could have been expected at
best to achieve a local career as a musiqa mizraḥit singer. Yet she succeeded
in becoming one of the most distinguished female singers of mainstream
Israeli pop, together and in competition with singers such as Yardena Arazi
and Rita. Eventually, Haza became the most globally successful Israeli pop
artist ever.

Her national breakthrough came in 1979, when she sang the provocative
"Shir ha-freḥa" (lyrics, Assi Dayan; music, Tzvika Pick; from the film
Schlager, directed by Assi Dayan). The song represented a vindication of the
pride of low-status mizraḥi females in an Ashkenazi-dominated society.

After *Schlager,* her early albums were marked by a conscious attempt to distance herself from musiqa mizrahit and by the embrace of simple, catchy, middle-of-the-road pop. This phase culminated in 1983, when she represented Israel at the Eurovision song contest and won second place with the song "Hay" (Alive; referring to *'am-Israel,* the Jewish people; lyrics, Ehud Manor; music, Avi Toledano).

In the mid-1980s she recorded three albums of SLI songs, arranged for her by Shem Tov Levy. It was only after she established herself as a mainstream pop singer that Haza reached back to her own family roots, as did Yehuda Polikar, but in a nonrock fashion. Her album *Shirei Teyman* (Yemenite songs [1984]) consisted of traditional Jewish-Yemenite songs, arranged to sound authentic and ethnic. Two tracks from that album—"Galbi" and "Im nin'alu"—were electronically remixed and became international dance-floor hits, making her a salient exponent of "world beat." Her international success was further consolidated with the albums *Shaday* (1988) and *Desert Wind* (1989), both produced abroad and including performances in English. Her low-key local career after 1986 did not diminish her popularity, because her global success became a source of national pride. At her occasional performances in Israel during the 1990s, however, she retained the Eretz-Yisraeli and MOR tone of her mid-1980s albums (see her triple compilation album, *Manginat ha-lev* [Melody of the heart], issued in 2000). Her untimely death in 1999 at the age of forty-one was a shock to the Israeli public.

Haza can be perceived as a new kind of mizrahi mediator, continuing the trend set by Bracha Zefira half a century before. The mainstream Ashkenazi Israeli public accepted Haza's Yemenite songs as belonging to Israeliness (as did the Yishuv with Zefira's), but not as a threat to its basically European identity. She opened the public's ears to the sounds of oriental Jewish tradition, but within the strict hierarchy of the mainstream popular-music industry. Her career demonstrated that mizrahi sounds and singers have a better chance of being accepted in Israel by the public at large and the dominant forces in the field when they come from a general pop position (and not from the core of musiqa mizrahit itself). This point was made even more explicitly in the work of the ethnic-tinged rock bands Ethnix and Tea-Packs.

Indeed, the last stage in the process of introducing ethnic sounds into the Israeli mainstream can be seen in the rock bands, especially Ethnix. Overtly dedicated to "Western dance and rock with mizrahi motives" (see *Ha-osef shel Ethnix* [The collection of Ethnix], 1995, liner note 6), Ethnix became a successful rock band during the 1990s. In some of the songs, the band combined Eastern instruments such as the bouzouki, the 'ud, and the darabuka and experimented with materials more akin to typical musiqa mizrahit than any previous Israeli rock band. In 1991, the band released the album *Masala*. It included the song "Kitorneh Masala" in which the already successful band collaborated with one of the then-rising female singers of musiqa mizraḥit, Zehava Ben. The appearance of Ben on an Ethnix album opened a new era of collaborations between rock musicians and bands and musiqa mizraḥit artists.

The path of Ethnix toward ethnicity accelerated in later albums. For example, the song "Yeled Marrakesh" (Marrakesh kid) released in 1993 (included on the album *Atah* [1994]) employs an electronically sampled bouzouki and heavy mizraḥi inflections by bandleader Ze'ev Nehama.

As Finegold (1996: 30) correctly observed, the ethnicity of Ethnix remained ambiguous in musical terms, reflecting the ambiguity found in the music of musiqa mizraḥit. In 1996 Ethnix began a series of collaborations with an until then unknown singer of musiqa mizraḥit, Eyal Golan. This move was the outcome of the belief held by Ze'ev Nehama and Tamir Kalisky, the two major authors within Ethnix, that musiqa mizraḥit was in fact an Israeli form of pop and, as such, had great commercial potential and deserved rock-inspired production. Indeed, Eyal Golan with Ethnix became a phenomenal success in the late 1990s, but rock critics as well as musiqa mizraḥit critics interpreted the move as yet another example of the hierarchical relations between Israeli rock and musiqa mizraḥit.

The proliferation of ethnicity as an expression of Israeli authenticity in rock resulted in other currents, besides that represented by Ethnix. Perhaps the most noticeable of these currents can be found in the rock bands that emerged from the southern development town of Sderot, which was inhabited mainly by North African Jews (until the 1990s wave of immigration from the former Soviet Union). The young people of Sderot made rock music fused with pop, Israeli songs, and the musical traditions of their parents, and this music became the hallmark of activities of second generation of Israeli-born North African Jews.

Of these bands, the most successful on a national level was Tea-Packs. This band combined the basic rock lineup with "ethnic instruments," that is, the accordion and the 'ud. The band also featured a full-time female mizraḥi vocalist. Unlike Ethnix, whose members were mostly Ashkenazi Jews, key members of Tea-Packs felt at home with performing techniques unique to Eastern music, such as singing and playing in unison for extended sections of a song, heterophony, vocal and instrumental improvisations in fluctuating rhythm, plugging quotations of traditional Moroccan songs, and the use of microtones and Arab rhythmic patterns. Another characteristic of the repertory of the band, which recalls the repertories of the early musiqa mizraḥit bands, is its eclecticism. Their third album, *Ha-ḥayyim shelkha ba-lafa* (Your life in a large pita bread [1995]), includes songs in diverse styles such as funk, rock, and a ballad reminiscent of the Shirei Eretz Yisrael style. The latter, "Ha-taḥanah ha-yeshanah" (The old station), is an elegy to the old bus station of Tel Aviv. It not only depicts the feelings of the youngsters from Sderot when they arrive in this "other world," but also expresses nostalgia for the old world of cassette music ("three cassettes for ten shekels," says one of the lines). A symbolic link is thus created between Tea-Packs's success in becoming an authentic expression of late 1990s Israeliness and the early, marginalized, and debased world of cassette music.

The model of Tea-Packs is just one of several cultural options taken by the bands from Sderot. Another band, Sfatayim (Lips), for example, almost exclusively performed rock arrangements of songs in Moroccan-Jewish Arabic, mostly based on a recognizable Moroccan beat. Unlike Tea-Packs, this band specifically addressed the local musical traditions of the immigrants of Sderot (for more on the Sderot bands, see Saada-Ofir 2001).

All the examples mentioned here—Ofra Haza, Ethnix, Tea-Packs, Sfatayim—represent different stages and reactions to the increasing influence exercised by musiqa mizraḥit on the Israeli field of popular music and on the general discourse on Israeliness of the 1990s. Recognition of the cultural impact of musiqa mizraḥit, and therefore of its market value, can be seen in the fact the managers of major record companies began to seek contracts with musiqa mizraḥit musicians and to produce joint projects with musiqa mizraḥit firms of long standing. Still, despite this apparent equalization of musiqa mizraḥit with mainstream Israeli pop, the success reflected a deep, hierarchical pattern of power relations. Thus Shmuel Sachar, chief executive of Hed Arzi, says in a paternalistic manner that his "dream is to someday record [rock singer/composer] Shlomo Artzi with [musiqa mizraḥit singer] Ofer Levy" (quoted in Finegold 1996: 37), implying that this would elevate Levy to the status of Shlomo Artzi. This pervasive attitude to musiqa mizraḥit shows that although much ground has been covered in terms of stylistic rapprochement, the battle over Israeliness in popular music is far from over.

THE "WINNERS": MUSIQA MIZRAḤIT IN 1998

The year 1998 was perceived by Israeli music journalists as the year in which musiqa mizraḥit attained its ultimate goal: to become consensual Israeli culture. This perception was expressed, for example, by journalist Amos Oren: "The local pop year was characterized by the victory of the

Eastern sound. . . . Most of us, who brew ourselves in the [Israeli] socio-cultural melting pot, know that this achievement is the apex of a long process" (Amos Oren, *Yedioth Ahronoth,* September 20, 1998). Oren analyzes the origins and stages of this process and concludes that in 1998 all public fronts, that is, mainstream pop charts, major prime-time talk shows, the festival of "Israeli" music in Arad, and so on, were dominated by musiqa mizrahit. This "victory" is especially related to the success of young mizrahi singer Eyal Golan (also of Yemenite origin).

However, the unprecedented success of Golan, a soccer player, in 1997–98, is perceived by some journalists as a departure from mizrahi authenticity or, in the opinion of Avihu Medina, as a token concession by the media to conceal its inherent bias against this music and to silence protests against its discriminatory policies (as told to Shimon Ifargan in *Kol ha-darom,* August 28, 1998). Journalist Adi Masubi interprets Golan's success as the result of a "plot" by the media establishment to de-ethnicize musiqa mizrahit:

> Eyal Golan is the singing result of the worrisome process that musiqa mizrahit in Israel is going through. On the surface, everything is fine. Golan cannot complain that he is closed in a ghetto. He cannot cry over discrimination or lament over the disregard of music editors. Ze'ev Nehama discovered for him the formula for gaining success, and he is hugged by national consensus, as if Ori Or [Labor Party Knesset member whose harsh remarks on Moroccan Jews in a newspaper interview a few weeks earlier stirred the media] does not exist, as if we arrived to the days in which the social, ethnic and other gaps were closed. Only "as if." Because Eyal Golan continues to do what Haim Moshe and Eli Louzon are doing: he pays a price for the love of the music editors of Galei Tzahal. He castrated his mizrahiyut. It's true, he still sings with guttural *het* and '*ayin,* and there is here and there a hint of a *silsul,* but besides that there is nothing.
>
> Where are the days in which Avihu Medina used to decode and present to the Western [public] ear the codes of musiqa mizrahit? The days in which Avner Gedassi sung authentic Yemenite materials are gone; Zohar passed away and we are left with Ha-brera ha-tiv'it, and there is even not a ghetto in the broadcast programming of the Israeli radio. . . . Eyal Golan and the ones like him *ya'ani* ["so to speak" in Arabic] progressed, left the ghetto, and what happened to them on the road [out] proves that it was preferable to have stayed in it. (Adi Masubi, "Zamar dika'on" [Depressing singer], *Kol ha-'Yir,* August 7, 1998)

This militant type of "new journalism" rejects the widespread public recognition of musiqa mizrahit and its embrace by the media, perceiving these as threatening its primordial authenticity. Since the cultural hegemony in Israel is Western oriented, musiqa mizrahit needs to retain, according to these critics, its status as an opposition. This ideal of musiqa mizrahit emphasizes ethnicity and social struggle against the latent discrimination of the Israeli establishment (both political and mass media).

Other journalists who analyzed Eyal Golan's success interpreted it as a process of appropriation of musiqa mizrahit by astute rock artists who wished to capitalize on the success of underprivileged mizrahi artists. This recalls the "domestication" of rock by the music industry in the 1970s. Alon Hadar reports on a summer concert by Ethnix and Eyal Golan under the title "Salute to the Residents of the *Shkhunot* [neighborhoods]," held at the Katamon Park in Jerusalem on September 6, 1998:

> Let's assume that the residents of the Katamonim [a working-class neighborhood of Jerusalem] are mostly mizrahim, and let's assume that the mizrahim like only musiqa mizrahit, and let's also assume that Ze'ev Nehama and Eyal Golan is musiqa mizrahit. This means that a salute to the residents of the Katamonim with Golan, Gili Argov, and Galit Sadan fit like a glove. But why deal with assumptions? Here is someone who says it to our faces. "We brought you your music," declared [Jerusalem Mayor] Ehud Olmert in his speech to the nation at the opening of the salute organized by the Municipality and the shekhunot Headquarters [a grassroots social organization] . . . and defined anew the boundaries of the ghetto, as if Golan does not belong to the First Israel, and as if there is a big difference between the pop of Ethnix and High Five [an Israeli version of Take That], the stage dolls of the record and public relations industry of Tel Aviv.
>
> Ethnix and Golan proved some assumptions: Golan has a voice that contributes a rare added value to each song; Ze'ev Nehama is a successful machine who succeeds in raising emotions like [notoriously apathetic] David Magen MP in a speech in the Knesset or Coach Abraham Grant after another draw of Maccabi Tel Aviv [soccer team]. Let him sing his successful pop, which is exciting in its boredom, and not stride in mizrahit. Nehama, who made the mizrahi [songs] close to the San Remo style and composed melodies that sound like the simple mizrahi songs written in the early 1980s, feels like Golan's patron. He sent him to greet the audience, paternalistically hugged him, and fixed and arranged the balance with the technicians. (Alon Hadar, "Sameah bagetto" [Rejoicing in the ghetto], *Kol Ha-'Ir*, September 11, 1998)

It is interesting that even mainstream rock journalists became concerned with the ability of musiqa mizrahit to appeal to wide audiences. In a review of *Ha-ossef ha-yam tikhoni* (The Mediterranean collection), a canonic four-CD pack compiled by radio editor Shimon Parnas, the chief exponent of musiqa mizraḥit in Kol Israel, Gidi Avivi asks whether "the 'culture war' of Israeli pop is over." And he answers:

> Whoever did not pass through the old Central Bus Station of Tel Aviv in the 60s, 70s, or 80s, will find a good introduction to the different trends and faces of this music in this collection, music that was called by names such as musiqa mizraḥit and musiqat qassetot before it earned its present name, *musiqa yam-tikhonit* [Mediterranean music].
>
> Musically, the songs [included under the title "singing in pairs" which couple mizraḥi with non- mizraḥi singers] represent the yearning of most of the creators of musiqa yam-tikhonit to find a good place in the middle. The history of musiqa yam-tikhonit in Israel is a short history of anger and offense, of longing for legitimacy and of the will to bond with the centers of power of the popular culture and of the Israeli society at large. The continuous coupling of "singing in pairs" has a fitting symbolic meaning: the songs reflect the will to connect, to contribute, to merge.
>
> All this is very nice and harmonic, of course, but for the sake of coming generations it is worth remembering that in less commercial circumstances, another anthology could have been made. The spirit of fraternity in this record cannot conceal either the critical relations between some of its participants, or what is excluded from it.
>
> The connection between rock and musiqa mizraḥit—one of the fascinating connections of local pop—is practically undocumented. . . . Also within the Mediterranean genre itself there is perhaps room to consider. In an era of longing for unity, there is something natural in the wish to locate "Yeladim zeh simḥah" by Ha-brera ha-tiv'it between "Ani Gedaliah" by Natan Alterman and Moshe Vilensky and "Ha-peraḥ be-ganni" performed by Zohar Argov.
>
> However, it seems that the tensions between these songs are more interesting than their relations. They appear here one after the other, but the split seconds that separate them conceal emotional dramas, social tensions, and musical experiments that reflect these dreams and tensions. (Gidi Avivi, "Mitga'age'im la-beyaḥad" [Yearning for integration], *Haaretz*, April 23, 1997)

The analysis of these recent approaches to musiqa mizraḥit in music journalism reveals a paradox. While celebrating what appears to be the acceptance of musiqa mizraḥit as an expression of a new and legitimate mizraḥi form of Israeliness, there is also a sense of a loss of authenticity. This loss derives from the "concessions" made by mizraḥi artists to the technological and aesthetic demands of the popular-music industry. Eyal Golan appears to represent this new synthesis of musiqa mizraḥit more than any other artist.

MUSIQA MIZRAHIT, MIZRAHIYUT, AND ISRAELINESS

Eyal Golan was not the only musician who successfully "crossed over" from the separateness of musiqa mizrahit to Israeli pop in general. Female singer Sarit Hadad soon followed him. She quickly moved from a young and aspiring musiqa mizrahit singer, who performed mainly translated and adapted Turkish songs in the mid-1990s, to a very widely popular performer. In fact, original songs such as "Ani lo Cinderella" (I am not Cinderella) and "Hayiti be-gan 'eden" (I was in paradise) made her one of the country's top pop singers in the end-of-year polls for 1998 and 1999.

Another example is Amir Benayun. After approaching rock musician Mikha Shitrit with tapes of his original compositions, he sprang from total anonymity to become a musician who was highly acclaimed by both rock and musiqa mizrahit critics. His first album *Raq at* (Only you [1999]), produced by Shitrit, was a declaration of authorial presence—words and music—rare in musiqa mizrahit. Also significant are the touches of orientalism in several songs on *Negi'ot* (Touches), rock musician Berry Sakharof's album. This indicates that by the late 1990s, the major and dominant media venues of Israeli popular music were extensively permeated by oriental sounds in general, and by the presence of musiqa mizrahit in particular.

Musiqa mizrahit emerged as the result of a particular sociopolitical conjuncture in which public expressions of a pan-mizrahi Jewish culture began to emerge in Israel. By the early 1970s, de-Arabization had been successfully implemented, and most mizrahi Jews came to perceive themselves as "Israelized," alienated from their own cultural roots and trapped as Israelis of generally low-socioeconomic status. Their relegation to the position of "others" led to various articulations of their grievances. On the one hand, there was the adoption and reinterpretation of Shirei Eretz Yisrael by early musiqa mizrahit bands, expressing a wish to assimilate Hebrewism; on the other hand, there was the revival of ethnic folk festivals, such as the Moroccan *Mimuna*, which emphasized transient cultural groupings possessing nonconfrontational folklore elements. Ethnicity was used instrumentally, mainly to protest their marginal social and economic position. The work of Shlomo Bar and Ha-brera Ha-tiv'it in the 1970s is testimony to such an approach.

During the 1970s, Middle Eastern and North African Jewish communities in Israel increasingly rejected the label of *'edot ha-mizrah* (Eastern ethnic groups), inflicted on them by Hebrewism, and began to consolidate their pan-ethnic sense of identity, the mizrahiyut. The rise of the right-wing

Likud Party to power in 1977, which was largely elected by working-class mizrahi Jews, empowered them politically for the first time since the mass immigration of the 1950s. This is sometimes perceived as a major factor in the rise in public attention to musiqa mizrahit. A feeling that "their own" were governing the country (although, ironically, most of the Likud Party leadership were Ashkenazim), gave mizrahi Jews a sense of added legitimacy and allowed them to express their ethnicity without endangering their status as Israelis. It was within this social and political context of the late 1970s and early 1980s that the original, authentic musiqa mizrahit fully emerged on the general public scene.

The evolution of labels used to refer to this music is revealing of this change in the eyes of the musiqa mizrahit producers themselves. They stopped referring to it as musiqa mizrahit yisraelit and began calling it musiqa yam tikhonit, in order to differentiate it from "other" musics, particularly Arabic music. By adopting this strategy, they avoided the tendency of European Israelis to confuse them with the Arabs, whom they resembled in musical tastes and other aspects of culture. Such a distinction also lent legitimacy to the claim that musiqa mizrahit was truly Israeli music.

In its initial stages, musiqa mizrahit was not specifically Israeli, but mainly imported. Prominent among its musical styles were Greek songs performed by singers such as Aris San, or the mellow Mediterranean style of singing characteristic of the San Remo festival. Some of the early bands did include Eretz-Yisraeli songs in their repertory. Still, musiqa mizrahit was essentially Greek, Arabic, or Turkish popular music adapted from records, cassettes, or radio performances and "made" Israeli by merely substituting Hebrew lyrics for the original ones.

By the 1980s the original songs in the specifically Israeli-hybrid mizrahi style began to outnumber the covers of foreign songs, while in the 1990s, the fusion of musiqa mizrahit with diverse forms of rock and mainstream popular music brought it to the center of national attention. Musiqa mizrahit, whether adopted whole cloth or originally composed by Israeli composers, became "Israeli" rather than ethnic music. From this viewpoint musiqa mizrahit is unlike the traditional music of the Jews from Islamic countries, that was either "museumized," "ethnicized," or simply rejected in Israel (see Cohen and Shiloah 1985; compare with Giladi 1990: 196 and 280 on the discrimination against traditional mizrahi immigrant musicians in Israel).

The growing "Israelization" and "rockization" (or "popization") of musiqa mizrahit, as exemplified by Eyal Golan, Sarit Hadad, and Amir Benayun, has differentiated musiqa mizrahit into at least two separate positions. On the one hand are successful "crossovers" like Golan or Hadad who became icons and models for others to follow. The cultural "cost," as exemplified above in the harsh criticism of Golan, was a certain dilution of the sounds and sense of identity with which musiqa mizrahit had long been associated. On the other hand are the orthodox musicians, who refused to melt down the "classic" musiqa mizrahit sound and spirit. In the late 1990s they still make musiqa mizrahit that sounds almost exactly like what was made in the early 1980s (performers such as Lior Farhi, Kobi Peretz, Liat Banai, and others). The "cost" here is remaining marginal and labeled inferior and "non-Israeli."

In a way, the split within musiqa mizrahit reflects the cultural dilemma of mizrahiyut in general. The story of musiqa mizrahit is sometimes depicted by media commentators in what can be described as a popularized version of the neo-Gramscian terms of "resistance" and "subversion." From such a perspective, musiqa mizrahit is viewed as the authentic assertion of the mizrahi identity and, therefore, as implicitly expressing criticism of and rebellion against the marginalization and inferiority of mizrahiyut within Israeli culture. In this view, the success and the "crossover" of musicians such as Golan and Hadad are interpreted as the appropriation of musiqa mizrahit by dominant Israeliness, its incorporation into the patterns and interests of Israeli rock. In other words, this reads Golan's and Hadad's success as a "failure" in terms of the subversive potential of musiqa mizrahit.

Given the essential commitment of musiqa mizrahit to Israeliness and national culture, the "crossover" phenomenon, and indeed the "mizrahization" of popular music in Israel, should be interpreted as a goal achieved. That is, musiqa mizrahit speakers have persistently argued that their music is Israeli, and that what they desire is to be recognized as legitimate and Israeli-authentic musicians. With musiqa mizrahit performers placed on center stage of Israeli popular music, with rock and pop musicians influenced by the sounds of musiqa mizrahit, and with classic musiqa mizrahit musicians such as Avihu Medina and Zohar Argov canonized as all-Israeli, one can hardly interpret the situation as a cultural "failure." The nationalist impetus that underlined musiqa mizrahit for decades has achieved its own self-declared goal of both bringing musiqa mizrahit into the mainstream of Israeli popular music and of affecting the sounds of all popular music in Israel. It should be emphasized, however, that success in culturally affecting Israeliness does not necessarily mean that a corresponding process is underway in regard to the socioeconomic situation of mizrahim in Israel.

Conclusion

Popular music can be considered "valorization of the banal, the everyday, the demotic" as well as a marker of social and individual differences (Middleton 1990: 251–52). In this book we have argued that in the Israeli case, these functions of popular music were intensified due to the particular circumstances under which Israeli nationhood and its invented culture evolved since the first Zionist settlers set foot on the Ottoman province of Palestine in the late nineteenth century. The field of popular music emerged at that time as a clear symbolic embodiment of Israeliness in its diverse forms, shades, and contradictions.

We have tried to show that the creation and reception of popular music in Israel was conspicuously affected by a commitment to the invention of an authentic "Israeli national culture." This commitment, in turn, was an integral part of a deep belief in the idea of "one nation-one culture" that dominated the discourse of mainstream secular Zionism and subsequently much of Israel's cultural practices during the twentieth century. The ongoing quest for a characteristic musical expression of secular Israeliness resulted, over time, in the consolidation of distinct popular-music cultures. The three most prominent of these cultures comprised the core of our text: Shirei Eretz Yisrael—the "folk" music of Israel; Israeli rock—the cosmopolitan, "globalized" form of Israeli music; and musiqa mizrahit—the "ethnic" popular music of Israel. These dominant cultures are the most significant in terms of their historical pertinence, quantitative presence in the media and public discourse, and relevance to large sectors of Israeli society.

What the examination of these three music cultures has unveiled is that no one unique sound idiom or indigenous type of music can exclusively be called "Israeli." Moreover, these three music cultures are not the only ones: an extremely diverse range of music styles and microcultures of popular music coexist in Israel. By focusing on music scenes that are conventionally perceived as the major actors in the field of popular music in Israel, we have only introduced the primary contestants for the designation of "Israeli music." Bringing into the picture additional music cultures would further complicate this question of Israeliness in music. It is perhaps helpful to recall that the attempt to construct an indigenous national music is not an exclusively Israeli endeavor. The quest for unique and indigenous "national music" is in fact shared by many different nation-states that have emerged on the world scene throughout the modern era.

As a direction for further study, we briefly examine two additional popular music cultures that exist in Israel; consider some possible answers to the question with which this book opened, namely, "Is there a unique sound idiom, a specific type of music, that can be properly called 'Israeli'?"; and discuss some theoretical implications of this study for the general understanding of popular music and national identity.

TWO OTHER POPULAR MUSIC CULTURES IN ISRAEL

This short discussion of two additional popular music cultures in Israel—we call them "religious" and "Arab"—is intended to indicate that a full understanding of the area of popular music in Israel, and indeed of the field of culture in Israel, must take into account actors that are often marginalized by the prevailing public and academic discourse.

Religious Popular Music

The first music culture consists of the popular music styles associated with the variant of Israeli culture we have called "Religious Israeliness." Forms of popular music, such as those distributed as "Hassidic" songs and some contemporary klezmer music that follows the path of the American klezmer revival, are created and disseminated primarily among the various branches of Israeli orthodox Jews. These types of popular music can be further subdivided into traditional, pop, and even electro-dance styles. This music is consumed especially by the two largest concentrations of Ashkenazi, partly Yiddish-speaking, ultraorthodox Jews, in the cities of Benei Berak and Jerusalem. Many of these products are made by a separate music industry, sold in specific music stores in the orthodox neighborhoods, and heard on local radio stations, many of which are illegal "pirate" stations. The deliberate limitations of this type of popular music reflect the oppositional stand of the ultraorthodox Jews, Hassidic and non-Hassidic, toward secular Israeli culture.

The situation is rather different in the Zionist religious community, the "modern orthodox" Jews of Israel. Their position of religious nationalism, which places them between secular culture and ultraorthodoxy, is reflected in their consumption of musical products from both music contexts: the religious and the secular. This sector of Israeli culture consumes variants of Hassidic pop and klezmer music and is one of the most avid and passionate audiences of Shirei Eretz Yisrael after this genre's decline from dominance. Their taste culture is best exemplified in the music programming of Arutz sheva' (Channel Seven), a quasi-legitimate "pirate" radio station strongly associated with the ideology of the national religious right-wing of Israeli politics. By playing music that ranges from hits by American-based Hassidic pop stars such as Mordechai Ben-David and Avraham Fried, to SLI songs by Naomi Shemer and Nurit Hirsh, to the soft Israeli rock of Arik Einstein, Arutz sheva' attempts to place traditional religious Jewish music and secular Israeli folk and popular song on one continuum.

In the case of the Hassidic Song Festival—a secular event that infused the field of religious popular music in Israel with much of the energy that fuels it to this day—the various religious popular-music styles tend to be perceived as "Jewish," and more specifically as "Ashkenazi Jewish," rather than "Israeli." Thus, by attempting to locate some Israeli rock hits, SLI songs, and Hassidic pop on the same continuum and in effect integrating them into one context, the cultural practices exemplified by Arutz sheva' tend to blur the difference between Israeliness and Jewishness—a crucial theme in mainstream secular Zionism during most of the twentieth century.

The situation is somewhat different among mizrahi orthodox Jews, whose repertoire of music consumption includes cover versions of musiqa mizrahit hits. Yet here, as in many other practices of everyday life, ultraorthodox mizrahiyut was susceptible to processes of "Ashkenazization." That is, just as Ashkenazi orthodoxy has exerted an influence on practices of apparel, prayer, and study among mizrahi orthodox Jews, so Hassidic and other religious popular music has entered their repertory; hence, in the case of mizrahi orthodoxy, one finds a slightly different mixture of popular music influences, one that juxtaposes cover versions of musiqa mizrahit hits and Hassidic pop.

Arab Popular Music

The second music culture in this context is one associated with Israeli Palestinians. Their exclusion for decades from the contest over Israeliness and their own commitment to Arab culture and Palestinian identity have left their popular-music culture quite separate from the dominant Jewish Israeli culture. This alienation implied, especially in the context of urban culture, the consumption of classic Arab popular music of the mid-twentieth century. The "great names" of Arab popular music, Mohamed Abd el-Wahab, Um Kulthum, Farid el-Atrash, Fairuz, and others, are admired by and central to Israeli Palestinians as much as they are in any other Arab nation. Since the 1980s, "lighter" forms of Arab pop and contemporary performers have made their way into the Israeli Palestinian market: Amr Diab, Hany Shaker, Majda Al Romi, and George Wassuf are some of those who have emerged as pan-Arab pop stars in the 1980s and 1990s (Regev 1993).

The popular-music culture of Israeli Palestinians is not, however, totally segregated. To begin with, their taste for classic Arab popular music is shared by many first- and second-generation mizrahi Jews, as well as by an intellectual niche market for "world music." Admiration for Um Kulthum or Farid El Atrash is shared, for example, by Israeli Arabs and at least some parts of the Israeli Jewish society. In addition, the sounds of recent Arab pop resemble in many ways those of musiqa mizrahit. This has enabled some musiqa mizrahit performers—Haim Moshe, for example—to gain popularity among Israeli Palestinians. Also, original music made by local musicians in the vein of Arab pop and musiqa mizrahit emerged in the 1980s; some of it has found receptive audiences in the musiqa mizrahit market. The most notable example is Samir Shukri, whose hit "Ronna" became a staple of musiqa mizrahit repertoire in the 1980s. Finally, Arab-Jewish cooperation has emerged in the 1980s and 1990s in various ensembles that cater to the "world music" local and international markets. Most exemplary is the Bustan Avraham Ensemble, which attained wide international recognition. The Arab and Jewish members of this ensemble are inspired by and mix together various Near Eastern art-music traditions, mid-twentieth-century Arab popular music influences, as well as jazz and some European folk traditions (including Jewish). It therefore stands at the foreground of music-making practices that blur the difference between "Arabness" as something not-Jewish and not-Israeli, and "Israeliness," as a non-Arab entity.

In other words, by being consumers of pan-Arab popular-music cultures, Israeli Palestinians have introduced Arab music into the field of popular music in Israel. In addition, by participating and cooperating in the creation of music of various types, some of them in Hebrew, Israeli Palestinians challenge the Jewish exclusiveness of national culture in Israel.

ISRAELINESS IN MUSIC

Returning to the question posed by Israeli public discourse on the occasion of the state's fiftieth anniversary—"Is there an indigenous Israeli music?"—

one is tempted to answer with a categorical "No." Indeed, given the plurality of genres and styles presented diachronically in this book, each one of them perceived as or claiming to be a representation of Israeliness, it is certainly impossible to point to a genuine sound, a unique idiom that can be called "typical Israeli." An all-Israeli sound or idiom has not been crystallized, but it is indeed possible to point to the existence of a body of songs—a canon—containing items from different music cultures and periods and believed by Israelis to represent their collective national identity in music.

On the Impossibility of "Typical Israeli" Music

It seems almost obvious, in retrospect, that the aim of inventing a single, typical, all-Israeli sound or musical idiom was impossible from the outset. Besides being an idealistic illusion inherited from romantic nationalism, two major factors were crucial in hindering the possibility of an indigenous all-Israeli popular music. One is the composition of Israeli society as an aggregate of communities and individuals from a wide variety of cultural backgrounds; the other is the intensification of the globalization of culture that occurred almost precisely at the time when Israelis were trying to invent a national culture.

Two phrases—*kur hitukh* (melting pot) and *kibbutz galuyot* (in-gathering of the exiles)—were located at the core of mainstream Israeli ideology of cultural integration for many years. They reflected the ideal that, ultimately, Israeli indigenous art and culture would come to consist of products based on a mixture of elements from Jewish Diaspora communities (mainly Eastern European), as well as local "native" (that is, Arab) or "authentic" (that is, Jewish Yemenite) ones. This idea runs like a thread throughout the history of cultural discourse in Israel. In the case of popular music, it is embodied in the fact that, deliberately or not, musicians have often attempted to construct East-West fusions, which were consequently hailed as exemplifying what Israeliness should sound like in music. Starting with early SLI composers and culminating with the work of Tea-Packs, the paradigm of East-West fusion is the music ideal to be embraced by national ideology as expressing "authentic Israeliness."

But it is precisely the ideological neatness of these fusions that gives them the connotation of being forced, sometimes fabricated efforts. They might fit a symbolic sense of Israeliness, but they cannot express the entire range of cultural and musical contexts that exist in the country. Thus music cultures associated with various sectors and factions of society in Israel might not find their own sense of identity in these East-West fusion formulas. This is true, even for musiqa mizrahit audiences, who sometimes feel that some types of fusion in effect dilute the authenticity of their music. It is all the more true for the newest immigrant communities of former Soviet and Ethiopian Jews, who feel distanced, if not alienated, from such fusions as an expression of their own local/national identity.

It is also true for adherents of pop/rock, for whom cosmopolitanism and participation in contemporary global culture is as important to their Israeli identity as any notion of "authenticity." Shalom Hanoch's quote about his commitment to "rock" and almost complete disregard for anything "ethnic" says it all (see Chapter 7). This brings us to the other factor that hinders the emergence of an indigenous Israeli music idiom—the globalization of culture.

Although the invention of Israeli "folk" music began relatively early in the twentieth century, the major effort and investment in the construction of musical Israeliness occurred in the second half of that century. This is precisely the period of global expansion of the media and culture industries, of the intensification of worldwide dissemination of cultural goods and contexts of meaning of Western origin. This is the era, in other words, when the processes known as "Westernization," "Americanization," "cultural imperialism," and "the globalization of culture" were dramatically enhanced and intensified (Tomlinson 1999). Obviously, these phenomena had an immense impact on culture in Israel as well. This impact is conventionally perceived to have disrupted the process of constructing of a unique, "pure" Israeli-Hebrew culture.

In the case of popular music, the globalization of culture, or "Americanization," supposedly interfered in the process that was already on its way to creating an authentic folk music (SLI) by bringing in pop/rock. In addition, it is argued, it made ethnic Jewish traditions of music susceptible to "impure" influences. This type of argumentation is extremely problematic, as it can be convincingly countered by arguing that the very notion of inventing or constructing an indigenous national music, an "authentic," present-day Hebrew-Jewish popular-music culture in Palestine/Israel, was itself an element in the larger phenomenon of the emergence of "world culture." That is, as Meyer and colleagues (1997) demonstrate, the spread and implementation of the nation-state as the elementary unit of collective identity, and within it the notion of "one nation-one culture," was at the core of the emergence of "world culture" in late modernity. The Jewish endeavor of establishing a nation-state in Israel, and of striving to construct a unique national culture, was in fact one of many similar phenomena that reflect the essential meaning of the process of globalization of culture. Moreover, the construction of the body of SLI songs was based on practices of hybridization, mixing and fusion of elements from various traditions—practices that make this type of music a product of intercultural exchange.

However, even if the notions of Hebrewism as "pure," authentic Israeli culture and of SLI as truly "folk" music are accepted, the fact that the attempt to consolidate it as the all-Israeli national popular music occurred after the 1950s doomed it to failure. Faced with the growing presence and influence of the transnational media and culture industries, the preservation of the original SLI spirit as the dominant music of Israel barely had a chance. The globalization of culture gave rise to types of music inspired by pop and rock, all claiming to represent some sort of Israeliness. In fact, the globalization of culture ushered in not only Hebrew variants of rock but also wider "rockization" of music practices—that is, standard and extensive use of electrification, amplification, and studio technology. These practices thus undermined tendencies toward "uniqueness," by causing Israeli popular music to share common sonic features with music from other parts of the Western hemisphere and elsewhere.

Consequently, given the plurality of music types that claimed local authenticity and representation of Israeli identity, one is tempted to settle for the somewhat naive postulation that the field of popular music in Israel simply reflects that Israel is a multicultural society. That is, there is no single "Israeliness," but rather a multiplicity of types and forms. Thus there are several Israeli "musics," in the plural, and not one type of all-Israeli music. That this assertion is somewhat simplistic, given the struggles between the various types of music over dominance, is something that we hope to have shown in this book. We therefore reaffirm our assessment that although the notion of Israeliness in music is as yet unsettled, it continues to be an issue to which many of the actors in the field still feel committed.

An Israeli Canon

Although we believe that the notion of "typical Israeli music" is probably impossible to realize, we do want to stress that during its history, through the complex incorporation of influences and the interconnections between its different positions, the field of popular music in Israel has produced a body of songs that can be called a canon that is widely accepted as all-Israeli. Its existence is best exemplified by the 1998 Jubilee hit-parades and the sizeable, retrospective sets of CDs released around the same year. The consolidation of this body of songs stems from the process of mutual appropriations of cultural elements between the different variants of Israeliness.

The struggle over recognition, legitimacy, and dominance among the different variants of Israeliness includes practices of borrowing, adoption, adaptation, appropriation, and co-optation of cultural materials between the different variants. As part of one variant's attempt to gain legitimacy, to claim continuity of heritage, and to demonstrate its commitment to the nationalist idea of integration, its cultural producers sometimes use works that originally "belonged" to another variant, in a mode typical of their own. With these practices repeated over time, a body of cultural works gradually emerged across different variants. This body of works, crossing the variants and existing within most forms of Israeliness, has come to be identified as "all-national," as the core of Israeli national culture.

In the case of popular music, the struggle over Israeliness has produced practices of borrowing, adoption, adaptation, and appropriation not only of stylistic elements from one music culture by musicians associated with another culture, but also of memorable songs. Thus songs, originally associated with one particular music culture, tend to gain some presence in the contexts of additional music cultures. They are adapted to the typical sound formulas and performance practices of those other music cultures and come to exist within two or more contexts.

This is most strongly the case with SLI songs that through the years were adapted to and performed by musicians working within either Israeli rock or musiqa mizraḥit. The tendency to "cover" SLI songs is obvious, given the status of these songs as the "folk" music of Israel and, therefore, as the songs most representative of the roots of Israeli society and love of country. Claiming recognition and legitimacy, musiqa mizraḥit performers have recorded various songs from the repertory of Shirei Eretz Yisrael. Rock musicians, claiming continuity of heritage and artistic supremacy, have also recorded many songs from the same repertory.

But such practices of covering songs exist in other directions as well. In the 1990s, musiqa mizraḥit performers began to record and perform various Israeli rock songs, especially ballads. Ḥavurot zemer and shirah be-tzibbur leaders, for their part, attempting to reinvigorate the Shirei Eretz Yisrael tradition, added songs from musiqa mizraḥit and Israeli rock to their repertory. These practices were possible because all three cultures shared much common musical ground: most of the songs composed and performed within them abided by the Western tonal system. Thus the weakest direction of borrowing seems to be from musiqa mizraḥit to Israeli rock. Almost no songs from the former culture were performed or recorded by musicians from the latter, probably reflecting the deep sense of artistic superiority that rock musicians still feel toward musiqa mizraḥit. The phenomenon here described cannot be considered a salient feature of the field. Yet it hints that there is some consensus that a body of "all-Israeli" songs from all music cultures is shared by audiences and musicians of Shirei Eretz Yisrael, Israeli rock, and musiqa mizrahit.

This body of song therefore amounts to a sort of national canon. It is exemplified by songs such as the 1982 musiqa mizrahit hit "Ha-perah be-gani" (The flower in my garden) by Avihu Medina, originally performed by Zohar Argov; the 1970 Israeli rock ballad "Ani ve-ata" (Me and you) by Miki Gavrielov and Arik Einstein, who also first recorded it; and the tradi-tional Eretz-Yisraeli song "Shnei shoshanim" (Two roses), written in 1945 by Yaakov Orland and Mordechai Zeira and an all-time staple of shira ba-tzibur events. This canon stands as an ingredient of the habitus that gives the individuals who possess it a sense of belonging to the collective identity of Israeliness.

To put this into a theoretical context that makes the Israeli case compa-rable to others, it is useful to refer to the discussion by Born and Hesmondhalgh (2001) of the four ways in which music represents and artic-ulates sociocultural identities:

> (1) When music works to create a *purely imaginary identification,* an imaginary figuration of sociocultural identities, with no intent to actual-ize those identities; . . . (2) When the music imaginary works to *pre-figure,* crystallize or potentionalize *emergent, real* forms of sociocul-tural identity or alliance; . . . (3) When the musical imaginary works to *reproduce,* reinforce, actualize, or memorialize *extant* sociocultural identities; . . . (4) When the musical representation of sociocultural iden-tity come, *after the fact,* to be reinterpreted an debated discursively and, out of this process, "reinserted" as representations into the changing sociocultural formation. (Born and Hesmondhalgh 2001: 35–36)

It is quite clear that initially SLI work fit the second category. It greatly helped to usher in the emergent identity of Israeliness in its formative years. The work of Israeli rock and musiqa mizrahit, by contrast, was essen-tially the one outlined in the fourth category. That is, both music cultures were "inserted" into Israeliness following debates and reinterpretations of the music and of Israeliness itself. Finally, as outlined in the third category, after the successful insertion of rock and musiqa mizrahit, the canon that includes songs from all three music cultures works to reproduce and rein-force the extant sociocultural identity known to its members as Israeliness. If, as Frith argues (1996: 274), "identity is always an ideal, what we would like to be, not what we are," and "music gives us a real experience of what the ideal could be," then the songs comprising the canon of Israeli popular music probably work for Israelis in exactly this way: they give them an experience of what Israeliness, as an ideal identity, could be.

POPULAR MUSIC, GLOBALIZATION, AND CULTURAL UNIQUENESS

Insofar as Israelis tend to perceive the body of songs just discussed as expressing their own local/national identity, many of them are well aware of the fact that the musical sources and influences of these songs lie elsewhere on the globe. Whether they are Russian pastoral ballads, American Tin-Pan Alley song craftsmanship, French chanson, Arab music vocal techniques, Yemenite rhythms, Greek laika music, Italian sentimental ballads, Latin beats, Brazilian samba, or the electric guitars, electronic synthesizers, samplers, sophisticated studio techniques, R&B-inspired vocal styles associated with "pop/rock"—Israeli popular music incorporates diverse traditional and late-modern global influences.

The field of popular music in Israel is not different in this regard from national fields of popular music in other countries. Its mixture of influences and plurality of music cultures is probably the standard rather than the exception in contemporary popular music around the globe. But popular music in Israel, because of its short and concentrated history, and therefore the clarity and perceptibility of its cultural and social processes, can be viewed as a sort of test case for understanding the connection between globalization of culture, the aspiration to national or local identity, and popular music.

Theoretical approaches to the globalization of culture tend to oscillate between notions of homogeneity and views of diversity. But as Robertson (1995) and Meyer (2000) argue, it seems that the two approaches do not necessarily contradict one another. Globalization seems to take the form of diversity within similarity, where diversity stands for the attempts of collective actors to either maintain or construct local cultural uniqueness, while similarity stands for organizational structures, "rationalized" culture (that is, science, managerial practices, and so on), technology, and what could be described, generally, as tools for constructing uniqueness. Put differently, contemporary cultural uniqueness is typically constructed within similar organizational frameworks (that is, the nation-state) and by using similar cultural and art forms.

Indeed, the construction of cultural uniqueness involves the use of cultural and art forms. The globalization of culture renders all mechanically and electronically reproduced art forms, as well as a plethora of styles and genres from different periods and eras, available for use practically everywhere. The same art and cultural forms thus become tools with which different collective actors—nations or others—produce diversity and uniqueness. Films and novels, for example, were adopted as contemporary forms of expression all over the world. Undoubtedly "Western" in their origin as art forms, and therefore initially alien to many national, local, and ethnic cultures, they were localized in order to create unique national and local styles and genres—not to mention individual works—of film and literature. Indian films, Japanese films, and French films all bear marks of Hollywood styles and genres and, in their turn, have influenced Hollywood films. Most importantly, they have all become components of the global art world of film.

Consequently, within the process of globalization, the circuits of production, dissemination, consumption, and interpretation of each art and cultural form become networks, in the sense discussed by Castells (2000), or Bourdieusian fields. The transformation, transmutation, and permutation of art and cultural forms are expressive tools used for the maintenance and invigoration of contemporary cultural uniqueness. Yet, at the same time, the works, genres, and styles of these forms, as well as their producers and audiences, remain interconnected and interrelated as components of social information networks and as actors in social spaces of power, hierarchy, and prestige.

In the case of popular music, this mainly means two things: the presence and availability for absorption into national music cultures of many "foreign" stylistic elements; and the "pop/rockization" of national popular music genres. That is, introduction and legitimization of electric and electronic instruments, studio technology (including techniques of sonic "collage" and "cut and paste"); and amplification as the conventional way for creating popular music, as well as the use of the star system and other managerial components as the standard way for packaging and marketing popular music.

National music cultures in countries like India, Japan, Congo (Zaire), Italy, and China—to name but a few—may come to include, in one way or another, stylistic influences of, for example, tango, salsa, samba and flamenco, hip-hop and reggae, swing, rock'n'roll and blues, sentimental ballads and operatic drama, country music, Arab and other "oriental" flavors, Central and West African rhythms—and many more. In addition, the sonic textures from which the music is made include the sounds of electric guitars, synthesizers, drum machines, the cleanliness and amplitude of sound, and the accuracy and punctuality in putting together sound fragments associated with studio techniques. "Pop/rockization" of world popular music seems to be the major factor in the intensification of the connectedness and aesthetic affinity of different national and local music cultures.

In fact, in light of the consuming presence of pop/rock genres, the preservation and reinvigoration of "pure" folk and ethnic genres should be understood as a response to pop/rock. That is, the proliferation of "world music," of styles and genres emphasizing traditional, premodern sonic textures, is to a large extent also a paradoxical outcome of "pop/rockization." Although often very different in terms of music structure and style, contemporary conservation and revival projects of folk and ethnic traditions in many countries do share the same cultural logic of existence; hence, they have also become elements of one world network.

Consequently, insofar as such music cultures are perceived by local audiences and commentators to represent cultural uniqueness and as being variants of national identity, they also stand as genres that have at least some affinity to popular music cultures and genres in other countries. In other words, the globalization of culture accelerates the connectedness of local and national music cultures from different countries. Cultural uniqueness in music can no longer be perceived in terms of total separateness of national music cultures. Popular and even "folk" and "ethnic" music cultures are no longer the distinct cultural entities that they were once thought to be. Instead, they are components of global networks, or indeed of one global network of popular music genres and cultures, interconnected by intricate stylistic influences, similar sonic textures, and conventional practices of music making.

The field of popular music in Israel superbly exemplifies all of this. Thus musiqa mizrahit, for example, with its self-image of local Israeli authenticity, is at the same time a music culture strongly connected to the stylistic contexts of Turkish arabesk, Greek laika, and Algerian/French rai. In addition, its typical instrumentation, which includes synthesizers, drum machines, and electric guitars, makes it a component of the global genre of "world beat," which is in fact part of the larger category of global "pop/rock." Musiqa mizrahit thus stands as an Israeli variant of a global music culture, an element of the world network of "pop/rock," sharing much common aesthetic ground with other genres or styles that are perceived, in turn, as signifying the cultural uniqueness of different collective identities. Israeli rock, needless to say, with all its subcurrents, also has close aesthetic and formal affinities to various styles and genres of Anglo-American rock, as well as certain variants of ethnic rock from around the world. Finally, Shirei Eretz Yisrael, in their current status of national "folk" music partially marketed as popular music, have become the Israeli equivalent of types of local music found in different countries in an increasingly shrinking, and yet diverse, world.

Select Discography

This discography collects titles of albums mentioned in the book. It is organized alphabetically by the performer's surname. Compilations consisting of songs by various performers are listed by their title. Unless otherwise noted, the entries relate to currently existing CDs and their distributing companies. When these are exact reissues of original vinyl LPs, the original year of release is given. Names and titles starting with "ha-" (the), are entered according to their actual name.

100 shirim rishonim (First 100 songs). 1981. Various Artists. NMC.
Aḥarit ha-Yamim. 1972. *Aḥarit ha-Yamim* (Apocalypse). NMC.
Alal, Corinne. 1989. *Antarctica*. CBS.
———. 1992. *Zan nadir* (Rare species). NMC.
Alberstein, Hava. 1975. *Kmo tzemaḥ bar* (Like a wildflower). NMC.
———. 1989. *London*. NMC.
Amar, Jo. 1999. *Greatest Hits* (originally late 1950s and early 1960s). Azoulai.
Argov, Zohar. 1980. *Elinor*. Reuveni.
———. 1982. *Nakhon le-ha-yom* (True for today). Reuveni.
———. 1983. *Kakh 'ovrim hayyai* (This is how my life goes by). Reuveni.
Artzenu ha-qtantonet (Our small country). 1989. Various artists. Ha-Taklit.
Artzi, Shlomo. 1970. *Ha-Taklit ha-rishon* (The first record). Hed Artzi.
———. 1978. *Gever holekh le-yibud* (A man getting lost). Hed Artzi.
———. 1984. *Tirkod* (Dance). Hed Artzi.
———. 1986. *Layla lo shaket* (Unquiet night). Hed Artzi.
———. 1988. *Hom yuli august* (July–August heat). Hed Artzi.
———. 1992. *Yareaḥ* (Moon). Hed Artzi.
———. 1993. *Ha-Osef ha-meshulash* (The triple collection). Hed Artzi.
———. 1996. *Shnaim* (Two). Hed Artzi.
Astral Projection. 1977. *Dancing Galaxy*. Phonokol.
Atari, Gali. 1986. *Emtza september* (Mid-September). NMC.

Avoda 'Ivrit (Hebrew work). 1998. Various Artists. Ha-kol Zahav.

Banai, Ehud. 1986. Ehud Banai ve-ha-plitim (Ehud Banai and the refugees). CBS.

————. 1989. Karov (Nearby). CBS.

Ben, Zehava. 1995. Super Golden Hits. Banai and Matana Productions.

Benayoun, Amir. 1999. Raq 'at (Only you). Hed Artzi.

Benzeen. 1982. Esrim ve-arba shaot (Twenty-four hours). NMC.

ha-Breira ha-Tiv'it (Natural Gathering). 1979. Eley shorahim (Origins). Tarbuton.

Caspi, Matti. 1974. Matti Caspi (I). CBS.

————. 1976. Matti Caspi (II). CBS.

Caspi, Matti, and Shlomo Gronich. 1972. Me-ahorey ha-tzlilim (Behind the sounds). Hed Artzi.

Churchills, the. 1968. Churchills. Hed Artzi.

ha-Click (The Click). 1983. Olam Tzafuf (Crowded world). NMC.

Daklon. 1992. Golden Hits. Reuveni.

Damari, Shoshana. 1994. Me-"kalaniyot" ad "or" (From "Kalaniot" 'til "Or"; 3-CD box set). Hed Artzi.

Einstein, Arik. 1966. Shar bishvilekh (Sings for you). Helicon.

————. 1968. Mazal gdi (Capricorn). CBS.

————. 1968. Yashan ve-gam hadash (Old and new). Hed Artzi.

————. 1969. Poozy. Phonokol.

————. 1970. Shablool (with Shalom Hanoch). Phonokol.

————. 1971. At Avigdor's Grass (with Miki Gavrielov). Phonokol.

————. 1971. Plastelina (with Shalom Hanoch). Phonokol.

————. 1972. Jasmine. Phonokol.

————. 1973. Eretz Yisrael ha-yeshanah ve-ha-tovah (Good Old Eretz Yisrael; vol. 1). Phonokol.

————. 1974. Sa Le'at (Slow down). Phonokol.

————. 1975. Shirim (Songs). Phonokol.

————. 1976. Ha-ahava panim rabot la (Love has many faces; with Yoni Rechter). Phonokol.

————. 1976. Eretz Israel ha-yeshana ve-ha-tova (Good old eretz Israel, vol. 2). Phonokol.

————. 1977. Eretz Israel ha-yeshana ve-ha-tova (Good old eretz Israel, vol. 3). Phonokol.

————. 1995. Yesh bi ahavah (I got love in me). NMC.

Elephant, Yossi. 1996. Osef Elephant (Elephant compilation). Nana.

Eretz tropit yafa (Pais tropical). 1978. Various Artists. NMC.

Erev shirey meshorerim (Poets' songs evening). 1974. Various Artists. NMC.

Ethnix. 1991. Masala. Helicon.

————. 1994. Atah (You). Helicon.

————. 1995. Ha-osef shel Ethnix (The Ethnix collection). Helicon.

Foreign Affair (Rami Fortis and Berry Sakharof). 1988. The East Is on Fire. Crammed (Belgium).

Fortis, Rami. 1978. *Plonter* (Tangle). NMC.

Fortis, Rami, and Sakharof, Berry. 1988. *Sipurim me-hakufsa* (Stories from the box). Nana.

———. 1990. *1900?* Nana.

Gadalnu Yahad (We grew up together). 1998. Various Artists. Hed Artzi.

Gedassi, Avner. 1991. *Greatest Hits.* Reuveni.

Geffen, Aviv. 1995. *Akhshav meunan* (It is cloudy now). Hed Artzi.

Golan, Eyal. 1997. *Bil'adaikh* (Without you). Ben Zur Productions.

Goland, Yossef. 1934. *Mi-shirei Eretz Yisrael.* Ahva (unavailable on CD).

Gov, Gidi. 1978. *Gidi Gov.* Hed Artzi.

———. 1983. *40:06.* Hed Artzi.

Gronich, Shlomo.1971. *Lama lo sipart li* (Why didn't you tell me). Phonokol.

Hadad, Sarit. 1999. *Kmo cinderella* (Like Cinderella). Goeta Productions.

ha-Ḥalonot ha-gvohim (The High Windows Trio). 1967. *ha-Ḥalonot ha-gvohim.* Hed Artzi.

Hanoch, Shalom. 1971. *Shalom.* DGC.

———. 1981. *Hatuna levana* (White wedding). NMC.

———. 1983. *Al pney ha-adama* (Face of the earth). NMC.

———. 1985. *Meḥakim le-mashiaḥ* (Waiting for messiah). NMC.

Hayo Hayu Zmanim (Once upon a time; special live concert). 1961. Various Artists. Hed Artzi (unavailable on CD).

Haza, Ofra. 1984. *Shirey teiman* (Yemenite songs). Hed Artzi.

———. 1988. *Shaday.* Warner.

———. 1989. *Desert Wind.* Warner.

———. 2000. *Manginat ha-lev* (Melody of the heart). Hed Artzi.

Hendel, Nehama. 1998. *Ha-shirim ha-yafim* (The beautiful songs; originally 1961–67). Hed Artzi.

Kaveret. 1973. *Sipurey poogy* (Poogy tales). Hed Artzi.

———. 1974. *Poogy be-pita* (Poogy in a pita). Hed Artzi.

———. 1975. *Tzafuf ba-ozen* (Crowded in the ear). Hed Artzi.

Kraus, Shmulik. 1982. *Galgal mistovev* (Turning wheel). Hed Artzi.

———. 1988. *Aharey esrim shana* (After twenty years). Hed Artzi.

Lehaqat geisot ha-shirion, lehaqat piqud darom, lehaqat kheil ha-yam. 1992. *Ha-lahitim ha-gdolim 1962–72* (The greatest hits of the Armored Forces, Southern Command and Navy Ensembles, 1962–72). Hed Artzi.

Lehaqat ha-naḥal. 1989. *Ha-lahitim ha-gdolim 1963–1972* (The greatest hits of the Nakhal Ensemble, 1963–72). Hed Artzi.

Lehaqat piqud ha-tzafon and lehaqat piqud ha-merkaz. 1990. *Ha-lahitim ha-gdolim 1963–72* (The greatest hits of the Northern Command and Central Command Ensembles, 1963–72). Hed Artzi.

ha-Lehaqot ha-tzvaiyot: ha-shanim ha-rishonot (The *lehaqot tzvaiyot:* The first years). 1988. Hed Artzi.

Louzon, Eli. 1988. *Ha-Neshama* (The soul). Ben Mush.

Mashina. 1985. *Mashina.* CBS.

———. 1989. *Gvirotay ve-rabotay* (Ladies and gentlemen). NMC.

————. 1990. *Ha-ʿamuta le-Ḥeker ha-tmuta* (Death-rate research association). CBS.

————. 1992. *Miflatzot ha-tehila* (Monsters of glory). NMC.

————. 1993. *Si ha-regesh* (Climax of emotion). Hed Artzi.

————. 1995. *Le-hitraʾot neʿurim, shalom ahavah* (Farewell youth, hello love). Hed Artzi.

Minimal Compact. 1986. *Raging Souls.* Crammed (Belgium).

Mitzʿad ha-Kohavim (Star Festival). 1968. Various Artists. CBS Israel.

Moshe, Haim. 1983. *Ahavat hayyai* (Love of my life). Reuveni.

————. 1985. *Kol nedarai* (All my vows). Reuveni.

————. 1986. *Todah* (Thank you). Reuveni.

ha-Osef ha-yam tikhoni (The Mediterranean collection). 1997. Various Artists. Media Direct.

Pick, Tzvika. 1972. *Zohi ha-derekh sheli* (This is my way). NMC (originally on Koliphone).

————. 1978. *Musiqa.* CBS Israel.

Poliker, Yehuda. 1985. *Eynaim shely* (Eyes of mine). NMC.

————. 1988. *Efer ve-avak* (Ashes and dust). CBS.

————. 1990. *Paḥot aval koev* (Less but still hurts). CBS.

————. 1992. *Le-eineikha ha-khulot* (To your blue eyes). NMC.

————. 1995. *Ha-yeled she-bekha* (The child in you). NMC.

————. 1997. *Live at Cesarea.* NMC.

————. 1998. *Meuhar oolay mukdam* (Late maybe early). NMC.

Qtzat Aḥeret (Something Different). 1975. Israedisc.

Ravitz, Yehudit. 1984. *Derekh ha-meshy* (Silk road). NMC.

————. 1987. *Baah me-ahava* (Coming from love). NMC.

————. 1993. *Ve-meod lo pashut le-hakot* (And it is not simple to wait). Helicon.

————. 1996. *Eizoh min yalda* (What kind of girl). Helicon.

Rechter, Yoni, and Avner Kener. 1975. *Arba esre oktavot* (14 octaves). Helicon.

Reichstat (Ofarim), Esther. 1961. *Hayu Leylot* (There were nights). Israphone.

Rita. 1985. *Rita.* Helicon.

————. 1988. *Yemey ha-tom* (Days of innocence). Helicon.

————. 1994. *Tzipor zara* (Foreign bird). Helicon.

————. 1999. *Tiftah halon* (Open a window). Helicon.

Sakharof, Berry. 1991. *Ha-kol o klum* (All or nothing). Nana.

————. 1993. *Simanim shel hulsha* (Signs of weakness). Nana.

————. 1995. *Ham al ha-yareah* (Hot on the moon). Nana.

————. 1998. *Negiot* (Touches). NMC.

San, Aris. 1993. *The Best* (originally 1968–75). NMC.

Saroussi, Nessim. 1999. *Golden Hits* (originally 1973–75). NMC.

Shemer, Naomi. 1998. *Asif Kahol* (Blue crop; various artists). NMC.

————. 1998. *Asif Zahav* (Golden crop; various artists). Hed Artzi.

Sheshet. 1977. Sheshet. CBS.

Shlishiat Gesher ha-Yarkon (The Yarkon Bridge Trio). 1965. *Ahava rishona* (First love). Israphone.

————. 1966. *Ha-tokhnit ha-hadasha* (The new program). Hed Artzi.

Tabory, Shimi. 1990. *Golden Hits.* Reuveni.

Tamuz. *Sof 'onat ha-tapuzim* (End of the orange season). 1976. NMC.

ha-Tarnegolim (The Roosters). 1989. *Ha-Tarnegolim* (originally 1961–63). Hed Artzi.

Tea-Packs. 1995. *Ha-hayyim shelkha ba-lafa* (Your life in lafa [a roll of pita bread]). Hed Artzi.

————. 1997. *Neshiqah la-dod* (A kiss to the uncle). Hed Artzi.

Tislam. 1981. *Radio hazak* (Strong radio). NMC.

Tsan'ani, Margalit. 1988. *Greatest Hits, vol. 1.* Reuveni.

————. 1992. *Greatest Hits, vol. 2.* Reuveni.

Tzlil Mekhuvan (Tuned Tone). 1979. *Tzlil Mekhuvan* (Tuned tone). Hed Atzi.

Tzliley ha-Kerem. 2000. *Be-zokhri yamim yemima* (Remembering old days; reissue of the first two albums, 1975–76, on one CD). Reuveni.

Tzliley ha-'Ud. 1975. *Qessem ha-Mizrah* (Magic of the orient). Koliphone.

Yarkoni, Yaffa. 1998. *Me-az ve-ad ha-yom: 1948–1998* (From then until now; 5-CD box set). Hed Artzi.

Yitzhaki, Yisrael. 1957. *Ahavati ha-rishona* (My first love). Hed Artzi (unavailable on CD).

Zefira, Bracha. 1960. *Bracha Zefira be-haqlatot meqoriyot 1937–1950.* (Bracha Zefira in original recordings 1937–50). CBS.

Works Cited

Adler, Haim, and Yohanan Peres. 1968. The Youth Movement and "Salon Society" (in Hebrew). In *Education and Society in Israel*, ed. S. N. Eisenstadt et al., 361–81. Jerusalem: Academon.

Aharoni, Reuben. 1986. *Yemenite Jewry: Origins, Culture, Literature.* Bloomington: Indiana University Press.

Alcalay, Ammiel. 1993. *After Jews and Arabs: Remaking Levantine Culture.* Minneapolis: University of Minnesota Press.

Almagor, Dan. 1996. Musical Plays on the Hebrew Stage. *Ariel* 103: 19–29.

Almog, Oz. 2000. *The Sabra: The Creation of the New Jew.* Berkeley: University of California Press.

Alter, Robert. 1994. *Hebrew and Modernity.* Bloomington: Indiana University Press.

———. 1988. *The Invention of Hebrew Prose.* Seattle: University of Washington Press.

Anderson, Benedict. 1991. *Imagined Communities: Reflections on the Origin and Spread of Nationalism.* Rev. ed. London and New York: Verso.

Appadurai, Arjun. 1990. Disjuncture and Difference in the Global Cultural Economy. *Public Culture* 2: 1–24.

Aran, Gideon. 1988. A Mystic Messianic Interpretation of Modern Israeli History: The Six-Day War in the Religious Culture of Gush Emunim. *Studies in Contemporary Jewry* 4: 263–75.

———. 1986. From Religious Zionism to Zionist Religion: The Roots of Gush Emunim. *Studies in Contemporary Jewry* 2: 116–43.

Armstrong, John A. 1982. *Nations before Nationalism.* Chapel Hill: University of North Carolina Press.

Baily, John. 1994. The Role of Music in the Creation of an Afghan National Identity, 1923–73. In *Ethnicity, Identity and Music: The Musical Construction of Place,* ed. Martin Stokes, 45–60. Oxford: Berg.

———. 1981. Cross-Cultural Perspectives in Popular Music: The Case of Afghanistan. *Popular Music* 1: 105–22.

Banerji, Sabita. 1988. Ghazals to Bhangra in Great Britain. *Popular Music* 7: 207–14.

Bar Haim, Gabriel. 1990. Popular Culture and Ideological Discontent. *International Journal of Politics, Culture and Society* 3: 279–96.

Bayer, Bathja. 1980. Creation and Tradition in Israeli Folksongs: Some Specimen Cases. In *Aspects of Music in Israel,* ed. Benjamin Bar-Am, 52–60. Tel Aviv: Israel Composer's League, National Council for Culture and Art.

———. 1968. Yithavuto shel 'maqam' ba-shir ha-yisraeli (The emergence of a "maqam" in the Israeli song). In *Eastern and Western Elements in Israeli Music,* ed. Michal Smoira, 74–84. Tel Aviv: Israel Music Institute.

Becker, Judith. 1981. Kroncong, Indonesian Popular Music. *Asian Music* 7: 14–19.

Ben-Ari, Eyal, and Yoram Bilu. 1987. Saints' Sanctuaries in Israeli Development Towns. *Urban Anthropology* 16: 243–72.

Ben-Eliezer, Uri. 1998. *The Making of Israeli Militarism.* Bloomington: Indiana University Press.

Ben Porat, Amir. 1999. *Heikhan hem ha-burganim ha-hem? Toldot ha-burganut ha-yisraelit* ("Where are those bourgeois?": A history of the Israeli bourgeoisie). Jerusalem: The Hebrew University, Magnes Press.

Ben-Porat, Ziva, ed. 1989. *Lyric Poetry and the Lyrics of Pop: The Israeli Popular Song as a Cultural System and a Literary Genre* (in Hebrew). Tel Aviv: Ha-kibbutz Ha-meuḥad.

Ben-Rafael, Eliezer. 1982. *The Emergence of Ethnicity: Cultural Groups and Social Conflict in Israel.* Westport, Conn.: Greenwood Press.

Benski, Tova. 1989. Ethnicity and the Shape of Musical State Patterns in an Israeli Urban Community. *Social Forces* 57: 731–50.

Ben-Yehuda, Nachman. 1995. *The Masada Myth.* Madison: University of Wisconsin Press.

Ben-Yehuda, Netiva. 1992. *Autobiografia be-shir va-zemer* (Autobiography in song). Jerusalem: Keter.

Berkowitz, Michael. 1990. Art in Zionist Popular Culture and Jewish National Self-Consciousness, 1891–1914. *Studies in Contemporary Jewry* (Special issue: *Art and Its Uses: The Visual Image and Modern Jewish Society,* ed. Richard I. Cohen) 6: 9–42.

Berlovitz, Yafa. 1981. The Image of the Yemenite in the Literature of the First 'Aliyot (in Hebrew). *Pe'amim* 10: 76–108.

Blacking, J. 1981. Making Artistic Popular Music: The Goal of the True Folk. *Popular Music* 1: 1–9.

Born, Georgina, and David Hesmondhalgh. 2001. Introduction: On Difference, Representation and Appropriation in Music. In *Western Music and Its Others,* 1–58. Berkeley: University of California Press.

Boskovich, Alexander U. 1964. Festival ha-zemer ha-israeli (The Israel Song Festival). *Haaretz,* April 24, 1964.

Bourdieu, Pierre. 1985. Social Space and the Genesis of Groups. *Theory and Society* 14: 723–44.

Bourdieu, Pierre, with Loic J. D. Wacquant. 1992. *An Invitation to Reflexive Sociology.* Chicago: University of Chicago Press.

Brandwine, M. H. 1997. *Reb Shlomele: The Life and World of Shlomo Carlebach.* Trans. Gabriel A. Sivan. Jerusalem: The Author.

Burnett, Robert. 1996. *The Global Jukebox.* London: Routledge.

Campbell Robinson, Deanna, Elizabeth B. Buck, and Marlene Cuthbert. 1991. *Music at the Margins.* Newbury Park, Calif.: Sage.

Carmel, Tuviya. 1980. Moʻadonei tarbut ve-ḥayyei ha-bohema (Culture clubs and the life of the bohemians). In *The First Twenty Years: Literature and Art in Little Tel Aviv* (in Hebrew), ed. A. B. Jaffe, 245–63. Tel Aviv: Keren Tel Aviv, Ha-kibbutz Ha-meuḥad.

Caspi, Dan, and Yekhiel Limor. 1998. *The In/Outsiders: The Media in Israel.* Cresskill, N.J.: Hampton Press.

Castells, Manuel. 2000. *The Rise of the Network Society.* Oxford: Blackwell.

Cohen, Daliah, and Ruth Katz. 1977. *The Israeli Folk Song: A Methodological Example of Computer Analysis of Monophonic Music.* Jerusalem: Hebrew University of Jerusalem.

Cohen, Eric. 1983. Ethnicity and Legitimation in Contemporary Israel. *The Jerusalem Quarterly* 28: 111–24.

———. 1972. The Black Panthers and Israeli Society. *The Jewish Journal of Sociology* 14: 93–109.

Cohen, Eric, and Amnon Shiloah. 1985. Major Trends of Change in Jewish Oriental Ethnic Music. *Popular Music* 5: 199–223.

Cole, Fred, and Michael Hannan. 1997. Goa Trance. *Perfect Beat* 3: 1–14.

Cushman, Thomas. 1995. *Notes from the Underground: Rock Music Counterculture in Russia.* Albany: State University of New York Press.

Danielson, Virginia. 1996. New Nightingales of the Nile: Popular Music in Egypt since the 1970's. *Popular Music* 15: 299–312.

DeBoer, Christine Adele. 1996. *Laika: Definition and Significance of a Greek Popular Music Genre.* M.A. thesis, University of California, Los Angeles.

Dellapergola, Sergio, and L. Cohen, eds. 1992. *World Jewish Population: Trends and Policies.* Jerusalem: The Institute for Contemporary Jewry, the Hebrew University of Jerusalem.

De Nora, Tia. 2000. *Music in Everyday Life.* New York: Cambridge University Press.

———. 1986. How is Extra-Musical Meaning Possible? Music as a Place and Space for Work. *Sociological Theory* 4: 84–94.

Deshen, Shlomo. 1978. Israeli Judaism: Introduction to the Major Patterns. *Journal of Middle East Studies* 9: 141–69.

Deshen, Shlomo, and Moshe Shokeid. 1974. *The Predicament of Homecoming.* Ithaca, N.Y.: Cornell University Press.

DiMaggio, Paul, and Walter Powell. 1983. The Iron Cage Revisited: Institutional Isomorphism and Collective Rationality in Organizational Fields. *American Sociological Review* 48: 157–60.

Druyan, Nitza. 1981. *Without the Magic Carpet: Yemenite Settlement in Eretz Israel (1881–1914)* (in Hebrew). Jerusalem: Ben Zvi Institute.

Dunevitch, Natan. 1959. *Tel Aviv* (in Hebrew). Jerusalem, Tel Aviv: Schoken.

Edel, Yitzhak. 1942. *Ha-shir ha-eretz yisraeli* (The Eretz Israeli song). Tel Aviv: Ha-histadrut ha-klalit, ha-merkaz le-tarbut.

Eisenstadt, Shmuel N. 1967. *Israeli Society.* London: Weidenfeld and Nicholson.

Eldan, Sari. 1989. Shir va-zemer bi-tenu'at ha-no'ar ha-Eretz-Yisraeli (Lyrics and song in the eretz Israeli youth movements). *Rav siah revi'i al mehkar toldot tenu'ot ha-no'ar, 29.6.1988. Shirei tenu'out ha-no'ar ve-ruah ha-tequfah – hashpa'ot gomlin* (The fourth symposium on the research of the history of the youth movements, 29.6.1988: The songs of the youth movements and the spirit of the time—mutual influences). Efal: Yad Tebenkin.

Eliagon, Talma, and Rafi Pesakhson, eds. 1981–94. *1,000 zemer ve-'od zemer* (1,000 songs and another song). 6 vols. Tel Aviv: Kineret.

Eliram, Talila. 2000. *On the Musical and Social Characteristics of the "Songs of the Land of Israel"* (in Hebrew). Ph.D. dissertation, Bar-Ilan University.

———. 1995. *Shirei Eretz Israel—Songs of the Land of Israel: The Creation and Meaning of a Popular Music Repertoire at the End of the Twentieth Century* (in Hebrew). M.A. thesis, Bar-Ilan University.

Even-Zohar, Itamar. 1981. The Emergence of a Native Hebrew Culture in Palestine: 1882–1948. *Studies in Zionism* 4: 167–84.

Eyal, Gil. 1996. The Discursive Origins of Israel Separatism: The Case of the Arab Village. *Theory and Society* 25: 389–429.

Featherstone, Mike, ed. 1990. *Global Culture: Nationalism, Globalization and Modernity.* London: Sage.

Finegold, Eliezer Moshe. 1996. *Musika Mizrahit: From the Margins to the Mainstream.* Harvard Judaica Collection Student Research Papers No. 2. Cambridge, Mass.: Harvard University Press.

Flam, Gila. 1999. Representations of the East in Hebrew Songs (in Hebrew). In *The Challenge of Independence, Ideological and Cultural Aspects of Israel's First Decade,* ed. Mordechai Bar-On, 248–61. Jerusalem: Yad Yitzhak Ben-Zvi.

———. 1986. Bracha Zefira—A Case Study of Acculturation in Israeli Song. *Asian Music* 17: 108–25.

Frith, Simon. 1996. *Performing Rites.* Cambridge, Mass.: Harvard University Press.

———, ed. 1989. *World Music, Politics and Social Change.* Manchester, Eng.: Manchester University Press.

———. 1981. *Sound Effects.* New York: Pantheon.

Fürst, Shifra. 1999. *The Popular Music Festivals as a Mirror of Changes in the Israeli Society* (in Hebrew). M.A. thesis, Bar-Ilan University.

Gambaccini, Paul, et al. 1998. *The Complete Eurovision Song Contest Companion.* London: Pavilion Books Limited.

Gammond, Peter. 1991. *The Oxford Companion to Popular Music.* Oxford: Oxford University Press.

Gans, Herbert. 1975. *Popular Culture and High Culture.* New York: Basic Books.

Geertz, Clifford. 1973. *The Interpretation of Cultures.* New York: Basic Books.

Gellner, Ernest. 1983. *Nations and Nationalism.* Oxford: Blackwell.

Gertz, Nurith. 1988. *Literature and Ideology in Eretz Israel During the 1930's* (in Hebrew). Tel Aviv: The Open University of Israel.

Giladi, Gideon N. 1990. *Discord in Zion: Conflict between Ashkenazi and Sephardi Jews in Israel.* London: Scorpion Publishing.

Gilroy, Paul. 1993. *The Black Atlantic: Modernity and Double Consciousness.* Cambridge, Mass.: Harvard University Press.

———. 1987. *There Ain't No Black in the Union Jack.* London: Hutchinson.

Gluzman, G. 1989. Fifty Years of Song: Basic Trends in the Israeli Song, 1930–1980 (in Hebrew). In *Lyric Poetry and the Lyrics of Pop: The Israeli Popular Song as a Cultural System and a Literary Genre,* ed. Ziva Ben-Porat, 9–19. Tel Aviv: Ha-kibbutz Ha-meuhad.

Goldberg, Harvey. 1977. Introduction: Culture and Ethnicity in the Study of Israeli Society. *Ethnic Groups* 1: 163–86.

Gracyk, Theodor. 1996. *Rhythm and Noise: An Aesthetic of Rock.* Durham, N.C.: Duke University Press.

Grinberg, Lev Luis. 1991. *Split Corporatism in Israel.* Albany: State University of New York Press.

Gronow, Pekka. 1998. *An International History of the Recording History.* London: Cassell.

Gross, Joan, David McMurray, and Ted Swedenburg. 1994. Arab Noise and Ramadan Nights: Rai, Rap, and Franco-Maghrebi Identity. *Diaspora* 3: 3–39.

Grossberg, Lawrence. 1984. Another Boring Day in Paradise: Rock and Roll and the Empowerment of Everyday Life. *Popular Music* 4: 225–58.

Hacohen, Eliyahu. 1993. The Hebrew Record, First Rounds: Chapters in the Discography of *ha-zemer ha-ivry* (in Hebrew). In *Ha-kol zahav,* ed. Yossi Mar-Haim and Yair Stav, 9–20. Tel Aviv: Sifriyat Maariv.

———. 1985. *The Songs of Tel Aviv 1909–1984* (in Hebrew). Tel Aviv: Dvir.

Hall, Stuart. 1996. New Ethnicities. In *Stuart Hall: Critical Dialogs in Cultural Studies,* ed. David Morley and Kuan-Hsing Chen, 441–49. London: Routledge.

———. 1991. The Local and the Global: Globalization and Ethnicity. In *Culture, Globalization and the World-System,* ed. Anthony D. King, 19–39. London: Macmillan.

Halper, Jeff, Edwin Seroussi, and Pamela Squires-Kidron. 1992. *Musika mizrahit* and the Realignment of Israeli Society: The Case of Haim Moshe. In *1789–1989 Musique, Historie, Democratie,* ed. A. Hennion 3:669–72. Paris: Editions de la Maison de Sciences de l'Homme.

———. 1989. *Musika mizrahit:* Ethnicity and Class Culture in Israel. *Popular Music* 8: 131–42.

Hannerz, Ulf. 1992. *Cultural Complexity.* New York: Columbia University Press.

———. 1990. Cosmopolitans and Locals in World Culture. In *Global Culture,* ed. Mike Featherstone, 237–52. London: Sage.

Harris, Keith. 1999. An Orphaned Land?—Israel and the Global Extreme Metal Scene. In *New Voices in Jewish Thought,* ed. Keith Harris, 2:1–21. London: Limmud Publications.

Hatch, David, and S. Millward. 1987. *From Blues to Rock: An Analytical History of Pop Music.* Manchester, Eng.: Manchester University Press.

Hatuli (Omer), Biniyamin. 1940. *Ḥag u-mo'ed* (Holiday and festival). Tel Aviv: Ha-kibbutz Ha-artzi.

Hajdu, Andre, and Yaakov Mazor. 1971. Hasidism: The Musical Tradition. *Encyclopaedia Judaica* 7: 1421–32.

Hennion, Antoine. 1993. *La passion musicale.* Paris: Metaille.

Hever, Hannan. 1987. Hebrew in an Israeli Arab Hand: Six Miniatures on Anton Shamas' *Arabesques. Cultural Critique* 7: 47–76.

Hirschfeld, Ariel. 1997. 'Al ha-shir ha-yisra'eli [1]: Ha-musika mefareqet mah she-ha-teqst menaseh le-ḥaber (Music deconstructs what the text attempts to construct). *Haaretz Literary Supplement,* December 19, 1997.

Hirshberg, Jehoash. 1998. Music Entries (in Hebrew). In *The History of the Jewish Community in Eretz Israel since 1882: The Construction of Hebrew Culture in Eretz Israel,* pt. 1, ed. Zohar Shavit. Jerusalem: The Israel Academy of Sciences and Humanities, The Bialik Institute. (Jewish Music in Europe, 69–70; Setting the Frameworks of Musical Life, 99–104; Development of Musical Performance Groups, 263–341; Concert Societies, Professional Unions, and the Struggle for Survival, 411–14.)

———. 1995. *Music in the Jewish Community of Palestine.* Oxford: Oxford University Press.

———. 1984. Bracha Zefira and the Process of Change in Israeli Music (in Hebrew). *Pe'amim* 19: 29–46.

Hobsbawm, Eric. 1990. *Nations and Nationalism since 1780.* Cambridge: Cambridge University Press.

Hobsbawm, Eric, and Terence Ranger, eds. 1983. *The Invention of Tradition.* Cambridge: Cambridge University Press.

Horowitz, Amy. 1997. Performance in Disputed Territory: Israeli Mediterranean Music. *Musical Performance* 1, no. 3: 43–53.

———. 1994. *Musika Yam Tikhonit Yisraelit (Israeli Mediterranean Music): Cultural Boundaries and Disputed Territories.* Ph.D. dissertation, University of Pennsylvania.

Jones, Andrew F. 1992. *Like a Knife: Ideology and Genre in Contemporary Chinese Popular Music.* Ithaca, N.Y.: East Asia Program, Cornell University.

Kadman, Gurit. 1969. '*Am roked. Toldot riqqudei ha-'am be-yisrael* (A people dances: History of the folk dances of Israel). Jerusalem, Tel Aviv: Schoken.

Katriel, Tamar. 1991. *Communal Webs: Communication and Culture in Contemporary Israel.* Albany: State University of New York Press.

———. 1986. *Talking Straight: Dugri Speech in Israeli Sabra Culture.* Cambridge: Cambridge University Press.

Kedar, Ran, ed. 1971. *Lehitim bo'arim* (Hot Hits). Tel Aviv: Ma'ariv.

Kedem, Peri. 1991. Dimensions of Jewish Religiosity. In *Tradition, Innovation,*

Conflict: Jewishness and Judaism in Contemporary Israel, ed. Z. Sobel and B. Beit-Hallahmi, 251–72. Albany: State University of New York Press.

Kemp, Adriana, Rebecca Reijman, Julia Resnik, and Silvina Gesser. 2000. Contesting the Limits of Political Participation: Latinos and Black African Migrant Workers in Israel. *Ethnic and Racial Studies* 23: 94–119.

Kimmerling, Baruch. 1999. Elections as a Battleground over Collective Identity. In *Elections in Israel—1996*, ed. A. Arian and M. Shamir, 27–44. Albany: State University of New York Press.

Kutner, Yoav. 1986. Habrera Hativ'it. *Ariel* 66: 37–44.

Lamont, Michéle. 1995. National Identity and National Boundary Patterns in France and the United States. *French Historical Studies* 16: 349–65.

Levi, Shoshana. 1998. *Eru'im u-dmuyiot be-hitpathut ha-zemer ha-yisraeli ha-mizrahi* (Events and personalities in the development of the Israeli mizrahi song). Seminar paper, Lewinsky College, Tel Aviv.

Levinson, Abraham. 1951. *Tarbut yotzeret* (Creative culture). Tel Aviv: Center for Culture and Education, the Workers Union of Israel (the Histadrut).

Lewis, Herbert S. 1989. *After the Eagles Landed: The Yemenites of Israel*. Boulder, Colo., San Francisco, London: Westview Press.

Liebes, Tamar, and Elihu Katz. 1993. *The Export of Meaning: Cross-Cultural Readings of Dallas*. Cambridge, Eng.: Polity Press.

Lomsky-Feder. Edna. 1998. *As if There Was Never a War* (in Hebrew). Jerusalem: Magnes Press.

Macan, Edward. 1997. *Rocking the Classics: English Progressive Rock and the Counterculture*. Oxford: Oxford University Press.

Mahanaimi, Gide'on. 1988. *Li kol gal 'ose mazkeret: Shirim rusiym* (Every wave stirs my memory: Russian songs). Jerusalem: Keter.

Manuel, Peter. 1993. *Cassette Culture: Popular Music and Technology in North India*. Chicago: University of Chicago Press.

———. 1988. *Popular Musics of the Non-Western World*. Oxford: Oxford University Press.

Margol, Ninah. 1989. Ha-zemer bi-tenu'at ha-no'ar "Tekhelet lavan" bi-Tchekhiyah (The song in the "blue and white" youth movement in the Czech Republic). *Rav siah revi'i al mehkar toldot tenu'ot ha-no'ar, 29.6.1988. Shirei tenu'out ha-no'ar ve-ruah ha-tequfah – hushpa'ot gomlin* (The fourth symposium on the research of the history of the youth movements, 29.6.1988: The songs of the youth movements and the spirit of the time—mutual influences). Efal: Yad Tebenkin.

Marom, Shulamit, 1997. *The Musical Activities of the Histadrut as a Propagation of Cultural Ideology* (in Hebrew). M.A. thesis, Tel Aviv University.

Maroz, Yael. 1990. *Processes of Institutionalization and Stratification in Cultural Systems: The Emergence of the "Alternative" Layer in Israeli Popular Music* (in Hebrew). M.A. thesis, Tel Aviv University.

Mattelart, Armand. 1979. *Multi-National Corporations and the Control of Culture: The Ideological Apparatus of Imperialism*. Sussex: Harvester Press.

Medina, Avihu. 1994. *Simanim shel Derekh* (Signs of a road). Petah Tikva: A.M. Productions.

Meron, Dan. 1981. *Miprat el 'iqar: Mivneh, janer ve-hagut be-shirato shel Natan Alterman* (From detail to essence: Form, genre and thought in the poetry of Natan Alterman). Tel Aviv: Ha-kibbutz Ha-meuḥad and Sifriat Po'alim.

Merriam, Alan P. 1964. *The Anthropology of Music*. Evanstone, Ill.: Northwestern University Press.

Meyer, John. 2000. Globalization: Sources and Effects on National States and Societies. *International Sociology* 15: 233–48.

———, et al. 1997. World Society and the Nation-State. *American Journal of Sociology* 103: 144–81.

Middleton, Richard. 1990. *Studying Popular Music*. Milton Keynes, Eng.: Open University Press.

———. 1985. Articulating Musical Meaning/ Re-constructing Musical History. *Popular Music* 5: 5–40.

Miron, Issachar. 1967. The Influence of Russian Jews on the Music of Israel. In *The Historic Contribution of Russian Jewry to Jewish Music*, ed. Irene Heskes and Arthur Wolfson, 47–53. New York: National Jewish Music Council.

Mitchell, Tony. 1996. *Popular Music and Local Identity*. London: Leicester University Press.

———. 1995. Question of Style: Notes on Italian Hip-Hop. *Popular Music* 14: 333–48.

Mizrahi, Mordecahi. 1983. *Views and Concepts of the Aims of Musical Education in Israeli Schools* (in Hebrew). M.A. thesis, Tel Aviv University.

Monelle, Raymond. 1992. *Linguistics and Semiotics in Music*. Chur, Switzerland; Princeton, N.J.: Harwood Academic Press.

Nathan, Hans, ed. 1994. *Israeli Folk Music: Songs of the Early Pioneers*. Foreword and Afterword by Philip V. Bohlman. Madison, Wisc.: A-R Editions.

Neeman, Amitai. 1980. Light Music and "Pop" in Israel. In *Aspects of Music in Israel*, ed. Benjamin Bar-Am, 61–65. Tel Aviv: Israel Composer's League, National Council for Culture and Art.

Negus, Keith. 1992. *Producing Pop*. London: Edward Arnold.

Nettl, Bruno. 1985. *The Western Impact on World Music*. New York: Schirmer.

———. 1978. Some Aspects of the History of World Music in the Twentieth Century: Questions, Problems, Concepts. *Ethnomusicology* 22: 123–36.

O'Brien, Lucy. 1996. *She Bop*. New York: Penguin.

Ofrat, Gideon. 1998. *One Hundred Years of Art in Israel*. Trans. Peretz Kidron. Boulder, Colo.: Westview Press.

Ohana, David. 1995. Zarathustra in Jerusalem: Nietzsche and the "New Hebrews." *Israel Affairs* 1: 38–60.

Oren, Amos. 1998. Ha-menatzḥim—ha-zemer ha-mizraḥi ha-davar ha-nakhon. (The winners—The oriental song [is] the right thing). *Yedioth Ahronoth*, September 20.

Pelinski, Ramón, ed. 1995. *Tango nomade*. Montréal: Tryptique.

Perlson, Inbal. 2001. *The Musical Institutions of Immigrants from Arab Countries in the First Years of Statehood* (in Hebrew). Ph.D. dissertation, Tel Aviv University.

Peterson, Richard. 1990. Why 1955? Explaining the Advent of Rock Music. *Popular Music* 9: 97–116.

Peterson, Richard, and David Berger. 1975. Cycles in Symbol Production: The Case of Popular Music. *American Sociological Review* 40: 158–73.

———. 1971. Entrepeneurship in Organizations: Evidence from the Popular Music Industry. *Administrative Science Quarterly* 16: 97–106.

Rabinowitz, Dan. 1997. *Overlooking Nazareth*. Cambridge: Cambridge University Press.

Racy, Ali Jihad. 1982. Musical Aesthetics in Present Day Cairo. *Ethnomusicology* 26: 391–406.

Ram, Uri. 1996. Memory and Identity: A Sociology of the Historians Debate in Israel (in Hebrew). *Teoria ve-biqoret* 8: 9–32.

———. 1995. Zionist Historiography and the Invention of Modern Jewish Nationhood: The Case of Ben Zion Dinur. *History and Memory* 7: 91–124.

Ramet, Sabrina Petra, ed. 1994. *Rocking the State: Rock and Politics in Eastern Europe and Russia*. Boulder, Colo.: Westview Press.

Ravina, Menashe. 1968. *Hatikvah: Origin, History and Comparative Analysis of the Jewish National Anthem*. Tel Aviv: M. Ravina.

Raz-Krakotzkin, Amnon. 1993–94. Exile within Sovereignty: Toward a Critique of the "Negation of Exile" in Israeli Culture (in Hebrew), pt. 1, *Teoria ve-biqoret* 4: 23–55; pt. 2, *Teoria ve-biqoret* 5: 113–32.

Regev, Motti. 1997a. Organizational Fluency, Organizational Blocks, Cultural Relevance: The Case of the Music Industry in Israel (in Hebrew). *Teoria ve-biqoret* 10: 115–32.

———. 1997b. Rock Aesthetics and Musics of the World. *Theory, Culture and Society* 17: 125–42.

———. 1997c. Who Does What with Music Videos in Israel. *Poetics* 25: 225–40.

———. 1996. *Musica Mizrakhit*, Israeli Rock and National Culture in Israel. *Popular Music* 15: 275–84.

———. 1995. Present Absentee: Arab Music in Israeli Culture. *Public Culture* 7: 433–45.

———. 1994. Producing Artistic Value: The Case of Rock Music. *The Sociological Quarterly* 35: 85–102.

———. 1993. *Oud and Guitar: The Musical Culture of the Arabs in Israel* (in Hebrew). Ra'anana: Beit Berl.

———. 1992. Israeli Rock or, A Study in the Politics of "Local Authenticity." *Popular Music* 11: 1–14.

———. 1990. *The Coming of Rock: Meaning, Contest and Structure in the Field of Popular Music in Israel* (in Hebrew). Ph.D. dissertation, Tel Aviv University.

———. 1989. The Field of Popular Music in Israel. In *World Music, Politics and*

Social Change, ed. S. Firth, 145–55. Manchester, Eng.: Manchester University Press.

———. 1986. The Musical Soundscape as a Contest Area: "Oriental Music" and Israeli Popular Music. *Media, Culture and Society* 8: 343–55.

Reshef, Yael. 1999. *The Hebrew Folksong in the New Yishuv: A Linguistic Investigation* (in Hebrew). Ph.D. dissertation, The Hebrew University of Jerusalem.

Ritzer, George. 1993. *The McDonaldization of Society.* Thousand Oaks, Calif.: Pine Forge Press.

Robertson, Roland. 1995. Glocalization: Time–Space and Homogeneity–Heterogeneity. In *Global Modernities,* ed. Mike Featherstone et al., 23–44. London: Sage.

Roniger, Luis, and Michael Feige. 1992. From Pioneer to Freier: The Changing Models of Generalized Exchange in Israel. *Archives Europèenes de Sociologie* 33: 280–307.

Rosenblum, Yair. 1988. Ha-lehaqot ha-tzvaiyot: mitosim ve-nitutzam (The army ensembles: Myths and their demolition). *Musica* 12: 32–36.

Rouhana, Nadim. 1997. *Palestinian Citizens in an Ethnic Jewish State.* New Haven, Conn.: Yale University Press.

Rubin, Judith Dena. 1981. *Israeli Folk Songs: Analysis and Implications for Music Education.* M.A. thesis, University of California, Los Angeles.

Saada, Galit. 1999. *Attitudes and Strategies of Action for Consolidation of an Oriental Identity: Musical Activity in Sderot* (in Hebrew). M.A. thesis, The Hebrew University of Jerusalem.

Saada-Ofir, Galit. 2001. Attitudes and Strategies of Action for Consolidation of an Oriental Identity: Musical Hybrids from the City of Sderot (in Hebrew). *Israeli Sociology* 3: 253–76.

Said, Edward. 1978. *Orientalism.* London: Routledge.

Schiff Wingard, Eileen. 1954. *Music Education in Israel.* M.A. thesis, University of California, Los Angeles.

Schweid, Eliezer. 1984. The Rejection of the Diaspora in Zionist Thought: Two Approaches. *Studies in Zionism* 5: 43–70.

Segev, Tom. 1999. *Yemei ha-kalaniyot* (Days of anemones). Jerusalem: Keter.

Seroussi, Edwin. 1999. Ḥanale hitbalbela (Hanale was rattled). In *Fifty to Forty Eight: Critical Moments in the History of the State of Israel* (special issue of *Teoria ve-biqoret,* vols. 12–13), ed. Adi Ophir, 269–78. Jerusalem: Van Leer Institute.

———. 1995. Reconstructing Sephardi Music in the 20th Century: Isaac Levy and his *Chants judeo-espagnols. The World of Music (Jewish Musical Culture—Past and Present)* 37, no. 1: 39–58.

Seroussi, Edwin, and Susana Weich-Shahak. 1990–91. Judeo-Spanish Contrafacts and Musical Adaptations: The Oral Tradition. *Orbis Musicae* 10: 164–94.

Shabtay, Malka. 2001. *Between Reggae and Rap: The Challenge of Belonging for Ethiopian Youth in Israel* (in Hebrew). Tel Aviv: Cherikover.

Shafran, Uchma. 1996. *A Repertory of Songs for Children in the Jezreel Valley Settlements Between the 1920s and the 1940s: A Reflection of Contrasting Ideological Trends* (in Hebrew). M.A. thesis, Tel Aviv University.

Shahar, Natan. 1998. The Eretz Israeli Song 1882–1948 (in Hebrew). In *The History of the Jewish Community in Eretz Israel since 1882: The Construction of Hebrew Culture in Eretz Israel*, pt. 1, ed. Zohar Shavit, 495–526. Jerusalem: The Israel Academy of Sciences and Humanities, the Bialik Institute.

———. 1997a. *Ḥavurot hazemer* in Israel: A Unique Sociomusicological Phenomenon. *Musical Performance* 1: 15–33.

———. 1997b. The *lehaqot tzvayiot* and their songs (in Hebrew). In *Ha-ʿasor ha-rishon*, ed. Tzevi Tzameret and Hanna Yablonka, 299–318. Jerusalem: Yad Yitzhak Ben Zvi.

———. 1994. *The Eretz-Israeli Song and the Jewish National Fund* (in Hebrew). Jerusalem: Research Institute for the History of the Keren Kayemet Leisrael, Land and Settlement.

———. 1993. The Eretz Israel Song and the Jewish National Fund. *Studies in Contemporary Jewry* 9 *(Modern Jews and their Musical Agendas)*: 78–91

———. 1989. *The Eretz-Israeli Song 1920–1950: Sociomusical and Musical Aspects* (in Hebrew). Ph.D. dissertation, The Hebrew University of Jerusalem.

Shaked, Gershon. 1987. Literature and its Audience: On the Reception of Israeli Fiction in the Forties and Fifties. *Prooftexts* 7: 207–23.

Shalev, Michael. 1992. *Labour and the Political Economy of Israel*. Oxford: Oxford University Press.

Shamas, Anton. 1989. Your Worst Nightmare. *Jewish Frontier* 55: 12–18.

Shamir, Ronen. 2000. *The Colonies of Law*. Cambridge: Cambridge University Press.

———. 2001. Jewish Bourgeoisie in Colonial Palestine (in Hebrew). *Israeli Sociology* 3: 133–48.

Sharma, Sanjay, John Hutnyk, and Ashwani Sharma. 1996. *Dis-Orienting Rhythms*. London: Zed Books.

Shavit, Yaacov. 1996. The Yishuv between National Regeneration of Culture and Cultural Generation of the Nation (in Hebrew). In *Jewish Nationalism and Politics: New Perspectives,* ed. Jehuda Reinharz, Gideon Shimoni, and Yosef Salmon, 141–58. Jerusalem: Zalman Shazar Center for Jewish History.

———. 1982. Hebrew Education and Hebrew Culture in Eretz-Israel: Frameworks and Context (in Hebrew). In *The History of Eretz Israel*, vol. 9: *The British Mandate and the Jewish National Home,* ed. Yehoshua Porat and Yaacov Shavit, 246–60. Jerusalem: Keter, Ben Zvi Institute.

Sheffi, Rakefet. 1989. The Development of the Poetics of the Israeli Popular Song (in Hebrew). In *Lyric Poetry and the Lyrics of Pop: The Israeli Popular Song as a Cultural System and a Literary Genre,* ed. Ziva Ben-Porat, 76–98. Tel Aviv: Ha-kibbutz Ha-meuhad.

Shenhav, Yehouda. 2002. Jews from Arab Countries in Israel: The Split Identity of Mizraḥim within the Realms of National Memory (in Hebrew). In *Mizraḥim in Israel: A Critical Observation into Israel's Ethnicity,* ed. Hannan Hever, Yehouda Shenhav, and Pnina Mutzaphi-Haller, 105–51. Tel-Aviv: Ha-kibbutz Ha-meuḥad.

Shepherd, John, and Peter Wicke. 1997. *Music and Cultural Theory.* Cambridge, Eng.: Polity Press.

Shiloah, Amnon, and Eric Cohen. 1983. The Dynamics of Change in Jewish Oriental Ethnic Music in Israel. *Ethnomusicology* 27, no. 2: 227–51.

Shimoni, Gideon. 1996. Summary. In *Jewish Nationalism and Politics: New Perspectives,* ed. Jehuda Rienharz, Gideon Shimoni, and Yosef Salmon, v–xxii. Jerusalem: Zalman Shazar Center for Jewish History.

Shmueli, Herzl. 1971. *The Israeli Song* (in Hebrew). Tel Aviv: Hamerkaz letarbut ulechinuch, Hasifria lemusika.

———. 1968. Tavniyot melodiyot ba-shir ha-yisraeli (Melodic motifs in the Israeli song). In *Eastern and Western Layers in Israeli Music,* ed. Michal Smoira, 68–70. Tel Aviv: Israel Music Institute.

Shohat, Ella. 1989. *Israeli Cinema: East/West and the Politics of Representation.* Austin: University of Texas Press.

———. 1988. Sephardim in Israel: Zionism from the Standpoint of its Jewish Victims. *Social Text* 19–20: 1–35.

Shokeid, Moshe. 1988. *Children of Circumstances: Israeli Immigrants in New York.* Ithaca, N.Y., and London: Cornell University Press.

———. 1971. *The Dual Heritage: Immigrants from the Atlas Mountains in an Israeli Village.* Manchester, Eng.: Manchester University Press.

Slobin, Mark. 1993. *Subcultural Sounds: Micromusics of the West.* Hanover, N.H.: Wesleyan University Press.

Smith, Anthony D. 1995. Zionism and Diaspora Nationalism. *Israel Affairs* 2: 1–19.

———. 1991. *Nationalism.* Oxford: Basil Blackwell.

———. 1986. *The Ethnic Origin of Nations.* Oxford: Basil Blackwell.

Smoira, Michal, ed. 1968. *Eastern and Western Layers in Israeli Music* (in Hebrew). Tel Aviv: Israel Music Institute.

Smoira-Cohen, Michal. 1963. *Folk Song in Israel: An Analysis Attempted.* Tel Aviv: Israel Music Institute.

Smooha, Sammy. 1992. *Arabs and Jews in Israel.* Boulder, Colo.: Westview Press.

———. 1978. *Israel: Pluralism and Conflict.* London: Routledge and Kegan Paul.

Snir, Reuven. 1995. "Hebrew as the Language of Grace": Arab-Palestinian Writers in Hebrew. *Prooftexts* 15: 163–83.

Soysal, Yasemin Nuhoglu. 1994. *Limits of Citizenship.* Chicago: University of Chicago Press.

Stokes, Martin. 1994. *Ethnicity, Identity and Music.* Oxford: Berg.

———, ed. 1992. *The Arabesk Debate: Music and Musicians in Modern Turkey.* Oxford: Oxford University Press.

Straw, Will. 1991. Systems of Articulation, Logics of Change: Communities and Scenes in Popular Music. *Cultural Studies* 3: 368–88.

Swedenburg, Ted. 1997. Saida Sultan/Dana International: Transgender Pop and Polysemiotics of Sex, Nation, and Ethnicity on the Israeli-Egyptian Border. *The Musical Quarterly* 81, no. 1: 81–108.

Swirski, Shlomo. 1989. *Israel: The Oriental Majority.* Trans. Barbara Swirski. Atlantic Highlands, N.J.: Zed Books.

Tagg, Philip. 1982. Analyzing Popular Music: Theory, Method and Practice. *Popular Music* 2: 37–68.

Talmon, Miri. 2001. *Israeli Graffiti: Nostalgia, Representation of Groups and Collective Identity in Israeli Cinema* (in Hebrew). Haifa: Haifa University Press.

Taylor, Timothy. 1997. *Global Pop.* London: Routledge.

Tessler, Shmulik. 2000. *Songs of the Military Entertainment Troupes of the Israel Defense Forces 1948–1979: An Expression of Consensus in Israeli Society* (in Hebrew). M.A. thesis, Tel Aviv University.

Thornton, Sarah. 1996. *Club Cultures.* Hanover, N.H.: Wesleyan University Press.

Tomlinson, John. 1999. *Globalization and Culture.* Chicago: University of Chicago Press.

Topelberg, Carmela. 2000. *The Popular Music of Tel Aviv from the 1920s to the 1950s* (in Hebrew). Ph.D. dissertation, Bar-Ilan University.

Wahlin, Moshe. 1998. *Yamim shel hol ve-kokhavim* (Days of sand and stars). Tel Aviv: Yaron Golan.

Vila, Pablo. 1987. Rock Nacional and Dictatorship in Argentina. *Popular Music* 6: 129–48.

Vilensky, Moshe. 1965. Gilui da'at 'al festival ha-zemer ha-yisraeli (Open letter on the Israel Song Festival). *Ha-ḥinukh ha-musikali* 8: 53–54.

Vinitzky-Seroussi, Vered. 1998. Jerusalem Assassinated Rabin and Tel Aviv Commemorated Him: Rabin's Memorials and the Discourse of National Identity in Israel. *City and Society* 10: 1–21.

Wallis, Roger, and Krister Malm. 1984. *Big Sounds from Small Peoples.* New York: Pendragon.

Weingrod, A., ed. 1985. *Studies in Israeli Ethnicity.* New York: Gordon and Breach.

Weitman, Sasha. 1987. Prenoms et orientations nationales en Israël, 1882–1980. *Annales—Economies, Societes, Civilisations* 4: 879–900.

———. 1982. Cohort Size and Onomasticon Size. *Onoma* 26: 78–95.

Wicke, Peter. 1990. *Rock Music: Culture, Aesthetics and Sociology.* Cambridge: Cambridge University Press.

Yaeger-Dror, Malcah. 1991. Linguistic Evidence for Social Psychological Attitudes: Hyperaccomodation or (r1) by singers from Mizraḥi Background. *Language and Communication* 11, no. 4: 309–31.

Yair, Gad. 1995. "Unite Unite Europe": The Political and Cultural Structures of

Europe as Reflected in the Eurovision Song Contest. *Social Networks* 17: 147–61.

Yair, Gad, and Daniel Maman. 1996. The Persistent Structure of Hegemony in the Eurovision Song Contest. *Acta Sociologica* 39: 309–25.

Yossef, Ovadia. 1954–55. *Sefer she'elot u-teshuvot yabi'a omer* (Book of responsa). Vol. 1. Jerusalem:Yeshivat Porath Yosef.

Zefira, Bracha. 1978. *Kolot Rabim* (Many voices). Ramat Gan: Masada.

Zerubavel, Yael. 1995. *Recovered Roots: Collective Memory and the Making of Israeli National Tradition.* Chicago: University of Chicago Press.

Zukin, Sharon. 1995. *The Cultures of Cities.* Cambridge, Mass.: Blackwell.

Songs Index

Albums Index

Names Index

Subject Index

Compositor:	BookMatters
Text:	10/13 Aldus
Display:	Aldus
Printer and binder:	Integrated Book Technology